IONA

*The living memory
of a crofting community*

1750–1914

To my father
DUGALD MACARTHUR
and to his father before him

IONA

The living memory
of a crofting community

1750–1914

E. Mairi MacArthur

EDINBURGH UNIVERSITY PRESS

© E. Mairi MacArthur 1990

Edinburgh University Press
22 George Square, Edinburgh

Set in Linotronic Garamond
by Speedspools, Edinburgh, and
printed in Great Britain by
Bell and Bain Limited,
Glasgow

British Library Cataloguing
in Publication Data
MacArthur, E. Mairi
Iona : the living memory of a
crofting community, 1750-1914.
1. Scotland. Strathclyde region. Iona.
Social life, history.
I. Title
941.423

ISBN 0 7486 0214 3

The publisher acknowledges subsidy from
the Scottish Arts Council towards
the publication of this volume

Contents

Acknowledgements

I have become indebted to very many people over the past few years of study and writing. In the first place, it is to the School of Scottish Studies in the University of Edinburgh that I owe the opportunity of taking the postgraduate degree which has led to this book. The initial enthusiasm of Dr Margaret Mackay and Professor John MacQueen provided the spur to get begun. Margaret Mackay, along with Donald Archie MacDonald, Director of the School, then devoted many hours of invaluable discussion and advice to the research as it progressed. Others within and outside of the University who kindly gave of their time and specialist knowledge were Ian Fraser, John MacInnes and Ian MacKenzie (School of Scottish Studies), Donald Meek (Department of Celtic), Hugh Cheape (Royal Museum of Scotland) and Ian Fisher (Royal Commission on the Ancient and Historical Monuments of Scotland).

I am grateful to the following for permission to reproduce illustrative material: Argyll Estates, plate 1 and figures 1 and 6; the Donald B. MacCulloch collection, in the care of Dugald MacArthur, Connel, plate 5; Murdo MacDonald, Lochgilphead, plate 7; the George Washington Wilson Collection in Aberdeen University Library, plate 12; the Royal Commission on the Ancient and Historical Monuments of Scotland, plates 2 and 4, figure 4.

I have met with courteous assistance from staff in the many collections and libraries I have explored, including: Argyll and Bute District Council Archives, Aberdeen University Library, Edinburgh University Library, General Register Office, the Mitchell Library, the National Library of Scotland, the National Trust for Scotland, the *Oban Times* office, St Andrews University Library, the Scottish Record Office and Strathclyde Regional Archive. I am particularly grateful to His Grace the Duke of Argyll for the privilege of access to the Argyll Estate papers. And Alastair Campbell, Archivist, was very helpful during my visits to Inveraray to consult the material.

For the loan of family papers, correspondence or books I wish to thank Robin Campbell, Mrs Iona Chatterton, Mrs Isabel Gillies, Angus Johnson, Jim MacDonald, John MacMillan, Mrs May MacKay, David Russell, Harold Troup. Through letters, useful information has come from descendants of Iona emigrants, namely Neil Cox (Australia), Shirley MacArthur Credo (USA), George

Cuming (USA), Kathleen MacArthur (New Zealand), Fay MacDougall (USA), Alan MacQuarrie (Canada), Deirdre Rowell (New Zealand), Ray Wylie (Canada). A special thank you must go to John MacInnes (London), also of Iona descent, who has generously shared the results of his own demographic study of the island.

The people of Iona have been central to the success of this project. They have supplied information, shared memories and given me hospitality on many occasions. Calum Cameron and Peter MacInnes have been especially generous with their time but all my conversations with islanders, whether short or lengthy, have made a useful contribution. My thanks go to: Molly Cameron (Oban), John Campbell (Bunessan), Colina Cooper, the late Mrs Annie Dougall, Helen Grant, Mary MacArthur (Gourock), Neil and Ena Mac-Arthur, the late Archie MacDonald, Colin MacDonald, Willie MacDonald, the late Donald MacFadyen, the late Angus MacKay, the late Mary Ann Maclean, the late Mary MacMillan (Balquidder), the late Ellen MacPhail, Morag MacPhail, Charles and Evelyn Mac-Phail, May Powell (Peterborough). I also appreciated the opportunity of talking with several people from the Ross of Mull, namely Jeannie Gibson, the late Donald MacFarlane, Attie MacKechnie and the late Donald Morrison.

All members of my family have continued to show unfailing interest and support. To my father, Dugald MacArthur, I owe the greatest debt of gratitude, however, for his role as principal informant – passing on a huge store of recollection and knowledge about Iona and its people. He has also been a tireless fellow-researcher, critic and proof-reader. Final responsibility for all errors and omissions, of course, rests with myself.

The history of a community is not stored in the record books alone. Toward the end of the research my father remarked that much of what I had dug out of libraries, papers and statistics confirmed what he remembered hearing from the older generation of his day. Some of that memory lives on, I hope, in this book.

E. MAIRI MACARTHUR

Notes to Readers

1. The name 'Iona' probably results from the confusion of the letters 'u' and 'n' in the reading of the manuscript 'Life of Columba', written by a later Abbot of Iona, Adomnan, about AD 690. He called the island 'Ioua Insula'. William Reeves argued this in the notes to his translation of Adomnan, published in 1857 and added that it was Adomnan's practice to put names of islands in adjectival form agreeing with 'insula'. Thus the nominative form may have been 'Io' or 'I'. Later scholars have concurred. The meaning of this root form is not known for certain but it has been equated with the Gaelic word 'I' for 'island'. Gaelic speakers refer to Iona as 'I Chaluim-Chille' (island of Columba of the church) or, very often, by the simpler form 'Eilean I'. 'Hii', 'Hy' and 'Y' are among other forms found by historians. Those recurring most commonly in sources used in this book are 'I' and 'Icolmkill'.

2. The Gaelic spelling of placenames adheres throughout to current local usage in Iona and may not always be consistent with standard Gaelic orthography.

Abbreviations

AE	Argyll Estate.
AEI	*Argyll Estate Instructions.*
AEP	Argyll Estate Papers.
BHMSS	Baptist Home Missionary Society for Scotland.
c.	circa.
CB or Central Board	Central Board of Management.
EE	East End.
f.	folio.
HIES	Highland and Island Emigration Society.
HLLRA	Highland Land Law Reform Association.
IC	*Inverness Courier.*
McNeill Report	Report to the Board of Supervision by Sir John McNeill on the Western Highlands and Islands.
ms.	manuscript.
Napier Commission	Royal Commission into the condition of crofters and cottars in the Highlands and Islands of Scotland.
NBDM	*North British Daily Mail.*
NLS	National Library of Scotland.
NSA	*New Statistical Account of Scotland.*
OPR	Old Parochial Register.
OSA	'Old' *Statistical Account of Scotland.*
OT	*Oban Times.*
PF	Procurator Fiscal.
PLIC	Poor Law Inquiry Commission.
PN	Place Name Survey (School of Scottish Studies).
PP	Parliamentary Paper.
RCAHMS	Royal Commission on the Ancient and Historical Monuments of Scotland.
RCRI	Royal Commission on Religious Instruction.
SA	Sound Archives (School of Scottish Studies).
SHS	Scottish History Society.
SRO	Scottish Record Office.
SSPCK	Scottish Society for the Propagation of Christian Knowledge.
TGSI	*Transactions of the Gaelic Society of Inverness.*
WE	West End.
WRH	West Register House.

Introduction

For centuries the island of Iona has occupied a special place in the history of Scotland. This book is about the people who have occupied that island and for whom it has first and foremost been their home. The chapters trace the economic and political events which, from the mid-eighteenth until the early twentieth centuries, affected the islanders' livelihoods, society and way of life. The course followed by this Hebridean community was not a particularly unusual one in a period of similar, and profound, change throughout the Highlands. The background against which their story unfolded, however, was by no means ordinary.

Adomnan records that on the evening before Columba died he climbed a knoll on the east side of Iona and spoke these words: 'On this place, small and mean though it be, not only the kings of the Irish with their peoples, but also the rulers of barbarous and foreign nations, with their subjects, will bestow great and especial honour'.[1] The saint's prediction has indeed proved true. Place of pilgrimage in Columba's own day, burying-ground of nobles and kings in early medieval Scotland, Iona became the destination of a steady stream of visitors whose numbers have swelled to countless thousands in modern times.

Historians, archaeologists, church scholars, geologists and naturalists have recorded what the island's soil, stones and structures tell us of its eventful past. Dozens of artists have committed to canvas the translucent hues and clear light for which Iona's land and seascapes are famed. The Cathedral and the Nunnery, the carved crosses and tombstones have all been engraved, photographed and documented down to the last detail.

By contrast, very little has been written about, or from the perspective of, the indigenous population. No study has been devoted primarily to the people settled there over many generations and to the farming and fishing economy that has supported them. Their existence has been overshadowed to such an extent that, even today, it is possible to encounter the erroneous belief that no one has *ever* lived there, outside of the former monastic orders and the modern Iona Community founded in 1938.

The wish to address this clear gap in the literature on Iona was a major reason for undertaking the research on which this book is based. Another incentive, closely allied to the first, arose out of my own family connections with the island. The pace of change continues on Iona, as elsewhere, and the generations move relentlessly onward. One of the vital sources for such a local study lies in oral tradition, those memories of land, people and custom that are preserved independently of any written history. It was thus important to tap the fund of knowledge possessed by the older Iona natives of today, before it slipped beyond recall.

The span of years from 1750 until 1914 saw changes of major significance in the circumstances and conditions of those who worked the land in Gaelic Scotland. The task of examining how one small community was influenced by, and responded to, those changes would, it was hoped, be a useful addition to the wider body of work on the social and economic history of the Highlands. The availability of source material also helped determine the chosen starting date.

Neither archaeological nor written records provide more than slender clues as to who lived on Iona prior to the eighteenth century. It is not certain when permanent human settlement there began. A few flints of Mesolithic date have been found, indicating transient fish or seal-hunting expeditions up to 3500 B C. Pollen analysis and a stone axe point to some farming after that date. There is one Bronze Age burial cairn, dating from about 2000 B C, and one Iron Age hill fort, at Dùn Bhuirg, which is thought to have been occupied between the first century B C and the third century A D. Larger numbers of Bronze and Iron Age sites have been identified in neighbouring Mull, Coll and Tiree and it is possible that Iona had more extensive pre-Christian settlement than the remaining traces suggest.[2]

It is not certain whether people were already living on the island when Columba arrived there from Ireland in 563 A D. A later Abbot of Iona, Adomnan, from whose *Life* of the Saint we learn much of what is known of the first monastic settlement, makes no specific mention of local inhabitants. As succeeding communities of monks maintained Iona as a great centre of religious scholarship and of missionary activity, its reputation continued to spread throughout Scotland and into Europe. It seems quite likely that a population will gradually have sprung up, alongside that of the monastery.

The existence of a parish church of St Ronan, within the Nunnery precincts, and the mention of a 'parsonage' by the fourteenth century, certainly imply a secular population by medieval times. The first surviving document to note rent paid by Iona tenants is dated 1561 and there are occasional references to income received during the seventeenth century, as for example at 13 January 1679: 'The ten pound land of Icalumkill pays of bear in bolls called boll-beg the number of 43½ bolls and of money £190.0.0 with twa stones cheese and 2 quarts butter'.[3]

By the mid-eighteenth century, however, a clearer picture of the tenantry begins to emerge. By then the island was in Campbell hands. After a series of earlier tussles over Maclean of Duart's possessions, the tenth Earl of Argyll landed a regiment on Mull in 1691 and seized the Duart territories including Iona. In response to land tenure reforms by both the second and third Dukes of Argyll, a number of reports, petitions and leases shed light on who their tenants were. An Estate map of Iona, drawn in 1769, shows the location of the original village and the pattern of pre-crofting agriculture.

In the fifth Duke of Argyll's time, two particularly useful documents have provided a solid factual basis for the main part of the study. These are: *Inhabitants of the Argyll Estate. 1779* and *Argyll Estate Instructions Mull, Morvern, Tiree 1771–1805*, both edited by the late Eric R. Cregeen. The former gives a precise population count, the earliest on record for Iona, and lists the male inhabitants by name. The latter is correspondence between the fifth Duke and his Chamberlain and covers many detailed aspects of estate management.

The aim of this book has been to build up as comprehensive a picture as possible, from both the inside and the outside, of the Iona people's history. To this end, a correspondingly broad range of documentary, oral and visual sources has been explored. At every stage all these types of material have been integrated and used to pose questions, one to another. For example, old photographs and maps have provided direct information, often correlating with that documented for topics such as housing, farming practices or land use. When the same items have been used as a tool, local informants have sometimes been able to fill out the picture. They may have been stimulated to tell an anecdote, relating to what a photo depicts; they may have been able to clarify the significance of a placename; or they may have recalled changes in where houses were built, crops grown or boundaries marked.

On the documentary side, the privilege of gaining access to the Argyll Estate papers has been invaluable. Much of use has been extracted from rent rolls, correspondence, petitions and accounts. It would not, however, have been possible to write this history from the Estate papers alone. In the first place, this vast archive is in the process of reorganisation and there are some gaps in what is currently accessible. For example, very little relating to the making of the crofts in Iona has come to light – no tenants' lists, leases or estate plans. It may be, of course, that this material never existed or was lost at an earlier date. It has been possible, fortunately, to reconstruct the number and layout of the first crofts from a combination of later rentals, visitors' observations and oral tradition. But even if the Estate records were complete, they could not be expected to illustrate all aspects of the society. They contain, for instance, virtually nothing on family history, on community ties or on culture and recreation.

Demographic changes in the island have been studied in some detail. The Argyll Estate population list from 1779 provided a starting point and this has been built upon with the help of the *Statistical Accounts* of 1795 and 1843, Census data from 1841 until 1891, travellers' accounts, tenants' rolls and Valuation Rolls. The minister entered baptisms and marriages in the Old Parochial Register (OPR) for Iona from 1804 until 1854 and entered deaths from 1835 until 1854. From 1855 these events were recorded in the Statutory Registers of Births, Marriages and Deaths. The main drawback of the OPR, deriving from the fact that it was not statutory, is the possibility of under-registration. Iona entries may have suffered even more in this respect as they depended on the minister's infrequent visits from Mull, at least up until 1829 when he became resident on the island. A detailed study of population change in Iona from 1800 to 1860 has cross-referenced the register with the Census returns of 1841 and 1851.[4] The author, John MacInnes, has concluded that marriage entries *were* generally well kept throughout the whole of the OPR, that baptism entries were also good up until 1840 but less complete thereafter. The death register was probably the least complete.

Using all of this population material, family trees for most of the long-established families on Iona have been constructed. But in many cases, due to the high frequency with which certain surnames and Christian names recur, it would not have been possible to complete these without details supplied by descendants, both in Iona and overseas. This genealogical information has helped to illustrate a variety of social patterns such as family size, intermarriage between families and in-/out-migration.

The fame of Iona has ensured a steady influx of visitors and, as a direct consequence, a very large number of written descriptions. This seam is particularly rich towards the end of the eighteenth century. By then a spirit of scientific curiosity had begun to replace the former suspicion of the Highlands as inaccessible and even barbarous. It was the Age of Enlightenment although, for some, the feeling that to explore those remote parts was to venture among savages clearly lingered still. After a tour in 1800, which included Iona, John Leyden noted in his journal upon reaching Perth: 'I may now congratulate myself on a safe escape from the Indians of Scotland, as our friend Ramsay denominated the Highlanders . . .'.[5]

Leyden was a friend of Sir Walter Scott, whose influence in popularising a romantic view of the Highlands was immense. Scott capitalised on sentiments that were already widely rooted. A George Douglas from Edinburgh, who in 1800 fulfilled his 'ardent desire' to visit the Hebrides, travelled first by the 'celebrated' Loch Katrine and the 'sublime and picturesque scene' of Loch Lomond.[6] By the time he reached Oban the inn was already crowded with other tourists and his is one of several journals which convey an impression that the route westward was indeed well trodden by the turn of the nineteenth century.

The most famous travellers to the Hebrides in the late eighteenth century were undoubtedly Samuel Johnson and James Boswell. Dr Johnson's account of the tour, published in 1775, was widely read and frequently copied. His passage on Iona which begins : 'We were now treading that illustrious island . . .' must be one of the most commonly quoted texts in Scottish travel writing. Those inspired to follow in his tracks usually did so out of admiration for the good doctor, although a desire to prove him wrong also surfaces from time to time as in the case of an anonymous diarist from 1806 :

> What is very remarkable, Doctor Johnson does not seem to have visited Staffa. . . . Could it be from narrow mindedness that he would not describe a place in Scotland to which England has no parallel ? . . . Though as Scotchmen we were at first ready to raise the war hoop against his journal, yet in the course of the tour we were forced to admit that in most cases his descriptions were just.[7]

A chance of geography also played its part. When Sir Joseph Banks recorded the fascinating geology of Staffa in 1772, he named the most spectacular cave 'Fingal's Cave', possibly confusing the Gaelic name Uamh Bhinn (musical cave) with Uamh Fhinn (cave of Fionn or Fingal). The two pronunciations are very similar. In any event, the adoption of 'Fingal's Cave' coincided with the enormous popular enthusiasm for James Macpherson's purported translations of ancient epic poems by Ossian, son of the legendary warrior Fingal. Published in the early 1760s, these had been read both in Britain and on the Continent and they undoubtedly contributed to the heightened romantic appeal of the Highlands in general and of Staffa in particular. The proximity of Staffa with its natural wonders to Iona with its man-made antiquities enhanced the reputation of both. In a number of cases, the only islands visited during a tour confined otherwise to the mainland were Staffa and Iona.

The 1820s ushered in the era of the paddle steamers and with them an increased number of travelogues and guidebooks, beginning with *Lumsden's Steamboat Companion*, designed to promote the new mode of travel along with the places that were now within easier reach. As the century progressed, many of these guidebooks tended to repeat each other. And most confined their comments about Iona to the sights which they judged of interest to the tourists, although happily not all were dismissive as the 1894 edition of John Murray's *Handbook for Travellers in Scotland*: 'Iona is a rather barren treeless island, 3 miles long by 1½ miles broad, belonging to the Duke of Argyll, and owes its interest entirely to its associations'.[8]

These 'associations' highlight a basic drawback of the travel literature on Iona. The very reason which drew the traveller to the island – the historic remains – then tended to dominate his or her full attention. The people were regarded by many as of peripheral interest, if of any at all. Even the account by Martin Martin concentrates on the ruins, the few local beliefs mentioned being those connected directly with the historic relics. By contrast, the rest of his Hebridean tour, made circa 1695, offers an absorbing assortment of observations on agriculture, fishing, diet, health, plant cures, superstition, social custom, stories and traditions. Moreover, Martin was not a stranger but a native of Skye and a Gaelic speaker.

The poor material conditions of Iona's inhabitants may even have been exaggerated by some writers, who hint that the destitute appearance of the people represented an affront to the sanctity and celebrity of the place where they lived. The vast majority of visitors, of course, landed for only a few hours, did not share the islanders' language and had little other experience of Hebridean life with which to compare Iona. Sir Walter Scott's remark in 1810 that the people were in a state of 'squalid and dejected poverty' is often quoted. Yet he himself admitted on a return journey four years later that they seemed better off than on other islands he had since visited and that his previous judgement may have been due to the shock of the unfamiliar.[9]

The large amount of material available in travellers' accounts must therefore be treated with some caution. This source cannot by itself provide a complete picture. Visitors' motivation ranged from objective scientific inquiry to romantic curiosity and any preconceptions or prejudices inevitably accompanied them. Writers about Iona to-day have been tempted to use this source selectively, quoting from travellers on the basis of their fame rather than on that of their actual accounts. The contributions of Scott, Keats, Mendelssohn and Wordsworth are thin and one-sided by comparison with, for example, such earlier men of science and letters as Dr John Walker,

Thomas Pennant or Thomas Garnett or with some visiting foreigners such as Necker de Saussure or Bernard Ducos.

A category of travel writing that has proved to be particularly interesting is that of personal journals. Perhaps because these records were not intended primarily for publication, they were often anecdotal, subjective and even irreverent in style. They were written for the author's own amusement and not to educate the public or promote tourism. An account by a visiting yachtsman in 1788 contains an unusually large number of facts and figures about the people of Iona, clearly jotted down on the spot. Other diarists shed a colourful light on their fellow travellers, for example Yorkshireman John Phillips who prepared to board the boat for Iona on 19 July 1826 after a night at Tobermory: 'Awakened at 5 by the music/noise? of the parading bagpiper, we soon entered the ready packet and set off at 5.30 with four Frenchmen, a gentleman who attached himself to us at Oban, two Cantabs, a blackguard Scotch writer, good hopes and bad weather'.[10]

The official papers drawn upon for this study comprise a wide variety of minutes, correspondence and reports. Government Commissions and Inquiries also yielded much of relevance in the testimony of ministers, factors and ground officers. The Royal Commission of 1883 into crofters' conditions was the first where the people themselves gained a platform on which to voice their views and feelings. Bad weather prevented that Commission from meeting in Iona, which was a pity as three people were ready to come forward with evidence. One of them, Malcolm Ferguson, was elected to represent the whole island at the final hearings in Glasgow and he did present a detailed and strongly argued case.

Even before this, the voice of the local community had begun to come through in the columns of the newspapers that served the south-west Highlands. The *Oban Times* began in 1866 and was read both in Iona and in emigrant communities overseas. News, features, letters and obituaries were submitted by various islanders over the years. In addition, during the 1870s and 1880s, Iona tailor Neil MacKay acted as local correspondent for the Glasgow-based *North British Daily Mail*. His regular despatches reveal a wealth of topical detail, often enhanced by the writer's own dry wit and pungent comments. Such newspaper contributions were presumably neither commissioned nor edited and thus can be taken as an authentic, first-hand account of what was considered important, interesting and entertaining to Iona folk of the time, at home and abroad.

Neither Malcolm Ferguson nor Neil MacKay can now be questioned further on the information they gave and the views they expressed in the Royal Commission evidence or the columns of the *Mail.* Yet the material they bequeathed in this way may in a very real sense be considered an oral, and not simply a written, source.

Oral tradition collected today has provided many useful details on family history, local customs, unmapped place-names and attitudes to past events, landlords or other personalities. None of this could have been derived from documentary sources alone. Recollections about school days, croft work or communal tasks along with ephemera such as old photographs, letters or notebooks, have helped deepen an understanding of the practical minutiae of people's lives.

What is absent from living memory in Iona today is any significant fund of Gaelic song and story. Yet in the eighteenth century John Walker, among others, mentioned the people's 'numberless' historical legends and Thomas Garnett talked of 'persons who can repeat several of the Celtic poems of Ossian and other bards'. In 1857 W. Maxwell wrote of supernatural tales 'by the hundred' recounted by the Ionians, as he called them, on long winter evenings.[11] And in the 1950s the School of Scottish Studies recorded several tradition-bearers from the Ross of Mull who knew tales either located in Iona or related to them by Iona people.

The art of storytelling was undoubtedly as vigorous a part of the Gaelic culture in Iona as it was everywhere in the Highlands at one time. But for reasons that are complex, and still not entirely understood, the tradition did disappear earlier or more completely in some places than in others. When John Francis Campbell of Islay was collecting folktales around 1860, he already found evidence of this process. In the introduction to the first volume of his *Popular Tales of the West Highlands* the contrast is made between the large numbers of heroic tales still heard in Barra and South Uist and their virtual disappearance in North Uist and Harris.[12] This was attributed partly to the stronger disapproval of the Protestant Church in the latter areas and partly to their higher rate of literacy. Access to books was thought to substitute, in some degree, for the entertainment value of storytelling.

These factors may have been at work in Iona. There are certainly references to discouragement by the minister of superstitious practices, of which magical legends were probably considered another form of expression. The school, and later the library, were flourishing institutions in Iona. The demise of storytelling and singing also accompanied the gradual vanishing of those occasions when people gathered together – droving cattle, rowing, waulking cloth, shoeing horses at the smiddy. It was also the case in many communities that particular individuals or families were gifted in these arts. Those who participated as listeners only were less likely to pass the songs or stories on to the next generation.

To all of this should be added the prevailing ethos of the late nineteenth century, particularly after the 1872 Education Act, that English was necessary for educational achievement and ultimate prosperity. The Gaelic language and culture was by association devalued. This attitude was forcibly expressed by a speaker to the Annual Gathering of the Mull and Iona Association in 1890, and reported in the *Oban Times*: 'He urged upon the youth in the Highlands that their stern duty was to acquire a commanding knowledge of the English language and not on any account if they could help it stay in the Highlands'.

Nevertheless, it is the oral material that, at many points, has illuminated and enlivened the documentary record in the course of this study. The evidence drawn from the people, and from the landscape where they live, are sources rarely tapped hitherto in references to Iona's secular history. Yet it is they that give that history one of its strongest lines of continuity.

The research for this book has delved into a very extensive range of sources. It has been necessary to remain aware of their differing origins in order to assess their reliability and value. They have been assembled and integrated with the aim of presenting a view of life on Iona across a wide spectrum of human interest. The narrative ends at the 1914–1918 War, thus bringing it into the present century and just within the memories of the oldest of my informants. Changes on Iona since then have been rapid and numerous. Their chronicle, however, must await another chapter.

Section I

1750–1802

I

The Land and the People:
Late Eighteenth Century

From the top of Dùn I, the highest point on Iona, the eye takes in a fine vista – southward to Islay and the Paps of Jura, eastward to the pink granite rocks of the Ross of Mull and to Ben More hunched above the dark crags of Burg. Sweeping north, if the day is clear you will see the distant blue shapes of the Cuillins and the South Uist hills.

At your feet spreads the diminutive panorama of the island itself. It is five and a half kilometres in length, two and a half kilometres at its broadest and the cairn at your back is a mere hundred metres above sea level. From the bottom of the hill fields slope gently towards the white silica sands fringing the north-east coast. To the south-west stretches rugged moorland, interrupted only by a green swathe of arable land cutting across its middle to meet the shelly shore of the western Machair. If tide and swell are right, a plume of spray will whoosh sporadically up from Uamh an t-Seididh (Spouting Cave), signalling where the rocky headlands and the jagged gullies of the southern coast begin.

Many of Iona's present-day dwellings are visible from the hill. A keen eye may also pick out the lines and bumps of former foundations, where houses, barns and stackyards once stood. Here and there, a grey latticework of old drystone dykes criss-crosses the island. These are some of the signs, to be read in the landscape itself, of where the people lived and how the land was used. It is an appropriate starting point.

In 1769 a man named William Douglas almost certainly stood on Dùn I. Little is known about him other than that he was a surveyor in the west of Scotland, making town, road and estate maps. He was employed by the Duke of Argyll to make a map of Iona that year. His careful draughtsmanship has left us with a detailed visual impression of the island in the eighteenth century.

The map shows the island's only settlement as a cluster of houses between Port Rònain and the Nunnery, with a few straggling along the track leading to the Cathedral. This corresponds to early descriptions, for example that of Thomas Garnett in 1798: 'All the huts in the island are grouped together in the form of an irregular village'. One other house is shown, above Port a'Churaich at the south end

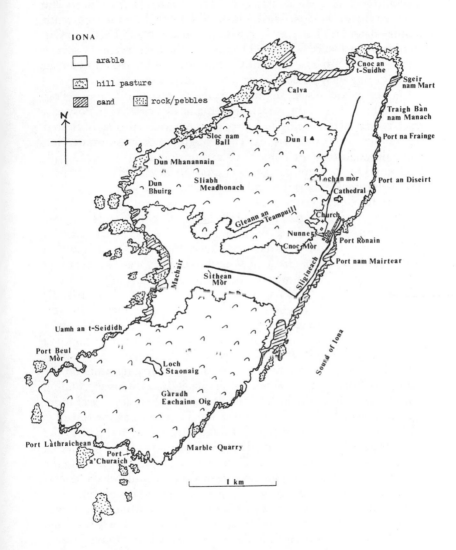

IONA

☐ arable

▨ hill pasture

▨ sand   ▦ rock/pebbles

N

Cnoc an
t-Suidhe

Calva

Sgeir
nam Mart

Traigh Bàn
nam Manach

Sloc nam
Ball

Dun I ▲

Port na Frainge

Dùn Mhanannain

Dùn
Bhuirg

Sliabh
Meadhonach

Lochan mòr

Port an Diseirt

Cathedral

Gleann an Teampuill

Church

Nunnery

Port Rònain

Cnoc Mòr

Machair

Sìthean
Mòr

Sligneach

Port nam Mairtear

Sound of Iona

Uamh an t-Seididh

Port Beul
Mòr

Loch
Staonaig

Gàradh
Eachainn Oig

Port Làthraichean

Port
a'Churaich

Marble Quarry

1 km

Map 1. Iona – topography including main placenames.

of the island near ground which the map notes was 'good green pasture part of which has been in tillage'. Traces of cultivation rigs and a small series of lazy beds are evident to this day, as are the remains of several turf-walled enclosures and three rectangular buildings. The rounded angles and opposed doors of the latter indicate an eighteenth century date. This flat grassy area is known as Gàradh Eachainn Oig (garden or enclosure of young Hector). A nineteenth century source claims this Hector as a cadet of the Macleans of Duart, implying an origin during their possession of Iona in the seventeenth century.[1]

On the raised beach slightly further to the south, above Port Làthraichean (bay of the ruins), are remains of a circular enclosure, a small rectangular building and three piles of stones, probably cleared from other walls or structures. The Douglas map does not mention these although they are considered earlier than the ruins at Gàradh Eachainn Oig, perhaps dating from post-medieval times. They may have been stock enclosures and seasonal shielings when cattle were brought for summer pasture.

Although it is clear that most of the population had long lived near to the Cathedral, and the earlier monastery, the occasional habitation of these outlying districts is very likely. Indeed, a local tradition holds that news of the battle of Waterloo in 1815 was first heard on Iona, from passing boatmen, by people living at Staonaig.

Today the name 'Staonaig' is mainly associated with the island's only loch, now the public reservoir. The Douglas map, however, marks the whole area south of the loch as 'Stenaig'. This had been part of the Nunnery lands in the sixteenth century and before and had long been designated a separate division. By the eighteenth century it formed part of the East End, one of the two farming units on the island, bounded by the Gàradh Dubh (black dyke) Staonaig running from either side of the loch to the coast. An alternative, and more accurate, term for the East End was the Two Ends as the rest of it took in the arable land of the north-east plus Dùn I and part of the moss or peat bog to its south. The mill stream below the Cathedral marked the continuance of the division which then curved round the ruins and graveyard to rejoin the stream above. A hill called Cnoc na Criche (boundary knoll) may well owe its name to its location close to this line. The West End extended over the centre of the island, from the eastern shore to the Machair and as far as Loch Staonaig. The Sliabh Meadhonach (middle moorland) was common grazing ground for both Ends.

At the time of William Douglas's survey Iona's land was worked under the system of agriculture then prevalent throughout the Highlands. It was called runrig. A farming unit generally consisted of some 'infield' and some 'outfield' arable land, plus an area of pasture. The infield strips lay closest to the settlement and were cultivated intensively. The outfield was planted less often, rotating some years as grassland. All these strips were allocated by drawing lots, usually every year, so that the better land was regularly redistributed among the tenants. The tenants' share of these strips varied, as did the number of beasts they possessed and thus the proportion of rent they paid. It is clear from one surviving lease for Iona, dated 1742, that a few tenants worked two or even three times the amount of land the majority did. At the other end of the scale were the cottars who did not have a share in the arable lots, and so did not pay rent, but generally worked for the tenants in return for a patch of potato ground and grazing for a few cows. Thomas Pennant, writing in 1772, specified that servants in Iona received a quarter of the crop plus pasture for three or four cows and a few sheep.[2]

On his map Douglas carefully drew in a compact pattern of ridged squares on the arable land, indicating the extent to which every possible spot was at some time cultivated. He also marked numbers at various points on both the arable and pasture land. No notebook or written comments by Douglas have yet come to light in the Argyll Estate papers and it is therefore hard to be sure what these numbers mean. But it is possible that they relate to the system of periodic lotting. The numbers run from one to seventeen in the East End, one to fifteen in the West End and there is only one number thirteen – the common pasture of the central moorland.

Today one can still walk the former East/West End boundary at Staonaig, tracing the moss-covered humps of the old dyke from either side of the loch. In low winter sunlight long rigs on the Machair, or tucked into the hollows around Dùn Bhuirg or Dùn I, are especially clear. Place-names too can reveal signs of the runrig system. Cnoc na Faire above Port a'Churaich means 'look-out hill' and was where the herds took turns to watch that cattle did not stray into the crops. One modern map shows Carn leth an Rathaid, meaning 'half-road cairn', where the southern hills rise behind the present-day Lagnagiogan croft. This name would have remained obscure had a local informant not recalled that there used to be a cairn around that area which was said to mark the mid-way point between the village and the farthest rig that was being cultivated.

Ten years after the 1769 map another document was drawn up which populates for us the landscape so meticulously recorded by William Douglas. This was a list of the inhabitants throughout the Argyll Estate and may claim to be one of the first such tables for any part of Scotland to identify the people by name. It is one of the achievements for which John, fifth Duke of Argyll is best remembered. From his succession in 1770 until his death in 1806 the fifth Duke displayed active interest in the management and improvement of his vast lands. He sought to introduce innovative forms of industry, he settled new villages and he was one of the first Highland landlords to pioneer the radical transformation of the agricultural system from shared holdings to individual crofts. The instructions to his Chamberlains in Mull, Morvern and Tiree reveal an energetic and ingenious mind bent on bettering the conditions and prospects of his tenants while seeking a sound return for the Estate. In 1779 the fifth Duke asked his Chamberlains in each district to compile a list of inhabitants. This was to supply precise information on the social and agrarian organisation then pertaining throughout his lands and so form a solid basis on which to plan future progress.

The 1779 list is the earliest known accurate record of the population of Iona. It gives the names and ages of the male inhabitants, including servants, and the number of females. It thus establishes which families were living in the island in the last quarter of the century, the size and structure of their households, how many of them were tenants and how many cottars. The total recorded was 249.

Sources prior to 1779 give only partial lists or rough estimates of the population. Twenty-four heads of families in Iona were among those named in letters of caption from the Earl of Argyll in 1675, which denounced as rebels a long list of occupants of the Duart lands which he had invaded the previous year.[3] There is no way of knowing, however, what proportion these were of the total population at that time.

In 1688 Dr Sacheverell was informed that Iona contained eighty families which, if an average household size of five is conjectured, implies there were around four hundred people.[4] This was probably an overestimate for that period, given the eighteenth century figures, although it is true that populations in many parts of Scotland were severely reduced by the harvest failures and plague of the 1690s. The minister for the parish that included the Ross of Mull and Iona referred to this in the old *Statistical Account* (OSA) in 1795. It was difficult to ascertain with any certainty the population of a hundred years earlier, but he *could* verify the increase during their own century from the low point of that disaster: '. . . and a famine and pestilence, in the time of King William, almost depopulated the whole parish. . . . Upon the whole coast of Brolas, it is said, two families only survived and very many parts of the other districts were waste. King William's days are still remembered with horror'.[5]

A document dated 2 April 1716, listing men obliged to give up their arms after the first Jacobite rebellion, contains twenty-five names from Iona.[6] Two surviving rentals from the mid-eighteenth century show a West End tenantry of twenty-three households in 1742 and twenty-one in 1744. To this would have to be added the family and servants working for the tacksman of the East End, the other half of the island, and any cottars who did not rent land.

In 1755 Dr Alexander Webster, an Edinburgh minister, collected population statistics from every parish in Scotland, largely from other clergymen. This was an enumeration rather than a nominal list and the returns did not separate out Iona from the larger parish of Kilfinichen and Kilviceuen of which it then formed part.[7] Estimates made by visitors up until the 1780s ranged rather erratically from the lowest of 150 inhabitants to well over 300. They were unlikely to gain accurate information on this subject due to the brief time they spent on the island, the difficulty of communicating with the Gaelic-speaking people, and the lack of a schoolmaster before 1774 or of a resident minister.

The Iona section of the 1779 list included no tacksmen. A few tacksmen were denoted on farms in the neighbouring district of Mull and in other parts of the Estate, but they were gradually disappearing, as part of a conscious policy by successive Argyll landlords.

After the Earl of Argyll had successfully ousted the Macleans from their Mull lands by the 1690s, the settling of his own tacksmen was necessary to secure his position. This was a continuation of the traditional order whereby chiefs placed loyal followers, usually kinsmen, on farms or 'tacks' in return for fighting men in time of war. 'Tack' is in fact the Scots word for lease. Tacks were worked either by the tacksman's own family and servants or, if he was not resident, by subtenants who paid part or all of their rent in produce and labour rather than money. Portions of an estate were also held by groups of joint tenants, directly from the Chief. Neither system was designed to generate hard cash.

In the early eighteenth century three large tacks in Mull were held by Campbells of the House of Dunstaffnage: northern Aros, south-east Torosay and Ross of Mull plus Iona. The latter was leased in 1694 to Archibald Campbell of Crackag, his brother Donald and Donald Campbell of Scammadale. The lease was renewed in 1716 to two of them, Crackag and Scammadale.[8] The tacks in Mull and Tiree were due to expire in 1735 but a period of low cattle prices and the wish for higher rents by the second Duke, who had inherited a family debt along with the Estate in 1703, were creating pressure for a change to the old system. The renewal of the tacks was postponed. Duncan

Forbes of Culloden was despatched in 1737 to both islands to report and to recommend improvements. The result was the introduction of open bidding for lots at a fixed rent and on a nineteen-year lease. This was intended to bring in a more reliable cash rental to the Estate, directly from joint tenants or from smaller, and thus less powerful, tacksmen. Payments in kind were to end, considered by Culloden as an 'unmerciful exaction' by the former large tacksmen on those who worked the land. The relationship between landlord and tenant was now primarily commercial, rather than one based on the rights and obligations of kinship. This was a move of far-reaching significance.[9]

It also meant that the automatic allocation of land to Campbells was no longer assured. In Iona, for example, the East End tack was leased for nineteen years in 1738 to one John Maclean and in 1742 the West End was leased for fifteen years to twenty-three joint tenants. It is not clear whether the former Campbell tacksmen had possession of the whole island or only of the East End. The question is posed by the wording of a memorial from the West End joint tenants when they came to seek a renewal of their tack in 1755: '. . . that the memorialists and their Forefathers have possessed the West End of Icolmkill time out of memory and have duly paid the rent thereof'. This implies that part of the island had been held collectively over a very long period. On the other hand, the phrase 'time out of memory' may have signified that for several generations they had worked that land, under previous tacksmen and then as joint tenants since 1742, and it was simply used to strengthen their case. This latter explanation seems more likely, as the existence of substantial Campbell tacksmen covering large areas was clear Argyll policy during the first fifty years of their possession of the Mull estates.

It is not known whether John Maclean, who took over the East End tack, was a local man but he was definitely the first resident tacksman on the island for some time. In a memorial to the Duke he mentioned that at his entry the dwelling house was 'in a ruinous condition'. One of the remains at Staonaig is known locally as 'John Maclean's House' and was probably erected for servants and herds in the southern part of the tack. It is more likely that his own permanent residence was in the village, perhaps the largest house on the Douglas map, just south of the Nunnery. The name Achabhaich (field of the byre), located south-east of Dùn I, is believed locally to have its origins as the spot where he had a byre for his East End cattle.

In 1753 John Maclean set out in a memorial the improvements he had effected, in support of his proposal to renew the tack from 1757. This was in line with a further modification in Estate policy. The third Duke had recognised that the competitive open auction

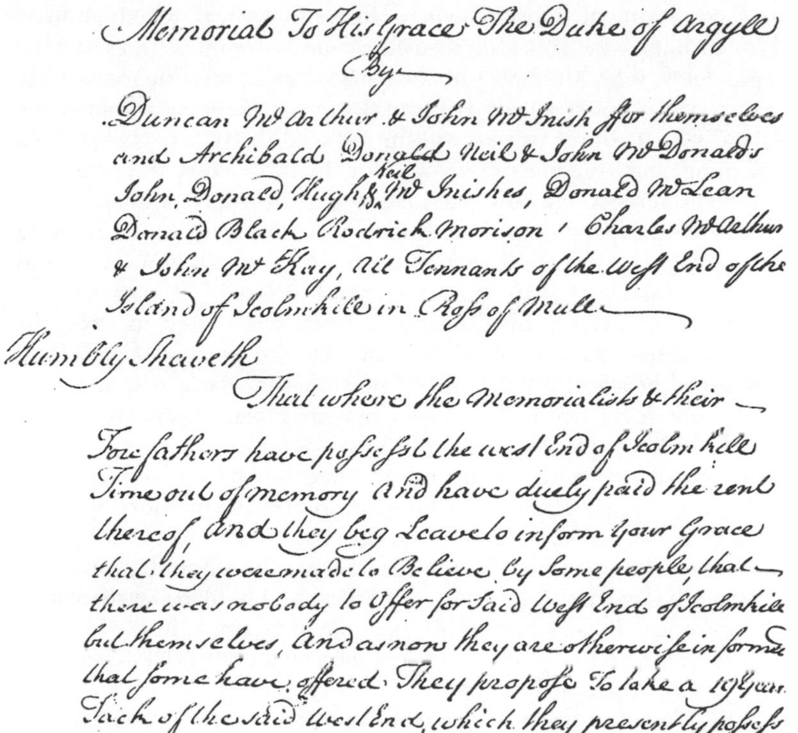

Memorial To His Grace The Duke of Argyll

By

*Duncan McArthur & John McInish for themselves
and Archibald Donald Neil & John McDonalds
John, Donald, Hugh & Neil McInishes, Donald McLean
Donald Black Roderick Morison, Charles McArthur
& John McKay, all Tennants of the West End of the
Island of Icolmkill in Ross of Mull*

Humbly Shaveth

*That where the Memorialists & their
Forefathers have possest the west End of Icolmkill
Time out of memory And have duely paid the rent
thereof, And they beg Leave to inform Your Grace
that they were made to Believe, by Some people, that
there was nobody to Offer for Said West End of Icolmkill
but themselves, And as now they are otherwise informed
that Some have offered. They propose To take a 19 years.
Tack of the said West End, which they presently possess
And to pay of yearly Tack duly for the Same Fifty One
pounds Sterling Includeing publick burdens Which is
£20..4..5⅓ over and above what it formerly paid —*

*May it therefore please Your Grace To sure ferr
the memorialists to a Tack of the above West End
of Icolmkill at the rent @ proposed Otherwise
the memorialists the greatest part of whom
Have numerous familys will Be oblidged to Go to
America —,*

*Which is humbly Submitted to Your Grace
By*

*Duncan D M A McArthur
John ∓ M ∓ McInish*

Figure 1. Copy of 1755 Memorial.

instituted by his predecessor risked pushing rents artificially high. He opted instead to invite private offers in writing which allowed him to judge the political, as well as the economic, fitness of the candidates. John Maclean had clearly been an industrious lessee. He had repaired his house and the enclosure at Staonaig, drained the island's only source of peat and introduced thirty wheels for linen spinning, resulting in extra income for the subtenants and prompter payment of rents. He now intended to slate the house, raise it to two storeys and expand the spinning industry. He applied not only for a renewal of the East End tack but offered to take the West End as well, at a total rent of £61.0.1, an increase of £9.6.9.

The Duke delayed his decision and two years later, in 1755, the West End tenants sent him a strong plea for the renewal of their tack. They had heard of another offer, presumably Maclean's, and such was their desire not to be outbid that they were prepared to pay nearly twice the present amount – £51.0.0 as opposed to £27.15.6.2/3. They concluded with a warning of what the alternative might be: 'May it therefore please your Grace to prefer the memorialists to a tack of the above West End of Icolmkill at the rent above proposed otherwise the memorialists, the greatest part of whom have numerous families will be obliged to go to America'. Highland settlement in America had already begun, for example in Georgia, in the Hudson River region and in North Carolina which had been the destination of 350 Argyll people in 1739.

The West End was a 'thirty boll land', that is it was estimated to yield thirty bolls of grain from the annual crop. The Duke did grant the joint tenants a new tack for nineteen years from Whitsunday 1757 at the augmented rent, but it transpired that some did not accept. The six boll lands thus left open were let to Donald Campbell of Scammadale, a son of the pre-1737 tacksman. Also at Whitsunday 1757 the East End tack was let to this same Campbell, at a raised rent of £35.

John Maclean's offer had therefore been unsuccessful and it may be that his activities during the Jacobite uprising had weighed against him. As far as is known he was the only Iona man to be arrested, after piloting a Spanish store ship to Barra in November 1745 with money and arms for the Prince. The local story is that he was in the house at Staonaig when soldiers landed to search for him and a young boy named MacInnes ran from the village to give warning. Together they hid in a cave and the troops departed empty-handed. The boy, when an old man, described the cave as large enough to conceal the whole population of the island but would not reveal its location even to his own son. A letter from a Justice Clark (sic) to the Duke of Argyll referred to the case of his tenant John Maclean 'whose crime is of a

singular nature and in my opinion of a deep die'. After successfully
evading capture, Maclean agreed to surrender himself at Inveraray on
condition that his family and effects would be protected up to the
time of his trial. This was in July 1746. There were insufficient
grounds to charge him with high treason and he was imprisoned in
London for three months in 1747.[10]

After 1757, therefore, a degree of Campbell prominence was restored to Iona. But Donald Campbell was also Bailie of Tiree and
although he sometimes accompanied visitors to Iona, for example
Bishop Pococke in 1760, he does not appear to have lived there. The
leases granted in 1757 were due to expire in 1776. There is no record
of Donald Campbell renewing his tack. It must thus be assumed that
after this date all tenants in Iona held their land directly from the
Duke.

Although the division into East End and West End continued,
appearing in accounts and other Estate papers, it is not mentioned in
the 1779 list. All the names appear consecutively, as if on one large
farm. Thirty-two tenants are followed by twelve cottars plus the
schoolmaster. The names, status and age of the 120 male inhabitants
are detailed but the 129 females are simply enumerated, with the
exception of two who presumably lived on their own. Analysis of
some aspects of the population's structure, therefore, may only be
made on the basis of the male inhabitants.

A certain amount of information may be gleaned, however, from a
close study of the list. Thirteen households included an extra family
member, usually a grandchild or a parent of the head. The mean
number of children was just over three for tenants and just over two
for cottars. This family size appears small compared to the early
nineteenth century, when a mean of seven and a half has been
calculated. But the list may be deceptive, as families of the younger
parents will not all have been completed and the elder offspring of
some families may have been absent temporarily, at seasonal work in
the Lowlands or on military service. These were certainly factors by
the 1790s when the minister described in the OSA the practice of
young men and women leaving home in the summer months to seek
employment. He mentioned too that 'numbers also inlist in different
Highland corps. Sixty men from Ross and I inlisted in the late West
Fencible regiment, raised by the Duke of Argyll, besides what inlisted in the 74th . . . and also in the 2d battalion of the 71st'. This
premise is strengthened by the dip in the population pyramid in the
twenty–thirty age band of the list, making that only six per cent of
the male population. Those from twenty to fifty years represented
twenty-three per cent of the male population in 1779 but this

contrasts with forty-two per cent in the same range of the total population when a detailed record was made by the schoolmaster twelve years later for the *Statistical Account.*

The Editor of the 1779 list notes that ages, especially for the older people, were probably not precisely known at this period. (The register of baptisms kept by the minister for Iona began in 1804.) There is no doubt, however, that the age distribution was weighted distinctly toward the young with eighty per cent of the male population under fifty. By 1791 this youthful proportion had grown to ninety per cent of the total population, which by then stood at 323. Observations in the *OSA* relevant to the age span of the community were that smallpox inoculation had greatly reduced the number of infant deaths and that, in contrast to the Ross of Mull, the people of Iona were not long lived : 'Few pass seventy years. The asthma is very frequent among them'. He attributed this to the odours from seaweed cast on the shore and the generally damp atmosphere of a seagirt island. The suggestion that the people were short-lived contrasts with observations during the following century about their renowned longevity, but that may have been the natural consequence of improvements in nutrition and medical care. In any case, the late eighteenth century trend was clearly toward a younger population with more surviving children. The basis was thus laid for a steady increase from the 1770s.

The first name on the 1779 list was that of Neil MacDonald. The size of his household, which included a workman, the latter's son as herd and more than one maid, indicates that he had a larger than average share of the farming land. This was probably the MacDonald to whom Johnson and Boswell were first taken by Sir Allan Maclean on their arrival in Iona : . . . the most substantial man among them. Sir Allan called him the Provost. He had a tolerable hut with higher walls than common and pretty well built with dry stone'. Johnson later referred to him as 'headman of the island' and his worth as no less than fifty pounds. A Neil MacDonald was also described as 'farm principal' by a visitor in 1788.[11]

MacDonald and MacInnes were the two most common names in 1779 and they were to continue to dominate numerically throughout the next hundred years. Of the sixteen surnames occurring in 1779, twelve were still present – mostly in greater numbers – at the Census of 1841. A core of nine names continued through to the 1881 Census and beyond. Only four names disappeared entirely before 1841 – Buie, McCallum, MacMillan, MacKay. (The last two reappeared by 1881 but came in from other districts and were not related to the earlier families.)

Tracing surnames backward, through the documents available for Iona, is more problematical. Those listed in the 1675 document were mostly identified by patronymic and are thus hard to link with specific family names, for example: 'Malcolm M'Finlay moir' (Malcolm son of big Finlay) or 'John M'Donald vic Ean' (John son of Donald son of John). The only surnames which may be clearly extracted are Maclean, MacIntyre and Fleger or Fletcher. All three are present in the 1716 list, the latter being by far the most numerous in its Gaelic form 'McInlester' which is equivalent to 'Mac an Fhleisdeir' (son of the arrow-maker). It appears that there were at least fourteen different surnames in Iona in 1716. By 1742 there was still a range of fourteen but only seven overlapped with those of twenty-six years before. Nearly half of these 1742 names disappeared in their turn by 1779. In the period of just over sixty years between 1716 and 1779 there seems to have been a notably higher turnover of family names than in the following sixty years up to 1841.

There was clearly some movement of people into and out of the island during the eighteenth century. A number may have emigrated. The memorial of 1755 indicated that this was being considered and it is known that a few did not accept the new lease. It is also possible that some names were simply changed. This was not uncommon in the Highlands, either due to a wish to identify with a more powerful family or because the Gaelic name was unusual, and difficult for a Chamberlain or Minister to write correctly. 'MacLucas' was readily interchangeable with 'MacDougall' in Tiree and Iona. A marriage entry in the Old Parochial Register for Iona in 1835 stated: 'John MacDonald commonly called MacKeorie', an interchange of names also found in Tiree. The high incidence of 'MacDonald' in Iona from 1779 onwards contrasts with the absence of this name in either 1716 or 1742. But four of those who petitioned for the renewal of that 1742 lease in the 1755 memorial were MacDonalds. It seems reasonable to assume that some changing of names to MacDonald did occur. The particular case of 'Henry McChruime', who appears in 1742 but not in 1755 or 1779, offers a further reason for this speculation. 'McChruime' is a little-known surname in Gaelic and 'Henry' an uncommon Christian name in the Iona family records. The one family where it does recur, however, is a branch of the MacDonalds and Donald MacDonald first appears in 1779 with a five-year-old son Henry.

There was much movement of people throughout the Highlands in the years following the battle of Culloden and the subsequent suppression of clan society by Government forces. Several Camerons, prominent Jacobite sympathisers, came to the Ross of Mull and

Iona from Lochaber between the 1740s and 1779. Three MacFarlane brothers are said to have come from Arrochar, one settling in the Ross, one in Iona and one in Tiree. It is thought that the Lamonts were brought into Iona by the Duke from Ulva in the late eighteenth century. One of the MacDonald lines also came from Ulva, having settled there after Culloden. It may be that the three Campbell tenants of 1779 were related to Donald Campbell, the last tacksman. Certainly, another Campbell family, who moved from Tirighoil in the Ross of Mull to Iona in the early nineteenth century, was originally from the Oban area and of the same Dunstaffnage line as Campbell of Scammadale. In the same way kin of John Maclean the previous tacksman may have remained, although the surname itself is not particularly numerous. This is perhaps surprising, given that the island had been in possession of Maclean of Duart for much of the seventeenth century.

Yet according to Johnson and Boswell, it was with the Macleans that the people's allegiance still lay rather than with the House of Argyll. They were accompanied to Iona by Sir Allan Maclean, with whom they had spent the previous two nights in Inchkenneth, and both visitors recorded the eagerness and respect with which he was greeted : 'The people are of the clan of Maclean ; and though Sir Allan had not been in the place for many years, he was received with all the reverence due to their Chieftain'. It was noted that 'MacGinnis' (a variant of 'MacInnes') was 'the name of a tribe of the Macleans'. One of them was reproached by Sir Allan for failure to send him some rum and declared afterwards that 'he had no design of disappointing him, "for" said he, "I would cut my bones for him ; and if he had sent his dog for it, he should have had it" '.[12]

The identification in 1779 of a core of family names, which were to last through into the early twentieth century, is one of the unifying threads of this book. As has been noted, three-quarters of them were still there in 1841 by which time the population was almost exactly double. Four surnames had been lost and nine gained. But of the fifteen households these nine new names represented, only seven were crofters. The other half included the minister, cottars and tradesmen, such as tailors, weavers and shoemakers, needed to serve the much bigger population. Those who worked the land were predominantly the long-established families. The 1779 list therefore records an agricultural tenantry who were to provide a substantial line of continuity through the period of major reorganisation in the late eighteenth and early nineteenth centuries.

The Local Economy:
Expansion and Reform

Rent was paid from the sale of cattle and surplus grain and as a rule Iona had the capacity to meet this without undue difficulty. Boswell noted: 'Icolmkill pays £150 of rent. They sell about 40 cattle and more than 150 bolls of barley'. And Heron stated twenty-one years later: '. . . such is its fertility that it affords a considerable exportation, as well of barley and oats as of cattle'.[1]

Visitors had long remarked upon the abundance of Iona's natural resources. Dean Monro in 1549 talked of: 'Sanct Colm's ile, ane faire mayne ile of twa mile lange and maire, and ane mile braid, fertil land fruitful of corne and store, and guid for fishing'.[2] There were three mentions of the island in MacFarlane's collection of topographical descriptions gathered in the seventeenth century, including: 'It is the most profitable and fertilest of all these Countries' and: 'The Ile is fruitful and has plaine arable ground in good measure . . . The product and chief commoditie is barley . . .'.[3] Dr John Walker's report on agriculture throughout the Hebrides gave a favourable account of Iona:

> A light sandy soil prevails over the whole island, which in some places however is very fertile. Upon the Sea Shore especially, there are some small Plains, exceedingly pleasant that afford good Crops of Bear and Oats. The Hills are covered with a fine Verdure and afford a very rich dry Pasture, for Black Cattle and Sheep. Some of the Hills are arable to the Top, but those on the South End of the Island are over run with Heath; yet the small Valleys interspersed among them are filled with Grass of finest Quality. The heat of the Summer, with the warm nature of the Soil proves sufficient to produce more early Crops than in most parts of Britain. For though the People are very late in sowing their Grain, they have always Harvested early in August.

Walker also noted that Donald Campbell the tacksman had experimented in Iona with bere or bear (an early four-rowed form of barley) and having found that it gained him a third more yield there he then introduced it to Tiree.[4]

Barley and bere were mentioned consistently by observers as doing well and it was the staple grain. Oats were sown also but to a lesser degree and, according to some, with less success as it was not a crop well suited to sandy soil. The remains of an 'àtha' or circular drying kiln for grain may still be detected in a field just north of Achabhaich, close to where the East End tacksman's byre stood. Potatoes had been brought from Ireland to South Uist in 1743 but it was not until the 1770s that they spread rapidly to their dominant position in the Hebridean diet. By the *OSA* of 1795 potatoes were described as 'the principal food of the inhabitants' in the Ross of Mull and Iona.

On 9 July 1772 Pennant described the land as he saw it in Iona:

> The soil is a compound of sand and comminuted sea shells, mixed with black loam; is very favourable to the growth of bear, natural clover, crowsfoot and daisies. It is in perpetual tillage and is ploughed thrice before sowing: the crops at this time made a promising appearance, but the seed was committed to the ground at very different times; some I think about the beginning of May and some not three weeks ago.

The swift growing season was also referred to in the *OSA*, along with the 'singular' method of sowing barley in Iona: 'The barley is sown before the ground is ploughed, and then they plough the ground over it. This prevents the grain being bared, by high winds drifting the sand off it. This mode was undoubtedly introduced by necessity and answers very well'.[5]

The stock reared was primarily cattle, the 'great herds of cows' feeding near the sea which Sacheverell saw in 1688. Pennant put the head of cattle in Iona at 108 and the number of sheep at 500 but this sounds like an overestimate of the latter. These proportions resemble the souming of a hundred years later when five sheep equalled one cow. ('Souming' was the process by which was determined the 'soum' or number of stock each tenant was allowed to graze on the common. One cow was equivalent to so many sheep, a calculation that varied from locality to locality and at different periods.) According to the *OSA*, the ancient souming of the parish had placed sheep on a one-to-one basis with cattle. In any case, up to the late eighteenth century sheep in this area were of the small native breed and kept, a few per household, mainly for wool and the occasional piece of mutton. Both the *OSA* in 1795 and J. Smith's report for the Board of Agriculture in 1813, refer to stocks of the larger, hardier, Lowland sheep having been 'lately' introduced into the parish.[6] The minister considered this 'among the improvements of the country' in 1795 but Sarah Murray's observations in 1802 imply that this change did not extend to Iona: 'Cattle are fed on I-Columbkill but sheep are forbidden by the proprietor, on account of the smallness of the island. A very few sheep are, however, reared on Iona; but it is in secret'.[7] This is a curious comment and the writer does not enlighten us as to how she became privy to such information. In any event, sheepwalks did not encroach upon Iona as they were beginning to do at this period in parts of Mull and elsewhere in the Highlands. Nor did the balance between the numbers of cattle and sheep kept on the island change until very much later in the nineteenth century.

Nine households in the 1779 list had extra help in the form of herds or maids, required for Iona's pastoral economy. The dietary main-stays of dairy produce and barley were sampled by several visitors to the island. The breakfast provided for Johnson and Boswell consisted of milk, cheese, eggs, bread and butter. At this period in the High-lands 'bread' meant the flat bannocks made on a girdle with barley-meal or oatmeal. When James Bailey visited Iona in 1787 he took bread with him from Mull, in case such an item was scarce, but he was pleasantly surprised: 'Milk at least we might calculate upon but we might have spared our solicitude as neither this nor many other articles were wanting. . . . Our hostess . . . made a large cheese-cake for supper after which we had plentiful beverage of milk'.[8] Many years earlier, in 1760, Bishop Pococke had been offered the traditional greeting of a drink of milk:

> In I-Colm Kill, when I went into a poor house with the Bailie of Terre-I a woman brought in a wooden vessel of new Milk and drank to the Bailie who performed the same ceremony to me and so it went round. After we had viewed everything, I was con-ducted to a house where Eggs, Cheese, Butter and Barley Cake were served and a large bowl of Curds.[9]

A rural society of this period was necessarily highly self-sufficient. There was little, if any, extra cash with which to purchase goods once the rent was paid and the only means of trading with other places was by sail, horseback or on foot. In 1773 Boswell was impressed by the people's ability to provide most of their needs:

> . . . and what is remarkable, they brew a good deal of beer, which I could not find was done in any of the other isles. I was told they imported nothing but salt and iron. Salt they might soon make. It is a very fertile island, and the people are industrious. They make their own woollen and linen webs, and indeed I suppose everything else, except for any hardware for which they may have occasion. They have no shoes for their horses.[10]

Fifteen years later, in October 1788, a visitor believed to be of the Marquess of Bute's family filled several pages of a journal with notes on many aspects of social and material conditions in Iona. The telegraphic style of his jottings gives the impression of a camera's eye, capturing a picture of life on the island at that particular moment. Although such a picture was in some respects limited and may have been embellished by the writer's imagination, the details recorded are numerous and vivid. Taken together, they do put some flesh on the statistical bones of the 1779 list, barely a decade earlier.

The journal stated that there were 'thirty-six tenants at will not all equally'. That is, their security depended on the will of the landlord and their share of the land varied. At Martinmas and Whitsun they went over to Mull to pay the Duke's steward their rent, which totalled £180. They ate little meat, lived on fish (especially salt ling and cod), barley bread and made good use of milk. The island could also yield lobster and crabs and wild geese in autumn but it had no game or fresh water fish in the two lochs nor fruits of any sort. People grew many potatoes but gave the small oats to the cattle. The drovers came for these at Whitsun, paying three or five pounds. Horses were bred in the island and the best were worth six guineas. Women made stockings and plaids, men brogues and belts and a tailor came from Mull when needed. As there was no shop, pedlars came too, from all quarters every month, to 'supply their other wants and drain the money'. An alehouse sold whisky, brandy and rum but no beer. (Whether this was because the people still brewed it themselves, as Boswell had found, or because the extra barley now went entirely for export is not known.) But there was great sobriety. One old woman had reached one hundred but the people commonly lived only to sixty or seventy years. There were no magistrates or medicines and sickness – fevers and consumption in particular – prevailed in Spring. But the women married at twenty, the men rather older and the village was already 'prolific' and the 'natives increasing'. Their fires burned peat fetched from Mull and their lamps oil from saith or seals, whose skin could be sold to pedlars. The turn of the seasons was orderly. In March they ploughed, in May and June they sowed and in September they reaped their crop with the sickle. And as the long dark nights of winter closed in, 'from 1st October to end January', the men seldom stirred from their hearths and the women never.

The journal did not describe the houses themselves but other travellers made passing mention of them as low, small and stone-built, with a roof of straw thatch or turf and the fire in the centre of the floor. The peat in the Lochan Mòr below Dùn I was largely used up in medieval times and then abandoned, although it served again for a few years after John Maclean drained it in the late 1730s. When Garnett arrived in 1798 and enquired for the schoolmaster, he was told 'that he had gone over to Mull to dig his peats'. All the islanders had to do this as Sarah Murray described :

There are no trees on the island, nor fuel of any sort. At the proper season the inhabitants cross over to Ross, where they find plenty of peat mosses. From these mosses or black bog, they cut, dry, and pile vast quantities of peat and let them remain in stacks upon the mosses until completely fit for use; they then set all their boats and hands to work to convey their yearly store of fuel across the sound to their houses.[11]

In 1752 the third Duke wrote to his factor: 'You are to make enquiry what farms of mine in Mull and Morven have valuable shoars of wreck for making kelp'.[12] The 1750s saw the beginnings of a kelping industry on the west coast, following its introduction on the east coast and in Orkney in the 1720s. The alkaline ash resulting from burned seaweed could be used in various manufacturing processes including glass- and soap-making. The boom years for Highland kelp were to come in the first two decades of the nineteenth century when foreign imports disappeared during the Napoleonic Wars and salt duties restricted the development of substitutes. By 1810 kelp was reaching £20 a ton and as the costs of labour and freight generally remained stable such prices brought spectacular profits to some landlords.[13]

Before this period, however, it was a less dependable enterprise. 'The price of no commodity in the country varies so much as that of kelp. It sometimes rises to £8 a ton and sometimes falls as low as 50/-' wrote the parish minister for Ross and Iona in 1795. But he also acknowledged its importance in the economy: 'Kelp is of great consequence to the Highlands in particular and of some to the kingdom in general. The manufacturing of it employs many of the natives; the price it draws brings money to the country, . . .'.[14] This summed up the attractions of the industry. It was very labour-intensive and could earn for the tenants useful extra cash for their rents. Maintaining a workforce, in order to maximise the potential of this abundant resource on their coastal estates, was a major reason why many landlords opposed emigration in the eighteenth century and seemed oblivious to the consequences of their burgeoning populations on limited areas of land.

In the absence of tacksmen, the Iona tenants dealt directly with the Estate in kelping transactions. According to Sarah Murray: 'The Duke of Argyle (I have been assured) suffers his tenants to burn, if they please, all the kelp on their farms for their own emolument'. The OSA explained that every farm in the parish, except for four small ones, had a share in the shore which was also of value for gathering seaware and shell sand as fertiliser and

Table 1.

West End Tenants:	East End Tenants:
1788 : 23 tons 4 cwt	1788 : 8 tons 19 cwt
1789 : 11 tons 4½ cwt	1789 : 8 tons
1790 : 7 tons 10½ cwt	1790 : 3 tons 16 cwt

for their cattle to eat wrack. James Maxwell, the Duke's Chamberlain for Mull and Morvern, set out the advantages to the small tenants :

> . . . they work their shore themselves and where these produce any considerable quantities of kelp the manufacturing of it furnishes employment to them at their doors during a time of the year at which the other labour of their farms does not require so much of their attention ; and if they can have the expense of their summer meal clear for their work it is a better object to them than if they got higher wages for working to another at a greater distance from home.[15]

The season was May or June until mid-August, months when the spring work of ploughing and planting was over. The previous year's store of meal was also probably exhausted and the new harvest not yet gathered. A source of ready cash will thus have been welcome, to buy meal for the summer. It was not, however, easy work. The weed first had to be cut from the rocks and dragged, wet and heavy, ashore. It was spread out on the grass to dry then placed in a kiln – an oblong stone trench or a circle – with a turf layer on the bottom. The burning might take four to eight hours and the weed had to be checked and raked constantly to keep a steady, intense flame at the heart of the mass. Finally it had to be pounded with clubs to form a pasty substance which, twenty-four hours later, had cooled sufficiently to break into brittle lumps for delivery to dealers. By this time it weighed only one-twentieth of the original seaweed, indicating the huge quantities that had to be gathered.

The weed itself varied in suitability. The *OSA* states that button wrack and lady wrack were the kinds used in the parish, producing the best kelp. And according to Maxwell, 'the kelp made upon the island of Icolmkill being chiefly manufactured from tangle and drift ware varies in quantity according as the season happens to be more or less favourable for throwing the seaware upon the beach'. Table 1 shows the amount made over three years on the island. Ships came from Oban to take away the kelp for merchants in Liverpool. No account was kept for 1791 but it was generally a year of very low prices. In 1790 a ton from Mull fetched £5–£6 but by 1792 this had dropped to £3–£4. In Iona in 1792 'the tenants have not made an ounce of kelp but used all the seaware for manure which is perhaps as profitable a way of employing a great part of it'. This may have been partly due to the fluctuating prices but it also fitted in with the general practice of not cutting every third year to allow the weed to grow again. Kelping certainly continued in Iona as an additional activity to agriculture. Both Garnett in 1798 and Leyden in 1800 observed kelp-makers at work on the shore as they approached, implying the east side of the island. The rocky gullies of the west coast were also productive, as Bailey noticed in 1787 : 'Kelp has of late years become a very lucrative article as the rocks on the back of the island are peculiarly abundant in the wrack from which it is manufactured'. A stone circle survives above Sloc nam Ball on the west coast, prob-ably the remains of a kelp kiln.

While embracing the opportunity which kelp afforded, the fifth Duke was anxious to diversify the economic base of his Estate in more reliable directions. In 1785 he issued clear instructions with regard to one of the obvious occupations of an island community : 'You must try to get a few good fishers to settle in Icolmkill and other parts of my property to instruct the tenants in fishing'.[16] The Cham-berlain acted promptly and was able to report the following year that John MacDonald, a skilled fisher from Uist, was settled in Creich, a new village of twelve lots set up on the Mull side of the Sound of Iona. He was given an advance of £25 sterling to purchase boat, lines and nets. The village is known today as Kentra.

It is reasonable to assume that the islanders had long fished in their immediate waters for their own consumption. It was probably a communal activity, as was traditional in the Hebrides, with four or six men sharing a boat and its catch. But the Duke's plans were of a more ambitious order. His aim to put fishing on a commercial footing in the area was supported by the recently established British Society for Extending the Fisheries, of which he was a Governor. After a tour of Mull, Iona and Tiree in 1785 their reporter wrote : 'Few places seem to me better situated for a fishing station than Iona. The banks all round the island, according to the accounts we received from the natives are well stocked with fish and the seas in general, especially towards the coast of Mull, much less turbulent than those parts on the West coast . . .'. The island did lack a natural, safe harbour but the two sheltered creeks on the Mull side of the narrow Sound would mostly remedy this disadvantage.[17]

Over the next two years Tobermory, Kinlochspelvie and Bunessan were identified by the Society as the best spots for the storehouses and Bunessan was considered especially suitable due to the herring shoals in Loch Laich each season. Initially the Duke was optimistic about the Sound of Iona fishery despite 'the aversion of the natives to the business'. He was determined to pursue the idea and if the locals continued refractory, then more people could be brought in from outside. Indeed, he approved of the action of Col. Campbell at Creich who had already removed three tenants as an example.

In March 1789 four Creich fishermen received £2.10.5 each from the Estate for their share of five hundred dried ling taken by their boat the previous summer. The same month, the Chamberlain asked the fishing agent at Creich to instruct the locals in the best methods of curing, drying and storing fish. He continued:

> You are to let it be known immediately, by an advertisement at the church doors, that all persons residing upon His Grace's estate who are willing to furnish themselves with fishing boats and tackling will be supplied with salt at Creich; and that all well cured, marketable dried ling fish which they shall bring to you in the course of the ensuing season will be taken off their hands at Creich at the rate of £14 per ton and whatever more the price which can be got for them at market will afford.

Fishing materials were to be supplied and, as further encouragement, up to one stone per week of oatmeal in proportion to the quantity of fish they lodged in the store. The Estate also employed James Lamont in Creich to make and repair fishing boats. Further attempts were made to attract experienced fishermen from elsewhere. In 1788 John Stout arrived in Creich from Shetland and remained. Two years later nine Shetlanders were brought to the area at the Duke's expense but they decided not to settle.

By this time the Chamberlain's reports were pessimistic about the poor return on the fishing investment. Despite all the incentives it had not become the thriving concern first envisaged. The parish minister corroborated this view in the *OSA* and dwelt at length on the problems encountered – distance from markets, low prices, the salt laws which obliged some to go to Oban to obtain salt, the severe weather, the conflict between the best cod fishing season and the busiest farming time and even the possibility that the local stocks had been overestimated. He praised the Duke and the Creich farmer Col. Campbell for their valiant efforts to develop fishing for the benefit of the community and regretted that it was now 'followed only as a by-job'.

Several travellers remarked that flax grew particularly well on Iona. Two place-names, unmapped but known in oral tradition, indicate that it must once have been cropped regularly – Strath na Lìn (vale or meadow of the flax) and Caol Lìn (narrow place of the flax), both in the West End of the island.[18] In 1750 John Maclean had set the tenants to spinning, for a type of coarse linen called Ozenburgh (after the German town of Osnabruck). But this ceased after he lost the tack. The fifth Duke decided that it might again be a useful form of employment for his increasingly populous island and in 1792 he wrote:

> I think much of the rent of that island Icolmkill should be paid in linin yarn or cloth as the land is fit to raise flax and there are many idle women. Another part should be paid in woollen yarn. Prepare a scheme for this and take measures for having it executed, and as the island cannot possibly support so many inhabitants without some industry of this sort, all who are refractory must be sent away.[19]

The following year the Chamberlain delivered to the schoolmaster in Iona two hundredweight of dressed flax and a list of twenty-six heads of families among whom it was to be distributed.[20] Twenty-five of them were named as tenants and one as cottar. Wheels and reels were loaned and one of each would be given to the best spinner as a premium. Wages would be one shilling for every four hanks of marketable yarn, paid either in cash or deducted from the rent. Although this wage might seem low, the Chamberlain urged the women to persevere. He explained that this experiment would be followed up by 'a more permanent and extensive plan' and that diligent work would bring the reward of useful additional earnings. By 1794 however he was obliged to report :

> It does not appear from the trial that has been made at Icolmkill that the buying of dressed flax and the employment of females to spin it, even on the most moderate wages, is a business that will defray its own expence. . . . there is a loss of about two Guineas by this experiment . . .

He suggested that for this enterprise to pay its way would require the provision of seed so that the islanders could grow and prepare the flax themselves, but there is no indication in the *Instructions* whether this was attempted. It appears more likely that the plan was abandoned.

Another short-lived commercial venture was the quarrying of marble. On the south-east coast of Iona is an outcrop of a forsterite tremolite-marble, mainly white but streaked with light-green serpentine. It has been quarried up to a hundred yards inland and is believed to have been worked sporadically from medieval times or earlier. The white marble altar which survived in the Cathedral up to the mid-eighteenth century was of local origin. The marble was hailed as a find in 1789, however, by Rudolph Erich Raspe who made a survey of mines and quarries on the Argyll Estate that summer : '. . . and with heartfelt pleasure I congratulate Your Grace to the discovery of a noble white Marble Quarry of which I submit

a plan and section . . . Success therefore to this new Scotch Carrara!'
He described it as of close and fine grain, of uncommon hardness and
rising in great blocks.[21]

The *OSA* recorded that the quarry was opened 'some years ago'
but had not lasted long: 'A considerable quantity of marble was
quarried and sent to Leith and London; but after much money was
laid out, the quarry was given up, for some time at least. The marble is
said to be of excellent quality'. The Marble Company, set up under
the Duke's patronage, may well have found the location – over
untracked hill ground and on a rocky coastline – too inaccessible for
efficient operation. There are no mentions of its fortunes in the
Instructions to the Duke's Chamberlain over these few years, except
for a retrospective one in 1794: '. . . and that the Marble Company's
store-house which is now not wanted for its original purpose, should
be repaired and fitted up for a place to teach in'. The foundations of a
building twelve by five metres lie on the slope leading down to the
quarry. It is called Tobhta nan Sassunaich (ruined buildings of the
lowlanders) and probably housed the workmen brought in, with
their specialist skills, from outside the island.

The twenty-five years after 1779 offer an unusually accurate
series of population figures. The *OSA* included two, one made by
the minister in 1782 and one by the schoolmaster in 1791. Visitors
played an important part as they always talked with the school-
master/guide, who was usually the only English-speaker and who
was in the habit of taking a census every two years on behalf of the
minister.

Iona was increasingly becoming a focus of interest for travellers,
particularly after the naturalist Sir Joseph Banks had measured, and
relayed to a curious public, the natural wonders of nearby Staffa. Dr
Johnson's account of his Scottish tour, published in 1775, became a
best seller and undoubtedly inspired many to follow in his steps.
One result of this attention, which concerned successive Dukes, was
alarm at the state of the ecclesiastical and historical remains. They
were subject to unrestrained weeds, wandering cattle, plundering
for building material, as well as the harsh elements of wind and rain.
In 1757 the enclosure of the ruins was a stipulation by the third
Duke on renewing the tenants' tacks. By the fifth Duke's time a
more substantial wall was required, as he instructed his chamberlain
in 1789: 'Get an estimate also of the expence of inclosing the ruins
at Icolmkill as you say strangers are much hurt at seeing them so
much neglected . . .'. And in 1797 a stern warning was issued:
'Inform the tenants of Icolmkill that I am resolved to put a stop to
the practice of carrying away stones from the ruins of the religious

houses in that island, and that all who shall hereafter transgress in this respect will certainly be removed'.

Removal was more commonly threatened than practised by the fifth Duke. The parish minister confirmed this: 'There is another reason why population should increase upon the Duke of Argyll's property. From his estate, small tenants are never removed, while they behave properly'.[22] There was one example, in 1799, of behaviour which the Duke did not condone:

> I cannot but greatly blame the people of Icolmkill for refusing to allow their sons to go into the militia . . . and as a mark of my displeasure I desire that Archibald McInnes and his son, Hugh McDonald and Donald McKillop, all of that island, who were concerned in beating and abusing Hector McPhail, employed to take up the lists of young men for the militia, be removed from their possessions at Whitsunday next, as I will suffer no person to remain upon my property who does not respect and obey the laws . . .[23]

Such disaffection, although rare, was clearly not allowed to pass unheeded and by the following October the Chamberlain reported that the three had been removed and 'fencible soldiers put in their place'. One of these is known to have been Coll MacDonald whose descendants possess a petition from Coll's son Alexander stating that his father had 'received half a croft in the West End of Iona for his services in the 5th Argyllshire Regiment of Fencible Infantry'. The others may have been an Allan Morison, entered in the parish register of 1804 as 'soldier' and, from the same source in 1806, a Malcolm MacInnes of the 'Private Argyleshire Militia'.

Neither compulsory nor voluntary removal were factors affecting the number of inhabitants in the late eighteenth century. The minister stated in the *OSA* of 1795 that 'a few families have emigrated to America within these few years', although he did not specify from which part of his large parish they left. He added that in 1792 several families had gone to seek work in the Lowlands, 'to cotton works etc' but most returned the next year having found the same 'want of employment' as at home and being drawn back by deep attachment to their native parish. Seasonal migration from the Highlands to Lowland mills and farms will be dealt with more fully in a later chapter. It was already significant by this period but not until the second half of the nineteenth century did it become a permanent movement.

The graph on page 36 illustrates the steady upward trend of the population from 1779. Between then and 1791 there was a thirty per cent rise in Iona as compared with twenty per cent in the same period

36

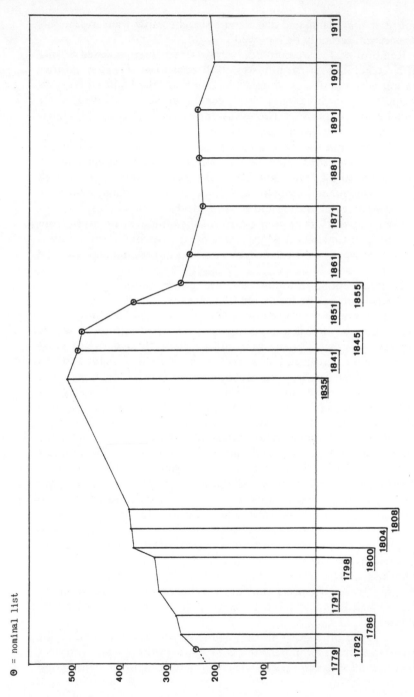

$\odot$ = nominal list

Figure 2. Population graph.

in the Argyll Estate as a whole. There was a particularly sharp jump of twelve per cent in just two years at the very end of the century. In the twenty-one years from 1779 to 1800 there was an increase of fifty-one per cent in the numbers of the inhabitants.

The minister noted that deaths from smallpox had been greatly reduced since the people of Ross, Brolas and Iona began to inoculate their children. He also attributed the growing numbers to natural increase and a benevolent attitude by the Duke toward his tenantry :

> The reason of the increase of population in this parish is common to it with the rest of the Hebrides. Few leave the country, if they can procure a house, which is easily built, with a spot of ground for crop and a cow's grass. All marry young, and being healthy, their progeny is numerous. The parents also, that their children might settle in the country and near them, often share their lands with them, whether male or female . . . It is no secret in the country that his Grace continued their farms to small tenants, at the former rent, though large augmentations were offered by gentlemen who were better able to pay their rents more punctually.

The minister was aware, however, of the vulnerability of such a populous area, dependent on subsistence agriculture. In 1791 the crops had failed, bringing severe difficulties to the parish and necessitating the importation of meal. 'Perhaps by a better mode of agriculture' he ventured, 'the parish might in general serve itself, particularly Ross and the island of I'.[24]

At the heart of the fifth Duke's zeal for improving his Estate was a reorganisation of the agricultural system. His attempts to broaden the economy in Iona, through kelping, fishing, flax spinning and quarrying had met with varying success but they had all been intended as adjuncts to, and not substitutes for, the basic activity of working the land.

One anomaly to be settled first was the division of the island, the two parts of the East End being still intersected by the West End :

> It is humbly Proposed,in order to accommodate the tenants of both farms and to prevent disputes which happen every day owing to the cattle of the one farm driving through the grass and corns of the other, that the island should be divided into two, as equal halves as possible and a march dyke built betwixt them.[25]

The correspondence over this new division lasted from 1785 until 1792, during which time the tenants gradually built a stone dyke running from the Machair shore west of Cùlbhuirg, through Gleann an Teampuill, over the north side of Cnoc Mòr to behind where the Church of Scotland Manse stands today. A narrow right of way leading through the present village to the shore marks the continuation of this boundary between the East End and the West End.

In 1783, a year of great scarcity due to crop failures, the rents received throughout the Mull and Morvern Estate were very low. A letter from the Chamberlain in 1789 about the dyke in Iona made clear that the tenants there, crowded together and working such small patches of land, would not bear any additional rent for the outlay 'as it is with difficulty they are able to pay what is laid upon them already'. These twin pressures of a steadily rising population and the Estate's continuing need for revenue lent urgency to the situation.

There was no lack of 'improving' literature aimed at the landlords of the time and the observers' principal target was what they regarded as an antiquated system of communal farming. Garnett's comments on Iona were an example:

> Where there is any arable ground, the farmers run-rig as it is called; . . . This mode of letting arable ground to several tenants . . . prevents those improvements which would otherwise be introduced. This island, from the nature of its soil, seems much more capable of improvement by cultivation than any part of Mull; but this can never take place to any considerable extent, till the tenants have leases and comfortable cottages, instead of the wretched hovels which they inhabit.[26]

The fifth Duke did not in fact need the advice. Along with the Earl of Breadalbane, he was already leading the way among Highland landlords in ordering the enclosure of land and its apportionment into separate lots or crofts. The process of improvement had been under way from the late 1770s in Tiree, where there was resistance at first to such a radical change from the traditional organisation, but eventual acceptance that to work the same piece of land each year was an advantage. Some years later J. Smith supported the progress that had been made in another part of the Duke's Estate:

> The Duke of Argyll has been for many years carrying on this system on his estate in Kintyre; and it has been attended with the happiest consequences. The land is better improved and the tenants are in a better condition. When everyone has thus his own division and all contiguous to him, a farm is made to produce more than double of what it did under the old run-rig system.[27]

The turn of Iona came in 1800, when the Duke wrote to his Chamberlain James Maxwell:

> Being satisfied that it will be of great advantage towards the improvement of my estates in Mull and Morvern if the small tenants were led to divide their farms, or at least the arable parts

IONA

<u>Township Divisions</u>

(1) <u>Pre-1795</u> :

☐ 1 East End

☐ 2 West End

▨ 3 Sliabh Meadhonach
       (middle moorland)
       held in common

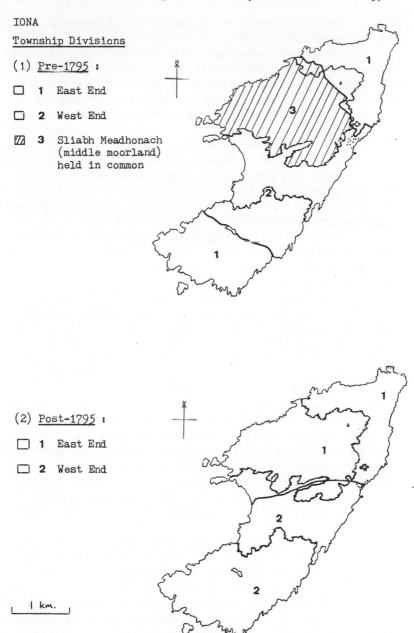

(2) <u>Post-1795</u> :

☐ 1 East End

☐ 2 West End

Figure 3. East/West End divisions pre- and post-1795.

of them, and every man to build his house upon his own particular lot, you will turn your attention to this object and report to me next year what farms you think may admit of this kind of management. I am aware that much cannot be expected from small tenants in this way whilst they possess from year to year, but I will agree to give leases for nine years and to help such of them as shall undertake to divide their farms and sit down upon the separate lots.[28]

In March 1802 a Decreet of Removing was served on the tenants by the Duke of Argyll and his Mull Chamberlain.[29] This was the legal step required before relocating the people on the new lots. From a later memorial it is clear that the first leases ran from 1802 until 1811. During 1803 and 1804 Maxwell reported that the tenants were gradually marking out the boundaries of their crofts and by 10 May 1804 he was able to write: 'The field labour of the season being now almost over I expect they will go on according to their abilities to finish what still remains to be executed of the fences necessary for completing the division of their farms'.

Contemporary accounts spoke highly of the fifth Duke's benevolence: '. . . I cannot, and ought not, to withhold my admiration of the noble proprietor of I-Ona, Ross of Mull etc for his goodness to his dependant people there, and elsewhere, who look upon him as a benign father rather than master; and well may they do so, for there cannot be a better landlord in every respect'.[30] Fully a generation had passed since Johnson and Boswell's observations that the Iona people were still loyal to the Macleans. It is surely no coincidence that their attitude to their Campbell landlords appears to have warmed and strengthened during the years of the fifth Duke's reforms. He was the first President of the Highland Society, founded in 1784, reflecting his status as a leader of the economic revolution in the Highlands. As Eric Cregeen noted, the fact that this revolution ultimately failed in its objective 'to preserve the southern Highlands from depopulation and decay' does not detract from the significance of what the fifth Duke was attempting to achieve.[31]

Three generations later, the eighth Duke recalled that his grandfather's consistent aim had been to bring his people into the age of improvement while keeping them on the land and to that end: 'He wished the tenants to live plentifully and happily'.[32] The making of the crofts was a central part of that effort and marked the opening of a new era. In Iona the pattern of land-holding thus established has lasted, in its essential form, up to the present day.

Section II

1802–1840

3

The Making of the Crofts

The term 'croft', meaning a small piece of land, occurs occasionally in
Argyll Estate Papers in relation to Iona prior to the reorganisation of
1802. From that date, however, it is consistently applied to the
smallholdings created under the new system and those tenants who
worked them become known as 'crofters'.

The croft divisions marked out in Iona between 1802 and 1804
remained intact until the late 1840s, when the potato famine was to
precipitate considerable emigration and some redistribution of land.
They were thus in place when the first nominal Census was taken in
1841 and when the Estate accounts began to feature lists of tenants
from 1846. Although by that period subdivision had resulted in a
greater number of crofters than there were individual holdings, these
sources do help to identify the original pattern. To this may be added
local knowledge of where the first boundaries ran and of surviving
dyke or house foundations.

From all of this evidence it may with confidence be assumed that
Iona was laid out into thirty lots. This is corroborated by two
visitors. Sarah Murray described the island in 1802 as 'subdivided
into about thirty farms' and the information obtained in 1893 by
Malcolm Ferguson, who used a local guide for much of his detailed
account, was that around the beginning of the century Iona was
'divided into thirty separate small farms or crofts'. This division is
reconstructed in Map 2.

There is no available Estate record of the total number of rent-
paying tenants, or crofters, in 1802. It may have been higher than
thirty as some crofts may have been shared by two or more families
from the start. A guide to the minimum number is provided by the
Old Parochial Register (OPR), in which the minister began recording
marriages and baptisms for Kilfinichen and Kilviceuen from 1804.
Up until 1811, which covers the period of the first crofting leases,
twenty-eight entries for Iona were designated 'tenant'. There must
therefore have been at least this number of couples, of marriageable
and child-bearing age, working the land. Registration was not, of
course, mandatory at this period but, as I have noted in the Introduction the Iona OPR is considered to have been fairly accurately kept in

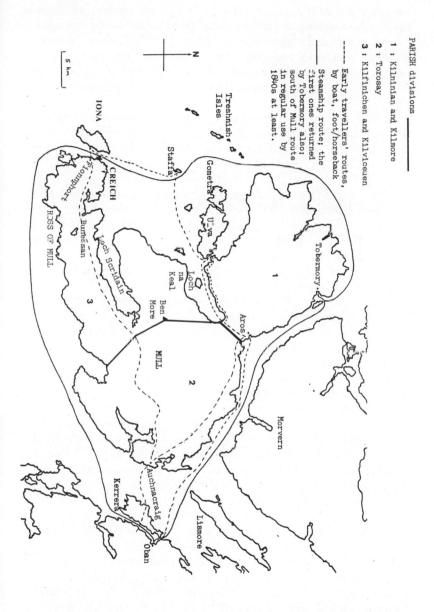

Map 2. Iona and Mull including part of mainland, showing parish divisions and travellers' routes.

the early part of the century. A sign that people *were* eager to have their children baptised may be gleaned from Sarah Murray's account, two years before the O P R began. After her party's dinner on Iona, the minister, who had accompanied them from Mull, was asked to carry out six baptisms since 'the poor folks were glad of the opportunity afforded them by Mr Campbell's unexpected appearance among them'.

From the Chamberlain's reports, it clearly took several years after the granting of the leases for the boundaries to be secured by stone dykes and then, after that, for the croft houses to be built. Necker de Saussure, in 1807, remarked on this:

> The houses, instead of being placed on the farm grounds, are all built in the form of a village in the eastern part of the island. Thus the inhabitants live very near each other and often at a considerable distance from the place they cultivate: this custom is justly considered as disadvantageous to themselves and to the prosperity of the isle in general.[1]

This disadvantage had probably been rectified by 1809 when the Chamberlain referred to the expense and effort of the tenantry throughout the Mull Estate in constructing their new houses.

The final stage in the physical reorganisation of the island was the relocation of the non-crofting inhabitants into one village street, laid out facing the sea above Port Rònain. An account in 1814 of '. . . a scattered village at the landing place directly above which are the ruins of the Monastery' is still reminiscent of the eighteenth century descriptions.[2] Not until the 1820s do contemporary reports clearly imply that the village houses were in their new layout.

The houses for two or more neighbouring crofts were at first built close together. The 1841 Census illustrates these clusters, particularly in the East End where the enumerator listed six out of the fifteen holdings by name with between two and five households on each. This pattern is backed up by oral tradition, for example that the MacFarlanes and the MacArthurs originally lived next to each other at Clachanach. There is also evidence on the ground, such as the traces of house foundations on Cnoc Cùl Phàil croft. These lie nearer to the Achabhaich house than do the present buildings.

One of the improvements expected of the new system was the construction of more substantial dwellings, to replace the 'wretched hovels' deplored by Garnett. A sketch of an original croft house at Clachanach has survived, drawn by Sir Henry Dryden, who was present during the repair work on the Cathedral in the mid-1870s. It was by then in use as a byre but the drawing and notes indicate that it was sturdily built, with clay-mortared walls of granite boulders and the traditional features of opposed doorways in the side walls, a central hearth and a smoke outlet in the ridge of the roof. There was no gable end and the hip roof was of straw thatch secured by straw or heather ropes. An early Valentine postcard shows a house at Sligineach, also of this older design.

During this first decade of the nineteenth century it is likely that a section of the population, who did not gain a foothold on the land during the agricultural reorganisation, was squeezed out. An examination of the O P R gives some indication of such adjustment. Between 1804 and 1811 a total of sixty-four couples were named. Twenty-eight were identified as tenants. The remaining thirty-six were either not identified or entered as cottar or by occupation – weaver, fisher, boat carpenter, herd. Out of this non-tenant category, thirteen were still on the island after 1811 and formed the nucleus of the new village population. But out of the total sixty-four couples, two tenants and twenty-three non-tenants disappear from the Register by 1811 after only one or two entries. Where these were older couples, of course, their families may simply have been completed, but the majority were newly married. In five cases the husband was from outside Iona and it is reasonable to assume that he returned with his wife to his own district. Six of the others have been traced to the Ross of Mull, where they reappear as crofting tenants.

Of the young tenant families identified over the same period in Iona, only two moved *into* that class from another occupation. Dugald Campbell was listed as boatman in 1804 but tenant in 1809. William MacFarlane was a cottar in 1807 and a tenant by 1814. In the two cases mentioned above, of tenants disappearing from the O P R, they were both couples already married before 1804 and the baptism entries may have been those of their last child. They did not necessarily leave the island.

The implication is that the tenantry was now stable but that a number of those *not* allocated crofts moved, to seek land or an alternative occupation elsewhere. One may have been the father of an Ayrshire weaver who, as a young man in the mid-1830s, was driven from that county for lack of work and 'wandered into this country [the Ross of Mull] because his father had been born in Iona'.[3]

Some movement in and out of the parish has already been noted in the previous section. The population was never entirely static during the period under study. The turnover of surnames between 1779 and the first years of the O P R was however very small, with the core names still overwhelmingly predominant. A few names had disappeared, such as Buie, MacCallum and MacKay. A few others came in, for example MacGilvra and MacPhail, and some made a

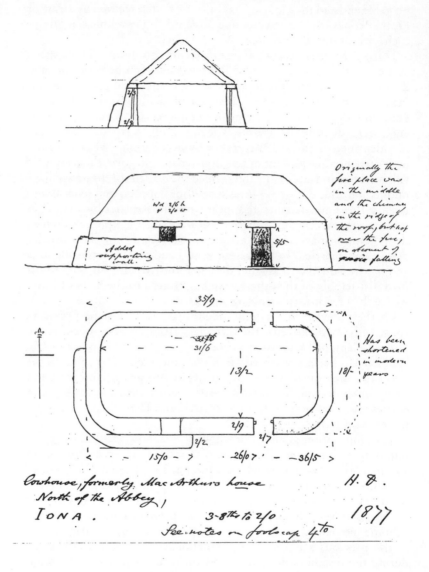

Figure 4. Dryden sketch of original croft house.

Table 2.

East End of Icolmkill	65 men	79 women	80 children	224 total
West End of Icolmkill	51 men	59 women	50 children	160 total
	116 men	138 women	130 children	384 total

brief appearance, such as MacNaughton and McFee. The last name might have been Irish. A visitor in 1806 mentioned a couple 'whom the rest of the company would not associate with. They were Irish of profligate character who had lately come to Iona and were held in detestation by all the old inhabitants'.[4] It was the perception of them as of low virtue, rather than the fact that they were incomers, which appeared to provoke hostility and they may have been travellers or pedlars.

The lack of a death register for Iona before 1835 prevents calculation of the natural increase over this period. But MacInnes's demographic study of the island has estimated the crude birth rate in the first half of the nineteenth century at just under forty births per thousand, implying a high fertility rate. The same study has revealed that between 1804 and 1840 a high proportion of the female population married. The mean age at which they wed was twenty-three and their mean family size was seven and a half, the number of children ranging from two to twelve. Birth intervals were generally two to two and a half years indicating uncontrolled fertility. Spinsterhood and childless marriages were rare.

A study of the OPR entries demonstrates this steadily rising number of births. Between 1804 and 1811 ninety-nine baptisms were recorded and in the next ten years up to 1821 there were 186. The youthful proportion of the population was also rising, significantly for future trends. By 1804 thirty-three per cent were under twelve years, as compared to twenty-five per cent under ten in the 1791 analysis by the Minister.

The 1804 figure comes from a series of population counts made by the Estate that year in Mull, Iona and Lismore. The total was very close to that noted by James MacDonald four years later, and so almost certainly included cottars along with tenants in each of the two 'Ends' or townships. Children were calculated at twelve years and under (see Table 2).

In June 1805 the Duke's Chamberlain reported that he had just returned from collecting rents in the Ross division of the Estate, which included Iona : 'I have had no cause hitherto to complain of the payments made by Your Grace's tenants'.[5] Rents were clearly being met by the new crofting tenantry, despite a recent depression in cattle prices mentioned in the same report. This temporary setback had so far been balanced by abundant yields of grain and potatoes and good fishing for cod and ling.

There are several references in the Chamberlain's correspondence of this period to the considerable effort and outlay incurred by the tenants in the building of their new houses and boundary walls. The changes had also led to some anxiety about their future relationship to the landlord. This is reflected in a long memorial from the Chamberlain dated 30 September 1809 and addressed to the sixth Duke, who had inherited the Estate in 1806. It refers to all parts of the Mull and Morvern Estate where divisions into crofts had taken place.[6]

In anticipation of the expiry of their nine-year leases at Whitsunday 1811, the tenants were first of all 'apprehensive that the benefit of their labours may then be in hazard of being transferred to others'. This insecurity arose from the crowded state of their own districts, possibly to be aggravated by 'many desperate and needy men' driven from neighbouring estates to seek land and compete in the offering of rents. The higher prices that might result would leave the tenants 'in impending ruin' or force them to embrace 'the harsh alternative of forsaking their country to seek an asylum in a foreign land'. The Chamberlain counselled caution in accepting such 'offers of adventurers' but was equally concerned about the risk of 'old tenants not coming forward so freely with offers of rent as His Grace has a right to expect from them' or of their claiming preference due to long possession, fencible service or recent improvements. His suggestion was to assess the capacity of each holding in the rearing of cattle, growing of crop and production of kelp and so calculate the average return. He then concluded : 'With this information before him His Grace will be able to lay such adequate rents upon these farms as the separate divisions of each may be found to deserve and as the tenants by industrious management and with a reasonable chance of markets should be fairly able to pay'.

The Chamberlain's approach was thus neither to grasp an opportunity to reduce the population, nor to encourage an escalation in rents. Indeed, he stressed that imposing either of these courses on the tenants would not only offend the Duke's sense of humanity but would also 'ultimately be adverse to the true interest of his affairs'. This interest was, of course, to maintain income from the Estate, particularly through the lucrative kelp industry which required a large labour force. The Duke approved this proposed method of setting rents.

The memorial underlines the impact of the agricultural reorganisation taking place throughout the Highlands in this period. Its significance was obviously not lost on the tenants themselves. The movement of potential new tenants into their district was ascribed to 'the general policy observed by other proprietors in the management of their Estates'. If there was not sufficient land to go round, the prospect of emigration, though unwelcome, was real enough. An incentive of the new crofting system was that it allowed a tenant to work and improve the same piece of land each year. This benefit was undermined, in the crofters' eyes, if they did not have the relative security of a fair and stable rent. Their ability to meet that rent, and thus keep their holdings, depended both on agricultural productivity and on extra sources of income.

The link between a healthy population and a healthy agricultural base was made by an anonymous traveller in 1806 :

> It is a general observation that religious houses were always situated in a fertile country. Iona is said to be remarkably so . . . we saw excellent barley growing close to the walls of the monastery. . . . The island is very populous more so in proportion than any other of the Hebrides, the best proof of fertility in a country where there is no commerce and where all the inhabitants must be supported by the fruits of their own soil.[7]

And James MacDonald's description of Iona in 1808 echoed earlier reports of the quality of its natural resources. He mentioned the fine spring water, the generally mild climate, the light sandy soil and the good pasture.[8]

MacDonald's fact-finding tour that year for the Board of Agriculture stressed the role of cattle as the principal livestock throughout the Hebrides, where he estimated there were over a hundred thousand head. A fifth of these were exported to the mainland each year, fetching an average of five pounds per beast. The remainder contributed to the subsistence economy of the islands through milk, cheese and butter, some meat consumption and manure for the land. Sheep farming, however, was 'still followed only in a very few districts. Hebridean farmers never thought of rearing sheep with any other view than merely supplying their own families with wool and mutton'.

MacDonald was pleased to note that 'the ancient prejudice against pork' was now vanishing and that the valuable and cheaply fattened pigs could now be found, at least in the Southern Argyll islands 'and especially in the little but celebrated island of Icolm-kill'.

MacDonald's extensive observations on all aspects of crop husbandry laid particular emphasis on the potato. He estimated that one
acre of potatoes could support the same number of people as seven
and three-quarter acres of oats and he urged landowners to encourage
the cultivation of this cheap and excellent food. He confidently
asserted that 'many thousand acres in the Hebrides might undergo
this change and many thousands of the natives bless those who
should accomplish it'. Neither he nor the grateful natives were in a
position to appreciate the irony of this prediction. By this time the
potato was firmly established as a staple food, in Iona as elsewhere,
underpinning the viability of the smallholding system.

There is no sign that the problems which had attended the late
eighteenth century attempt to establish a commercial fishery in the
Sound of Iona were resolved. Between 1804 and 1840 only five men
were specified as fishers in the OPR and three of them moved away
from the island before 1810. Eight others were identified as boatmen
or boat carpenters but those skills were required for a greater range of
purposes, including the ferrying of peats from Mull and the transport
of people and livestock. Older inhabitants may have been partly or
fully employed in fishing but the smaller number of younger men,
with families to support, suggests that it was not a reliable means of
earning a livelihood.

Fishing for domestic consumption will have undoubtedly continued, however. Necker de Saussure, in 1807, noticed that some of
the people '. . . are attached to fishing, the environs furnish a prodigi-
ous amount of fish'. And a few years later John MacCulloch considered that they '. . . display an industry unusual in this country' in
the taking of fish.[9]

Self-sufficiency in basic foodstuffs was thus still evident in the
early part of the nineteenth century. Sale of stock contributed toward
the rents but additional sources of cash income were essential to
maintain payments.

Kelping continued to be of importance, until the end of the
Napoleonic Wars brought the lifting of duty on imported barilla for
glass- and soap-making and the collapse of the domestic industry. In
June 1805 the Mull Chamberlain wrote to the Duke: 'The price of
kelp is not yet ascertained but as the supply of barilla must be
circumscribed by the war with Spain this article of Highland produce
should be of greater value than it was last year'. In November that
year, in correspondence over accounts for kelp from his island
Estates, the Duke stated with satisfaction: 'If others do not receive
their rents by such prompt payments it is only because they do not
consist of kelp which by the diligence of the Chamberlains and the

good will of the merchants might be turned into money in the month of July'.

In 1806 visitors riding across Mull to Ulva Ferry were struck by visible signs of this activity: 'The rents are paid from grazing and kelp. This was the season for burning the kelp and the West side of the island seemed enveloped in one continued cloud of smoke'. And when Dugald Sinclair, the Baptist missionary, visited Iona in July 1814, he stayed an extra few days as 'many people were manufacturing their kelp' and could not attend the service when he arrived.[10]

In 1802 Sarah Murray mentioned 'the putrid fevers brought from the low countries' by harvesters returning to Iona and Ross. This was an unwelcome side-effect of what was another major source of income, seasonal harvest work in the Lowlands. She went on: 'A traveller in June will continually meet groups of Highlanders trudging south; the women with cloth cloaks on, bare feet and legs, their petticoats pinned up, their sickle on their arm...'. Twenty-five years later a Highland newspaper reported that in two weeks of August 'upwards of 2,500 Highland shearers passed through the Crinan Canal for the South, in the steamboats *Ben Nevis*, *Comet* and *Highlander*, from the islands of Mull, Skye etc'.[11] The temporary migration southward, from the late eighteenth century until well into the nineteenth, was particularly associated with Highland women at harvest time. But other farm work such as hoeing and weeding turnips, road and railway construction, fisheries and domestic service also provided short-term employment opportunities for both sexes.

The OSA writer attributed a rapid rise in labourers' wages in the parish since 1780 to competition from this source:

> Such was the rage that seized young fellows to leave the country at that period; that it was with utmost difficulty servants could be got at any wages. The common practice is to go off in April or beginning of May, some to the Low Country of Scotland and some to England. They generally come home again to their parents and relations in November ... Numbers also go to the harvest and return again in the latter end of October or beginning of November. ... The wages of servant-maids are very low ... Numbers of them, as well as of the men, go to the Low Country to the harvest and also engage in family service and other works.

A tragic accident in 1822 confirmed the extent to which Iona and the Ross of Mull contributed to this migrant labour force.[12] On the night of 10 August a smack from that area was struck by a tug in the Firth of Clyde. Her stern severed, she sank at once. 'Of forty-six persons on board, all of whom except the master and one seaman were shearers on their way to the low country harvest, and most of them women, only four, two men and two women, were saved . . .'. The *Glasgow Herald*, the *Greenock Advertiser* and the *Inverness Courier* gave full coverage to the disaster, which aroused considerable public sympathy, particularly as it involved the sudden deaths of so many young women. The event lived long in local memory. In the late 1880s John MacCormick, from the Ross of Mull, and the Mull and Iona Association in Glasgow, tried to raise money for a memorial to the victims of 'Bàthadh nam Buanaichean' (the drowning of the harvesters), whose graves could at that time still be pointed out in the old kirkyard at Greenock.

In one of his articles MacCormick noted that although contemporary press accounts had called the smack the *Katherine of Iona*, 'according to Iona and Ross of Mull tradition the name of the boat was the *Mary of Iona*'. It was thought there had been a mix-up in the names of two smacks which sailed from the district on the same day. The existence of two boats, presumably both carrying harvesters, is also implied in the story that one woman saw a 'sgart' or cormorant on the fated vessel and, as this was a sign of bad luck, changed to the other one at the last minute.

It has been argued that income from temporary migration helped maintain high levels of population in the Highlands by supporting the people's established way of life. Absence for a period fitted in with the cyclical pattern of the crofting year and eased food supplies at home during the crucial time before the new harvest was secured.[13] The human loss from the *Mary of Iona* tragedy was undoubtedly deeply felt but the economic repercussions must also have been considerable, as an important extra source of money for a section of the community suddenly disappeared that year. Several families clearly sent more than one member to the harvest. Three sets of sisters were among the drowned and two sets of a brother and sister. One of the men saved lost his wife, mother-in-law and a sister-in-law. The list of victims and their dependants was published and most of them had children or aged parents to support.

The practice of going south for the season undoubtedly continued, despite the tragedy, and was helped by the improved communications of the 1820s. Lowland farms may well have been the destination of the extra passengers for the return journey of the *Highlander* packetboat on 19 July 1826: 'From this poor heath-roofed village of Iona some pretty, gay and even coquettish damsels came aboard'.[14]

Seasonal employment also served to consolidate the gradual change toward a cash economy, as products from the Lowlands became more familiar and desirable, although the trades and crafts of the old self-sufficient society were still much in evidence early in the nineteenth century in Iona. Up to 1840 the OPR includes mention of six shoemakers, twelve weavers, four tailors and a turner who made spinning wheels.

Horizons were, however, widening. Even before the steamship era facilitated communication with the mainland, the sea route to the Clyde and its towns, although long, was by no means insuperable. Sailing smacks and open skiffs brought the purchase and trading of goods within scope. Writing about the early years of the nineteenth century, John MacCormick said: 'Generally at Martinmas a boat left for the Nollaig's (New Year) supply of grog and if the journey was accomplished before the 12th of January it was considered a smart one'.[15] One Iona native recalls hearing that people usually sailed to Islay for the New Year whisky. And Donald Cameron (born in 1862) told Dugald MacArthur that before his day the people used to sail as far south as the mainland of Lorne to get housing timber.

A few early travellers' accounts mention an alehouse but no shop selling food or other articles. In the 1830s a Hugh Maclean came to Iona from Mull, married an Effy Maclean and set up as merchant on the island. This family business was to last through three generations until the mid-1960s.

The factual observations and subjective impressions of visitors continue to provide glimpses of life in Iona during the first part of the nineteenth century. The route was well established and Oban was 'the great disembarking port for Mull, Staffa and Icolmkill', as Sir John Carr called it in 1807. He hired a boat there for Aros in Mull for a guinea and a half.[16] The previous year a Mr Brown and his companions were immediately accosted by a sailor on arrival in Oban:

> He told us he had a good stout boat . . . This was no other than the famous Peter McIntyre, one of those worthies to whom this journal is to be dedicated. . . . The hyre of his boat of four hands to Arros was 30/- and 2/- a day as long as we kept the crew besides feeding them.

The fame, or notoriety, of this particular mariner was later to be revealed when the party arrived back at Aros for the return journey and found him in such 'a state of complete intoxication' that they had to pilot the boat themselves for part of the way.[17]

The entrepreneurial spirit demonstrated by the boatmen of Oban, in response to the evident demand, did not meet with the approval of one P. B. Homer in 1803:

> The demands for the use of a boat to carry you to Aros in Mull and the other expenses of visiting Staffa are very shameful and exorbitant. . . . It has become so much the custom among the

nobility and gentry of England to include Staffa in their northern excursions that the boatmen consider it as a very good
market and consequently have raised considerably the price of
their commodity; and to show their impartiality they have
levied the same tax upon their own countrymen.[18]

Some travellers used the stepping stone of Kerrera, crossing the
short distance from a spot two miles south-west of Oban and then
taking a second ferry from the other side of the island to Auchnacraig
in Mull. This was the droving route, when cattle were taken south
from the islands to mainland markets. John Keats struck a fine breeze
when crossing from Kerrera in 1818, covering the distance in forty
minutes. He then continued on foot all the way down the Ross of
Mull, the most arduous route over rugged and untracked terrain and
indeed described by him as 'a most wretched walk of 37 miles'.[19]

The more popular journey via Aros left the traveller with a short
distance on foot or by pony across the narrow neck of land to the
head of Loch na Keal and thence either by boat or along the lochside
to Ulva Ferry (see Map 3).

Ulva was another lively junction point. Mr Brown's party found
that the landlord of the inn, who was also the skipper of the boat that
was to take them to Staffa and Iona, had just returned from there with
another group. The following year Sir John Carr stayed with the
Laird of Ulva and noted: 'For several days, during which fresh
arrivals reached the hospitable roof of Ulva house, on their way to the
islands of Staffa and Iona, it never ceased to rain but for a few
minutes'. It is hoped that he had taken his own advice to the Hebridean tourist, to travel equipped with changes of clothes, linen and
boots, as unfavourable weather could frequently extend a short trip
to a lengthy undertaking.

The hard trek by land and small boat was largely relieved when the
steamship era opened in the 1820s. The first West Highland steamer
was the *Comet*, from the fleet of Henry Bell, Thomson and others,
which in 1819 began a service from Glasgow to Fort William via the
Crinan Canal. A second *Comet* was commissioned in 1821 and she
may have been the first commercial steamship to visit Iona. The
Inverness Courier reported her sail from Fort William to Staffa and
Iona in July 1822 with upwards of fifty ladies and gentlemen. The
writer praised the 'ease and comfort' of the voyage and the fine
scenery of the 'Hebridean Archipelago' now opened up for excursions. By 1827 four different operators were offering West Highland
steamship services. In June 1835 the *Inverness Courier* carried
advertisements for J. G. Burns' *Helen MacGregor* and *Rob Roy* and
for Daniel Wright's *Staffa* and *Maid of Morven*, all including 'the

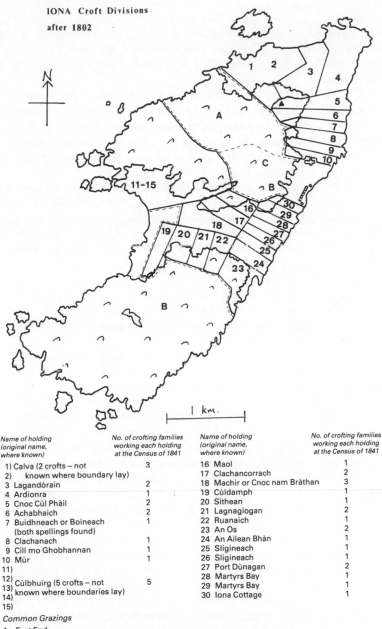

IONA Croft Divisions
after 1802

Name of holding (original name, where known)	No. of crofting families working each holding at the Census of 1841	Name of holding (original name, where known)	No. of crofting families working each holding at the Census of 1841
1) Calva (2 crofts – not	3	16 Maol	1
2) known where boundary lay)		17 Clachancorrach	2
3 Lagandòrain	2	18 Machir or Cnoc nam Bràthan	3
4 Ardionra	1	19 Cùldamph	1
5 Cnoc Cùl Phàil	2	20 Sithean	1
6 Achabhaich	2	21 Lagnagiogan	2
7 Buidhneach or Boineach	1	22 Ruanaich	1
(both spellings found)		23 An Os	2
8 Clachanach	1	24 An Ailean Bhàn	1
9 Cill mo Ghobhannan	1	25 Sligineach	1
10 Mùr	1	26 Sligineach	1
11)		27 Port Dùnagan	2
12) Cùlbhuirg (5 crofts – not	5	28 Martyrs Bay	1
13) known where boundaries lay)		29 Martyrs Bay	1
14)		30 Iona Cottage	1
15)			

Common Grazings

A East End.
B West End (included Cnoc Mòr above Port Ronain).
C Baile Mòr – part of this area was hill grazing for the village people.

Map 3. Iona – 1802 croft divisions including names.

celebrated islands of Staffa and Iona' on their various routes. The same newspaper noted with approval this increased competition and the swiftly expanding facilities it brought, attracting visitors not only from within Britain to the West Highlands but from Europe and America.

A visitor in 1825 was well pleased with the service from the *Highlander*, which had begun to sail the previous year from Glasgow to Tobermory, setting passengers ashore for the night before taking them on to Staffa and Iona the next day. The price he quotes for the whole trip compares very favourably with the cost of getting only as far as Aros from Oban twenty years before.

> Before we take leave of the *Highlander*, I cannot help express-
> ing the satisfaction and pleasure we uniformly received, both
> from her excellent accommodation and from the civility and
> intelligence of the captain and the steward during the whole of
> the voyage, a distance of 284 miles. The passage money
> amounted to £2.8.0 for each of us, including the boats which
> were provided at Staffa and Iona. . . . These steam vessels have
> opened so frequent, so expeditious and so easy a communication
> between Glasgow and the whole of the Hebrides and the West-
> ern coast of Scotland that they are effecting considerable changes
> in those remote places.[20]

A few years later Felix Mendelssohn's companion Carl Klingemann reflected on the impact which the twice-weekly influx of day trippers might have on a small and remote community :

> If I had my home on Iona and lived there melancholy as other
> people do on their rents, my darkest moment would be when in
> that wide space . . . suddenly a curl of steam should appear,
> followed by a ship and finally by a gay party in veils and frock
> coats, who would look for an hour at the ruins and graves and
> the three little huts for the living and then move off again.[21]

He considered this a 'highly unjustifiable joke', an intrusion into a tranquil and secluded way of life. But this was a romantic view. It is at variance with many other travellers' accounts which indicate that visitors were welcome and were received with politeness and hospit- ality. The sale of souvenir pebbles to those crowding off the steamers must have brought in a small but useful amount of extra cash every summer. The same people brought desirable items too, as *Lumsden's Steamboat Companion* reported : 'When a stranger lands the first thing they solicit is tobacco, which is esteemed a great luxury. They are polite ; and one of their customs is, when passing a person who is in the act of milking a cow, a quantity of milk is offered gratis'.[22]

The contrast in material conditions between the world of the visitor and that of the islanders was of course striking. Most simply remarked in passing on the poor housing, or the ragged clothing of the children. A Frenchman named Bernard Ducos, however, found his attention caught by a tall young woman whom he described as beautiful, with Greek features, dark eyes and a melancholy appearance. Her hair was caught up on top of her head. She wore a shawl over her blouse, a short skirt and no shoes or stockings. He asked permission to step inside her house:

> It is just a single room between four walls of mud, straw, branches and clumps of dried turf. There is no window or paving. Daylight comes in by the door. In the centre, set against two stones, clods of peat burn without flame. The smoke goes out through the roof made of heather roots and reeds, bound with sea grasses and held down with pebbles. The length of this rustic home, on two pallets strewed with bracken and I don't know what other brittle plants, trail scraps of woollen blanket. An old woman crouched on her heels gives a little grain to hens and ducks. In a corner pigs are eating vegetable peelings. All dwellings are like this, it is the equality of misery. I gave some money to the young woman who showed extreme gratitude.[23]

This is a typical description of the dwellings of the period throughout the Highlands and visitors from more sophisticated societies doubtless found it hard to conceive of happiness in such a context. There is a tone of mild surprise in some of the observations on this point. J. E. Bowman, in 1825, entered a hut to request a drink of water and noted: 'It was smoky, dark and squalid in the extreme yet its poor inhabitants wore the smile of content and were civil and obliging, according to our wishes'. James Johnson, in 1832, saw the village as 'a line of sordid huts' but also admitted that 'Both the minister and doctor assured me that the inhabitants of Iona are remarkably happy and contented'.[24]

Two accounts in particular hint at the rich culture and sociability of the Gael, which had long coexisted with a life of meagre resources and austere surroundings. In 1807 Necker de Saussure rewarded the boatmen who had brought him to Iona with a dance in the evening, 'as dancing is the favourite amusement among the Hebrideans of all ages'. He supplied toddy and the islanders brought forth a fiddler. He wrote with admiration of the liveliness of the dancers, neatly avoiding holes in the earthen floors, and of the 'iorrams' (rowing songs) and 'oran luathaidh' (waulking songs) sung in full chorus. He went on:

> The men and women seated themselves in a circle and joined hands or held, in couples, the end of a handkerchief, with which they kept time during the chorus. Two of our boatmen . . . made

all kinds of grimaces and apish tricks whilst singing . . . while the rest of the company were convulsed with laughter. This scene greatly amused us and we were astonished to see, under so foggy an atmosphere, in so dreary a climate, a people animated by that gaiety and cheerfulness which we are apt to attribute exclusively to those nations who inhabit the delightful countries of the South of Europe.

In 1806 the party which included a Mr Brown from Edinburgh, a Liverpool merchant Mr Wilson and a sea captain variously referred to as 'a mulatto gentleman' and 'the black prince', had travelled by the Ulva route where the boatman persuaded them to take along a local piper: 'He would cost us no great sum and would afford much amusement. We were afterwards very happy we took his advice'. This was almost certainly Archibald MacArthur, piper to Mac-Donald of Ulva. He had been a pupil of the celebrated Donald Mac-Crummin of Skye and is mentioned in several accounts of this period as playing for visitors to Ulva and while accompanying them by boat, including inside Fingals Cave. As the boat neared Iona the piper struck up, drawing people out of their houses to the shore. Still playing, he then marched the visitors single file behind him through the village to where the schoolmaster lived. The writer of this journal whose name is not revealed, simply drew on Dr Johnson's famous description of the antiquities. He was more interested in recording, in vivid detail, the scene which followed. The music had brought more than two hundred people to the shore:

> They became at last so exhilerated that they began to 'trip it on the light fantastic toe' and when we returned dancing was 'the order of the day'. One of our boatmen a nice young man of the name of Allan MacInnes was master of ceremonies and to do him justice he did his duty most dexterously. We looked on for some time but at last observing four ladies proposing to dance a reel by themselves our gallantry took the alarm and we immediately joined the jovial crew. With this frankness added to the roving commission with which we had despatched Allan to the Ale-house for whisky the villagers seem'd much pleas'd. It is amazing how many good looking girls there were in the company, several of them would have done honour to the streets of Edinburgh. . . . There was one girl in particular very pretty Miss Effy Maclean to whom Wilson and I paid great court. . . . We concluded each reel in the good old fashion of kissing our partners, a fashion that I am sorry to see has in our part of the country gone into disuse.

After various incidents and another round of grog the visitors eventually departed:

The inhabitants seemed vastly taken with us and as we were
going off gave us three cheers which salute we returned by a
discharge of our musquet. . . . Will we be accused of presump-
tion if we hint that the year 1806 will be long cherished in Iona
under the title of the year that strangers from Ulva treated them
with a ball.

Most travellers contrasted the wretchedness of the people with the
former glory and importance of the monastic buildings. On their
brief visits, concentrating primarily on the ruins whose fame had
attracted them, they saw the local inhabitants as little more than a
passing curiosity. The accounts of Necker de Saussure and the anonymous journal stand out for the degree of interest they displayed in
the people, although there is no reason to assume that the merrymak-
ing they describe were rare events. It was clearly not the first visit of
the Ulva piper. The journal's author even placed the experience on a
par with the historical and natural sights he had seen during the long
round trip from Ulva:

This was one of the pleasantest and best spent days of my life. I
had seen more of the wonders of nature and got more insight
into the character and behaviour of the lower orders of society
than I had ever done before in the same time. It is but few days in
a lifetime that you meet with an assemblage of such interesting
objects as what this afforded. Nature upon the most magnificent
scale in Staffa and MacKinnons Cave. Splendid remains sacred
to religion and virtue in Iona and the native simplicity and rustic
happiness of its present inhabitants.

Visitors were sometimes pressed into service for medical help, as in
a case reported in 1827. A steam vessel's crew provided medicine for
an Iona fisherman whose arm was swollen from the prick of a gurnet
fin and they undertook to alert a surgeon in Tobermory.[25] The
quotation from James Johnson in 1832 indicated that a brother of Mr
Campbell the minister was the doctor for the parish, but he almost
certainly resided in the Ross of Mull where he had been brought up.
The 1831 edition of Lumsden's guidebook had stated: 'It is an
extraordinary fact that there is neither a midwife nor any medical
person on the island; which is deeply felt and is the cause of the loss
of many valuable lives'.

The registering of deaths in the OPR did not begin for Iona until
1835. By then the island had a resident minister, following the
building of a Parish Church and Manse in 1828. The cause of deaths
was seldom entered, however, and it cannot be assumed anyway that
all deaths were scrupulously recorded. It is therefore almost impossible to say what the average life span in the community was at this

period or whether the islanders were vulnerable to particular illnesses or, indeed, if the lack of ready medical help *was* a significant factor. What *had* continued to flourish healthily, without a doubt, were the overall numbers of those living on the island.

4

Population Growth and
Economic Decline

During the autumn of 1835 the minister, the Rev. Donald McVean, and an elder went from house to house throughout the parish in order to count the population for the Royal Commission on Religious Instruction, Scotland. The total for the island of Iona was 521, the highest figure recorded up to that date.

Between that year and the first nominal Census of 1841 natural increase, calculated from the baptism and death registers, shows a continuing rise to 554. The unreliability of the death entries suggests the figure was probably never quite as high as that and any movement of people into or out of the island would also have affected the numbers. In 1841 there were 496 inhabitants, thus implying a net disappearance – through out-migration or unrecorded death – of fifty-eight people during the previous five years.

In any event, the island's population had risen inexorably since the making of the crofts, with a peak at the very end of the 1830s. There is no evidence of any attempt by the Estate to reduce numbers by eviction during the first half of the century. Some voluntary movement out of the district did occur. When the funeral of the victims of the *Mary of Iona* disaster took place in Greenock in 1822, the newspaper mentioned the attendance of 'a number of persons residing here and from Glasgow who had originally come from the islands we have mentioned'. And when the major waves of emigration began in the 1840s, there were several references to relatives of Iona people already settled in Canada and Australia. But none of this was on a significant enough scale to affect the steady upward rise of the numbers who remained. Indeed, rather than remove, the tendency clearly was to stay and share out the land as Sir Walter Scott had observed with some foreboding in 1814: 'This little fertile island contains upwards of 400 inhabitants, all living upon small farms which they divide and subdivide as their families increase, so that the country is greatly over peopled and in some danger of a famine in case of a year of scarcity'.[1]

A comment applying specifically to such a year has survived in a letter from a David Pitcairn to a Colonel Callander of Craigforth, dated 4 October 1822.[2] A few months earlier, on 13 June, a report in the *Inverness Courier* had highlighted severe scarcity in the West Highlands, and particularly the Hebrides, due to the loss of potatoes and other crops grown in sandy soil, following a prolonged drought the previous year. The people were described as having 'neither money nor credit to procure provisions, in consequence of the low price of cattle and their famished condition'. Pitcairn's letter may have been referring to the effects of this general situation on Iona or it may have been inspired by the special cases of need resulting from the *Mary of Iona* smack tragedy two months before. In either event, it represents an early example of outside interest in the islanders' material conditions and an effort to assist them:

> I enclose you the notice respecting the poor sufferers in Iona and shall be happy if you can enlarge the list of subscribers. It may be interesting to mention to your friends that the schoolmaster whose pious labours for about thirty years have done great good and completely gained the respect and affections of the people, is the richest man on the island from which it may readily be inferred that so poor a population have little internal means of relief. The Duke of Argyll is the sole proprietor and the embarrassed state of his finances leave little in his power.

The 'embarrassed state' of the sixth Duke's finances was largely due to his own profligate spending. Parts of the Estate were sold off to try to meet mounting debts. In 1819 the rental from Mull and Morvern together was over £5200. By 1825, after the sale of Morvern and parts of Mull, this income dropped to £2475.[3]

Individual rents in Iona parish ranged between £3 and £16, with the exception of the minister and teacher and one large farm in Ross. The Estate accounts throughout this period are not complete, but they do show for several years' income from rents a sum for the preceding year's arrears. Whereas these amounted to just under £250 in 1826 by 1836 they were over £1000, four times as much.

There are other indications that times were difficult. An entry in the school returns for 1837 stated that 'all the fees paid since more than two years only four barrels of potatoes'.[4] Collections made at the church door, at that time the basis of support for the poor of the parish, fell from £5.4.7 in 1836 to around £3 or £2 in the following few years.[5] Those temporarily in need, for example due to illness, could receive assistance at the discretion of the Kirk Session from the other half of the church collection not reserved for those legally on the poor roll. In Iona it was noted that the fund for this 'occasional' category was not distributed in 1837 and 1839 'in consequence of the smallness of the sums at the disposal of the Kirk Session and also because the poor were liberally supplied from other sources these years'. This statement reflected two key aspects of the crisis of the late 1830s : the reduction in cash incomes available within the community and the external help, which was itself a response to the gravity of the situation.

Food shortages are known to have occurred intermittently in the Highlands, notably in 1806/7, in 1811 and in 1817, when the Government intervened with supplies of grain. Lean times alternating with periods of sufficiency was an accepted pattern for communities whose subsistence agriculture was subject to the vagaries of season and weather. But the crop failures of 1835 and 1836 led to a crisis of more severe proportions. The famine which resulted was in itself widespread and harsh and the Highland economy was now less able to cope with it.

Early in 1837 Robert Graham, Secretary of State for the Home Department, was commissioned to enquire into the state of the poor in the affected districts of the Highlands and Islands. The report at the end of his tour noted : 'The oldest resident in any portion I have passed through were unable to call to their recollection any year which equalled the present one'. Although the immediate problem had stemmed from late planting and small crops following two unusually cold, wet springs, Graham was very clear that: 'Other causes have been long and silently in operation'. He identified the great increase in populations along with a decline in incomes from sources such as military service, kelping, road and canal construction, seasonal farm work. There had also been a steady fall in the price of black cattle and a slump in the herring fishery.[6]

With regard to kelp Graham noted : 'In Mull this has been considerably spoken to' and a few years later the writer of the *New Statistical Account (NSA)* claimed that the discontinuance of the industry in Ross and Iona had been 'much to the loss of the population'. Another significant source of income for people from this area was temporary work in the Lowlands. Graham spoke of 'great failure of harvest work in the low country last year'. The large influx of Irish labourers had begun to depress wages in this sector. There had earlier been fluctuations in earnings, as in August 1822, the same month that the harvesters from Mull and Iona lost their lives :

The shearers' wages are very low this season. Several hundred persons were engaged at the cross of Paisley at the rate of 1s 6d a day. This was a reduction of 6d a day, those labourers having got

2s on the previous days. Some refused to go at this rate and found much fault with others for having agreed work at the reduced wages.[7]

But by the 1830s it threatened to be a permanent decline, as a Midlothian farmer testified to the Agricultural Inquiry of 1833: 'It used to be considered the chief means of subsisting the Highlanders in winter, if they came and got £3 or £4 by harvest work to take home'. But now, he continued, 'the Irish labourers have nearly cut our Highlanders out of the Lowland market' and wages had been halved.[8] Along with the reduced return from their principal export, cattle, it is therefore clear that less money must have been coming into the economy of Iona in the 1820s and 1830s than in the first two decades of the century.

Robert Graham made a thorough investigation of the areas he visited and spoke directly with ministers of the parishes and with people affected by the crisis. He was accompanied by a Mr Stewart of Ardvorlich, who spoke Gaelic. In the Mull district it was estimated that over 6000 people, a quarter of the population, were in distress. It was even more serious in Skye where three-quarters of the population were destitute and in the Long Island where the figure was thought to be four-fifths.

The Ross of Mull and Iona were considered to be in particular hardship. Iona was included in a list of the ten most needy districts in a memorial to the Government of 27 March 1837 and Graham's impressions from his visit the same month were pessimistic:

> . . . it may almost be generally termed a pauper population. . . . the minister and elders whom we saw estimate the destitute families at present at 87 over the whole parish and within a month there will be many more. 57 able-bodied men cannot find any kind of work. If they had boats and fishing implements many could support themselves.

It was estimated that fifty-nine bolls of seed oats were required for the parish.

On 24 March 1837 a list was drawn up of families in Iona, with the number of souls in each, who needed immediate supplies of food.[9] There were thirty-eight names, representing 191 individuals, more than a third of the population. They were predominantly from the non-tenant class. Of the twenty-seven who can definitely be identified, only four were crofters. The rest were cottars or tradesmen and they included two sets of orphans and several widows. It was thus those without access to land who were most quickly reduced to destitution level and it was also they who were least able to move out of the predicament themselves.

Two of the crofting families on the list, totalling seven people, embarked on the *Brilliant* at Tobermory in September 1837, bound for Australia.[10] The 315 emigrants were assisted by Government funds and they had been selected on grounds of youth and ability. There was a proportionately high level of assisted passage to Australia during the next few years, largely due to the efforts of the Reverend J. D. Lang, who had arrived in Sydney from Scotland in 1823 and become an energetic promoter of the need for skilled labour in the colony. On his frequent trips home, Lang circulated parish ministers with information about Australia, supervised the recruiting of emigrants and the chartering of ships, and in 1836/7 talked with Government officials about the desirability of his adopted land as a destination for destitute Highlanders. The *Inverness Courier* described the sensation created in Mull by the arrival of the *Brilliant*, the largest and most splendid vessel ever seen in the area. The West Highland passengers were, it continued: 'decidedly the most valuable that have ever left the shores of Great Britain; they are all of excellent moral character and from their knowledge of agriculture, the management of sheep and cattle, must prove a most valuable acquisition to a colony like New South Wales'.

The reporter also noted that the departure of the *Brilliant* marked the third embarkation of Highlanders for Australia that season. There were further local opportunities in 1838 when the *British King* left Tobermory and the *St George* left Oban and again in 1839 with the sailing of the *George Fyfe* from Tobermory and the *Glen Huntly* from Oban.[11] Others may well have followed the example of Hugh and Christina Campbell and John and Marion MacDonald, the Iona emigrants on the *Brilliant*. Certainly, by 1841, a further eight households, or twenty-one individuals, had gone from the island. Death accounted for at least three heads of those households and, very probably, for several more. There is a marked rise in the number of deaths registered between 1837 and 1840 including, in the last two years, a high proportion of infants and young children. If malnutrition, or weakened resistance to infection, were to blame for any of these fatalities, however, the proportion of the population affected was happily quite small.

The majority named in the list, twenty-eight households totalling 161 individuals, were still in Iona at the 1841 Census. The emergency food supplies had tided them over and better harvests were gathered in the early 1840s. A relief fund set up in Glasgow raised £50,000 and this assistance alleviated the immediate crisis in all the affected areas.[12] It is worth noting, however, that thirteen of these

families were definitely to emigrate within the following two decades and a further eight disappeared from Iona by 1851, their
destination unknown. When famine struck the Highlands again in
1846 and the years beyond, many of the problems underlying the
1837 distress had still not been effectively resolved. The effects were
to be significantly more damaging and permanent.

Plate 1. Map of Iona, drawn for the Argyll Estate in 1769 by William Douglas.

Plate 2. Traces of cultivation marks and drainage ditches at Calva on the north-west side of Iona. The foundations of two croft houses and enclosures are also visible in the centre foreground.

Plate 3. Dyke built by the islanders to mark division of the East End and West End townships. Completed by 1795.

Plate 4. The Lochan Mòr, south-east of Dùn I. The island's only source of peat, used up by the late 18th century. In the 1840s, it was drained as part of the improvement programme following the potato famine.

Plate 5. The Marble Quarry, showing the derrick used to load the marble during the 1906–1915 period of operation.

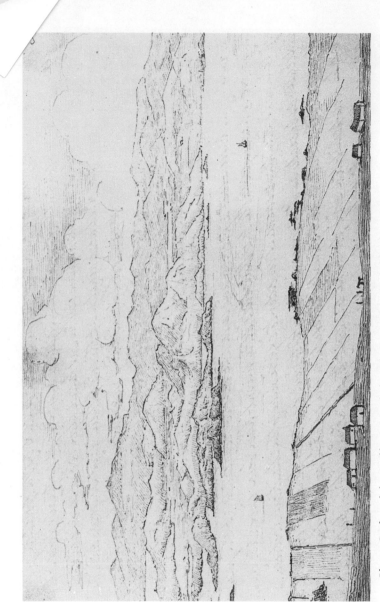

Plate 6. Crofts and clustered houses at Clachanach, Boineach and Achabhaich, East End of Iona, as sketched by Henry D. Graham between 1848 and 1852.

Plate 7. Thatched croft house at Sligineach, West End, c.1879/80. Peat-stack, cart and creel in the foreground. The older style of house, with no gable end, may be seen in the background.

Plate 8. House at Clachanach around 1905/06, just after it had been built up to two storeys by Archibald MacArthur and his father Dugald. They are standing to the left of the picture.

Section III

1840–1860

5

The Early 1840s: Material Conditions and Population Mobility

Of the 496 people living in Iona in 1841, nearly two-thirds were in the two crofting townships of the East End and the West End. Not all of them, however, were tenants. Scattered among the households listed in the 1841 Census as 'farmers' (i.e. the crofters), were a few weavers and agricultural labourers. These formed part of the cottar and tradesman class, the bulk of whom lived in the village and included shoemakers, tailors, merchants, carpenters and a mason. Apart from the small gardens attached to their cottages, the villagers did not hold land and did not at this period pay rent. They were charged a nominal sum of 5/- for their house and plot by the Estate.

The average family size of the cottars was smaller than that of the crofters. From the numbers actually recorded at the Census it was three, as opposed to four, although this does not account for children working as herds or maids with other families nor for older ones absent from the island. The reconstitution of family trees for thirty cottars and thirty crofters from this period shows a mean of five children for the former and eight for the latter. This ties in with the high fertility rate identified by MacInnes, who found a mean of seven and a half children in thirty-two families between 1804 and 1830.

The cottars represented forty-two per cent of the total inhabitants. It was thus fifty-eight per cent who contributed to the agricultural economy of the island and provided the Estate with its return. The distinction between the rent-paying tenantry and the landless proportion of the population was to be a significant one when the impact of the potato famine was felt.

The population was balanced almost equally between male and female but it was predominantly youthful. Fifty-two per cent were under twenty years and only twelve per cent were over fifty. The Census enumerator noted the temporary absence of five men and ten women. Although the date, 9 June, appears a little too early for the annual outflow of harvest workers to the Lowlands, other farming or domestic work could have drawn some of this number away. The minister was to comment to the Poor Law Inquiry Commission in 1843 'that the young people are generally inclined to go to the low country as servants'.

The Poor Law Inquiry Commission (PLIC) was established to assess the need for changes to the operation of the Poor Law in Scotland. The system, which had evolved since the late sixteenth century whereby voluntary contributions were administered by the Kirk Session of each parish, had come increasingly under attack as outmoded and inefficient in an age of growing industrialisation. A whole new class of urban poor were now often reduced to destitution by lack of work or epidemics of disease, yet they were not entitled to claim relief. Critics wished to see a uniform, legal and more substantial assessment.

In order to gather information on which to base their deliberations, the Commissioners sent out a questionnaire to all parish ministers in 1843 and then toured the country, examining them further in person and making first-hand observations of conditions.[1]

The evidence to the PLIC, along with other contemporary sources for Iona, serve to confirm the land- and sea-based economy of the community, still highly self-sufficient with an adequate, if monotonous, diet. The picture was neither one of abundant wealth nor of dire poverty. Apart from three families the whole population was said to 'depend more or less on their agricultural labours'. The principal food throughout the parish was 'potatoes and fish'. Arable holdings averaged five to eight acres with access to common grazing, and rents ranged from nine to fifteen pounds, although the *NSA* placed the lower level at four pounds.[2]

In 1844 a visitor to Iona found no difficulty in bringing back to his yacht 'a supply of eggs, potatoes, milk and oatcake'.[3] Indeed, not only self-sufficiency in food but the ability to export surpluses continued to be the norm through the first half of the 1840s. The Duke of Argyll's Chamberlain, speaking some years later recalled:

> Previous to the failure of potatoes, they were exported in large quantities from the Ross and Iona. In one year during which I kept the account, upwards of 6000 barrels were sold from the Kirkpatrick estate and the Duke's including Iona at 5s per barrel. That same year there was an export of barley of from 1000 to 5000 bolls, from the Duke's estate alone. I think this was in 1844 and 1845 . . .[4]

When the PLIC visited a number of houses in Iona in June 1843, their findings were on the whole positive. Notes included: 'Family in no unprosperous condition' and 'Parents and children healthy to appearance'. A few indicated a relatively good degree of ease and industry:

John MacFarlane . . .
Crockery and crockery-stand rather better than in the two

immediately preceding houses. His wife, a heartsome woman, engaged in boiling sorrel leaves to dye cloth of their own spinning and weaving.

John MacDonald, Senior . . .
Inhabits a house far superior to the other. It consists of two apartments. The kitchen, one of them, seems to be well provided. Fire-place had a chimney in the ordinary form. The other room was plastered. Bedsteads and bedding seemed neat and comfortable. There was a mahogany tea table and other articles indicating a very superior degree of comfort.

Two picked out as plainly poorer and overcrowded were both examples of sons-in-law who had built an extra house on a family croft : Alexander Lamont who married Betty MacKillop, Lagandòrain and Alexander MacDonald who married Catherine MacArthur, Achabhaich. Both subsequently emigrated.

Comments on cases of those considered 'poor' bears out the evidence from various sources that those with little means were looked after by the mutual support system of the community. The *NSA*, for example, stated that 'The poor are supported by the charity of their neighbours and the collections made at the church door'. Thus one widow visited, Flora MacKinnon, 'Spins a little for the neighbours and they give her food in return. Depends on neighbours'. And a MacArthur was said to be '. . . the poorest man in the parish, but he is able-bodied and works at potatoes upon a bit of ground he has and works for the farmer from whom he has it and a bit of barley ground, instead of paying him rent'.

In reply to a question from the PLIC the minister stated that twenty-three were on the permanent poor roll in Ross and Iona. When a Parochial Board was set up in 1845, following the Poor Law (Amendment) Scotland Act of that year, they drew up a new roll divided into three classes. None of the fifteen in the first, most needy, class were from Iona; only three out of twenty-seven in the second and one out of thirty-two in the third class were from Iona. The board also noted 'that the great proportion of paupers have free houses and potato ground or live with relatives and that they are all very liberally assisted by friends and neighbours'. According to the minister in 1843, the three shillings distributed to each pauper was 'generally applied in purchasing a pair of shoes', underlining the assumption that the needs of food and shelter were largely catered for through the help of friends and family.

The initial impression of the islanders' economic circumstances at the turn of the decade is that it was not one of desperate hardship.

Nor was the social fabric that held the community together seriously weakened. The same sources for this picture, however, also reveal signs of the vulnerable base on which these circumstances stood.

The minister confirmed to the PLIC that seasonal migration for work now brought a lower return than before: 'A considerable number of the people of Iona go to the low country in harvest and, after deducting the expense of travelling, the average remaining does not, in his opinion, at any time exceed £2'. He added that there was no manufacturing establishment in the parish and that 'there are a considerable number able and willing but unable to procure work'.

The decline in the kelp trade since earlier in the century was still keenly felt, meriting a strongly worded paragraph by the writer of the *NSA* on behalf of the parishioners throughout the Ross of Mull and Iona who had borne the economic loss:

> Kelp. This manufacture has entirely disappeared, with the exception of a very little made at Inchkenneth and Gribun . . . there were no less than 150 tons annually manufactured in this parish and of course it, in common with the Highlands in general, have felt, and do still feel, the loss ; . . . In previous years this manufacture employed and gave bread to many thousands in the Highlands and Islands, and the price it drew brought money to the country . . . which now goes to enrich the foreigner at the poor Highlander's expense ; a measure of policy which cannot be too strongly condemned . . .

The decline of these sources of cash income, to supplement the subsistence economy, had been identified by Robert Graham in his analysis of the underlying causes of the 1837 destitution crisis. The emergency food supplies had tided the people over that period but his proposed forms of employment, to engender a spirit of industry rather than the passive acceptance of charity, had not yet been put into effect. At least, the specific suggestions relating to Iona had not been taken up, such as the building of a new quay and the clearing and enclosing of the Cathedral ruins.

Iona did have the advantage over more remote and less famous places, of growing numbers of tourists flocking with the now thrice-weekly steamships from Glasgow. They did inject a certain amount of cash into the local economy during the short summer season in return for the pebble and shell mementoes proffered relentlessly by the native children. Between two and six pence per item was the selling price in 1835, according to visitor Robert Carruthers.[5] There was a small benefit to the house which served as inn for the occasional overnight guest, and to the official guide to the ruins. From 1840 this was Angus Lamont, paid five pounds a year by the Duke for his services. But the significant economic impact of tourism was not to come until a demand for accommodation, in hotels or cottages to let, arose in the latter part of the century.

Graham's report had also presaged the critical effect of high population levels throughout the Highlands. Permanent improvement in conditions, he believed, could only come about with a reduction in the numbers trying to gain a living from the limited resources of the available land: 'The most effectual mode of preventing a recurrence of the present distress and one which was suggested everywhere as being almost a necessary remedy would be by emigration. . . . to give effectual relief it must be done generally and on a great scale'.

In the previous chapter it has been argued that Iona's population probably reached its highest point in the late 1830s. In the PLIC questionnaire the minister gave the average ages for marriage in Iona as twenty-five for men and twenty-three for women, consistent with those calculated by John MacInnes in his study of the OPR from 1804 to 1841. The minister also stated that early marriages appeared to be 'getting on the whole less frequent' although the question did not, unfortunately, specify what 'early' signified. Over the ten years from 1840 until 1849, inclusive, nineteen marriages and ninety-six baptisms were registered in Iona. But in the previous three decades the average had been twenty-six marriages and 166 baptisms. This high rate of fertility in the first forty years of the century coincided with a lack of permanent out-migration on any significant scale. It was these two factors that left the legacy of a densely populated island just at the point of its most severe economic difficulties.

That there was some out-migration from Iona before the serious crisis of 1846/7 may be gleaned from a variety of sources. It is known from local tradition, and confirmed by the absence of their names from the 1841 Census, that particular families or individuals did leave in the 1830s or earlier. For example, Camerons were said to have gone from the croft next to Clachanach to Australia and the foundations of their house and outbuildings are still visible. From family correspondence it is clear that a Neil MacArthur settled in Australia and that his brother Charles left for America with his wife Catherine but he died on the passage. The name of Archie MacCulloch lives on in that of a field in the West End croft nearest to the village – Liana Mhic-Chullaich (MacCulloch's meadow) – and oral tradition holds that he was the first to be evicted from a holding, although the circumstances are not remembered. A later newspaper article recalls him as an emigrant forced from his home to die of a broken heart across the Atlantic. Evidence from the Rev. Donald McVean to the PLIC in 1843, and correspondence between him and the Duke in March 1847,

mentioned that Iona people had received good accounts from relatives who had already emigrated both to America and Australia. And a
list of adherents to the Established Church, drawn up in 1845, noted
that the previous year four families had left the island for America.[6]

The 1836/7 crisis had stepped up the official momentum to promote emigration in an organised manner and with assistance, where
necessary. A 'Report on the Applicability of Emigration to Relief of
Distress in the Highlands', dated 29 July 1837, stated: 'It must be
admitted that few cases could arise to which the remedy of emigration on a great scale would appear more appropriate than to this of the
distress in the Hebrides'. The landlords should be involved in the
emigration schemes and the ultimate aim would be '. . . a more
rational system of managing their lands'.[7] In 1841 the 2nd Report of
the Select Committee on Emigration, Scotland included evidence
from the Duke of Argyll who was quite clear as to what such a system
might be: 'No doubt my object is to get the farms divided into large
proportions and have proper tenants on them, and the rest of the
tenants to be provided for by emigration or induced to go to the low
country'.[8]

The movement of tenants and the redistribution of their lots were
to be twin factors of significance over the following two decades,
underlying all Argyll Estate policy. The Duke also indicated that on
his Mull Estate, which included Iona, there were one thousand
people willing to emigrate. The general picture, however, is that up
until the late 1840s out-migration from Iona was a trickle rather than
a flood. Between 1835 and 1845 there was a net drop of thirty-four
people. Taking into account recorded baptisms (131) and deaths
(seventy-seven) over these ten years, the number who may have left
the island was eighty-eight. In the decade from 1845 until 1855 it was
to be over two and a half times that figure.

The minister's assessment of the population's mobility in 1843 was
that, apart from the trend for some young people to seek work in the
Lowlands, '. . . he thinks that families would be unwilling to remove.
That he does not think there is generally an inclination to emigrate to
the colonies'. A little later, however, he did state that this 'aversion to
emigration' had been lessened by the good reports from relatives
already settled overseas.[9] The implication is that the dominant factor
was still the 'pull' of better prospects rather than the 'push' of
intolerable circumstances or outright eviction.

6

The Year the Potato went Away

1846/1847

On 4 September 1847, John Campbell the Factor wrote to the Duke of Argyll that 'Iona looked really well'. The occasion which he was reporting with such satisfaction was the visit of the Royal Yacht, on the tour which was to endow the Western Isles with even greater appeal for the travelling public. The Queen did not land but, according to one guidebook, Prince Albert was greeted enthusiastically by well-dressed islanders waving 'tufted willow wands' and saluted on departure with a farewell song.[1] Indeed, Campbell had selected 'constables' from among the most respectable to control the crowds.

The Iona people were well used to receiving visitors, even from among the nobility, and would have had no difficulty in rising to the importance of the Royal visit. A footnote to the Factor's letter, however, reveals what was for them an event of deeper significance that day. Immediately after the Prince had left, Campbell had set out for Oban to secure the sale of horses belonging to emigrants from the Mull estate.

1847 was a key year within a period which itself marked a turning-point in Iona's economic and social history. On 1 February 1847 the Reverend Alexander MacGregor wrote to the Duke, following a meeting of all his parishioners in Iona and the Ross of Mull to discuss the grave circumstances facing them: '. . . and I am aware my doing this has had the effect of arousing them to consider more fully their calamitous situation and I believe has all but determined a number of them to emigrate . . . Many see it as their only alternative'.[2]

Between the Census reports of 1841 and 1861 the population of Iona fell from 496 to 263, a loss in just twenty years of the numbers built up steadily over the preceding eighty. These two decades saw the most dramatic change in the size and structure of the island's residents. The underlying causes have been traced in the previous chapter. The critical factor proved to be the failure of the potato crop in 1846.

The fungus *Phytophthora infestans* originated in North America where it was first recognised in 1843.[3] It appeared in Scotland, Ireland and several countries on the continent of Europe in 1845, causing partial loss of the potato crop. But in 1846 it struck with full force. In Iona, as in some other Highland communities, this date was long referred to as 'A'bhliadhna a dh'fhalbh am buntàta' – the year the potato went away. The first signs were blackened and withered leaves, followed by rotting of the tubers, which succumbed even if dug out quickly and stored above ground. Affected plants gave off a pervasive and evil stench.

The suddenness and ugliness of the blight contributed to a popular view, shared by sections of the clergy, that it represented a judgement from on high. The Synod of Argyll of the Church of Scotland appointed a Day of Humiliation to seek forgiveness, since: 'In as much as the dispensations of Providence by which we have been visited with the failure and are threatened in the total loss of the potatoes indicates the wrath of God against us for sin . . .'. On a more practical level they also appointed a Committee to make approaches to the Government for assistance.[4] The Free Church, through its newspaper *The Witness*, voiced strong concern about the impending crisis and devoted a long editorial on 19 September to the need for action: 'The potato failure may be described in two words, total, universal, in Scotland. . . . The public voice must come forth to demand that a remedy be applied to a state of suffering unparalleled we believe in modern times'.

On 29 July 1846 Alexander MacDonald wrote from Mull to the Chamberlain of Argyll:

> I consider it my duty as Ground Officer to say that since you have left the place the disease in the potato crop has made an alarming progress both in the Ross of Mull and Iona. The fields that then appeared beautiful and in full bloom and promised an abundant harvest to the consumer are this day as if overrun by fire. I tremble at what may be the consequence from the complete failure of this staple article of consumption on this district and unless some means may be advised (and that without loss of time) of providing for the starving population, the issue will be most appalling.

On 1 September 1846 a public meeting in Salen, Mull, reviewed the serious straits to which the bulk of the small tenant population were now reduced, due to the total failure of the potato crop throughout the island.[5] A plea for urgent aid was prepared for the Government and a standing committee appointed to take immediate measures. Convened by Francis Clark of Ulva, it included the Rev. Alexander MacGregor of the Church of Scotland in Iona parish. The following day, in Campbeltown, the provincial Synod of Argyle of the Free Church identified districts in their area most needful of assistance by declaring:

That such is the overwhelming nature of this calamity, it is absolutely necessary, to prevent starvation, that immediate relief be afforded to certain localities, such as the islands of Tyree, Iona, Islay, Lismore and Mull and the parishes of Ardnamurchan and Morvern, on the mainland.[6].

The Free Church had made an early and efficient response to the crisis, raising funds and distributing meal from the end of 1846. A letter from one of their ministers in Mull (unnamed), dated 13 November 1846, spelled out the scope of the disaster.[7] The potato, he explained, was not just a major food item. It was also a source of income from exports, both directly as a commodity in itself and indirectly through the pigs and poultry fed on it. The consequent scarcity of money meant that most people could no longer purchase meal.

It was this loss of a staple part of the diet, combined with the loss of a further cash source on top of already reduced earnings over the preceding period, that precipitated a calamity of far-reaching proportions.

Government action was also swift when alerted to the gravity of the situation. In September 1846 the Treasury instructed Sir Edward Pine Coffin to tour the affected parts of the Highlands and Islands and a Treasury minute dated 20 November recorded that 'The Belvidera frigate is now on his voyage from the Thames to Tobermory in the island of Mull with a cargo of barley-meal, oatmeal and peas'.[8]

From the outset the Government approach was not merely to ensure emergency relief. It was determined that the landlords shoulder the main burden of costs and that means be found for the permanent improvement of economic conditions in the Highlands and Islands. These strands were brought together very clearly in the effort to extend and support fishing. The maritime districts and the islands were the areas most drastically affected by the potato famine and the sea was an obvious source of food.

In October 1846 the Board of Fisheries surveyed the Ross of Mull, Iona, Tiree, Coll and Ardnamurchan, where they had been advised that present and anticipated destitution was most pressing. In Iona twenty-four boats were examined. They belonged to both crofters and cottars and represented just under one-third of the total households recorded in the 1841 Census. But as each boat had five or six hands, totalling 124, most of the adult male population must have had access to regular fishing. The basic equipment was generally good but it was the lack of extra money that prevented it being fitted out to best advantage : '. . . a few of them requiring repair in the hull but nearly all in need of oars etc. None of them use great long lines as they cannot afford to purchase them but would gladly do so could they afford them'. The districts targetted by the Board of Fisheries included the Duke of Argyll's insular estates and their report made mention of 'the most unproductive population' he had to deal with there. His was a case, it continued, where Government support for the long-term improvement of fisheries was merited provided, as with all the proprietors concerned, he bore half of the costs. The expenditure needed for Iona was £268.0.6. Added to the larger sums for Tiree and Ross, the total was £2199.19.10 and the Duke's share was thus about £1100. A protracted correspondence between the Board and the Marquis of Lorne, however, illustrates the latter's doubts about the scheme. He believed that a good white fishing required a body of men devoted solely to it. It was indeed true that one reason for his predecessors' lack of success in establishing fisheries in the late eighteenth century had been that the two occupations of small-scale landholding and commercial-scale fishing did not easily combine. On these grounds the Marquis argued, on his father the Duke's behalf, for a smaller operation. He also hoped that many would emigrate anyway before the following spring. It was eventually proposed that the Board confine its trial of a new system to Tiree with Government aid and leave the Duke to assist the men of Iona and Ross who were already dependent on fishing. The Duke did in fact provide £500 towards the Tiree scheme, as despite his qualms he believed the Board would not act at all without some outlay from the proprietor. And a small sum of £14.7.4 appeared in the Iona accounts for 1846, spent on 'lines and hooks for poor fishermen'.

This correspondence over the fisheries plan is indicative of the Estate's general approach to the destitution crisis. The key elements may be summed up in a letter from Lorne in December 1846 : 'But at present my hope is that with the employment to be given under the Drainage Act and the meal that has been sent and what may be done by general subscription, we shall scramble through the winter and that all the money we can command should be kept for assisting in emigration'.

The Drainage Act provided grants by which landlords could employ labour to drain land and so improve or reclaim it for agricultural use. In the potato blight years it was seized upon as a mechanism for offsetting the costs of relief by receiving work in return. This double benefit was recognised by someone who was to be an influential figure in the Argyll islands for the next thirty years, John Campbell of Ardmore in Islay, the Duke's new Factor. The first accounts under his name are from September 1846 until January 1848. They include the sum of £880 spent on drainage in Ross and Iona. Writing in

November 1846 to John Stewart, Head Chamberlain at Inveraray (who was also his brother-in-law), Campbell urged him to apply for a loan under the Drainage Act for the Duke : '. . . Sufficient to keep the Tyree, Mull and Iona poor from starving and enable the crofters to pay the rent, as they might make the drains on their own possessions and receive the benefit, a double benefit would accrue'.[9] John Campbell was to play an energetic and controversial part in the management of the Duke's estates and something of his own ambition for his new post comes through at the end of the letter. Stressing again that drainage was 'the only salvation for the property' and that the Duke would save money, he added : '. . . and the factor will gain credit by it which I am sure you would wish, at least so think I'.

Neither Campbell nor the Duke were impervious to the very real plight of their tenantry. In the same letter Campbell asked that meal be sent to Bunessan at once, as the people were on the point of starvation. The estate accounts show payment to a Glasgow supplier, in November 1846, of £296.2.2 for meal for the poor and an undated expenditure of £524.1.2 for seeds furnished to tenants. On 18 January 1847 the Rev. Alexander MacGregor wrote from Iona to the Duchess, thanking her for clothing she had sent and for the fifty bolls of meal received from the Duke since the previous September. Although the destitution was 'great and daily increasing', this support had rendered the situation of the poorest less desperate.

Throughout the famine years, however, the Factor's consistent policy was to give food relief only in return for work. He applied this with quite deliberate severity, believing it the only way to induce the necessary spirit of industry for the people's own long-term benefit : '. . . nothing but harshness and dread I find will do, they are so naturally slothful and indolent. . . . I am doling out the meal in as small quantities as possible and only in cases of urgent necessity to keep soul and body together. . . I shall take barley in exchange for the meal from the crofters and labour at draining from the cottars'.

Another consistent thread in the Estate's argument about the long-term solution to the famine crisis was the need to reduce overall numbers and in particular the small tenants. Writing on 7 August 1846 on the subject of Government assistant, the Marquis of Lorne added :

> I cannot help thinking that it might be accompanied with such a well directed measure of emigration as would in great measure remove the possibility of such necessity again, by reducing that number of that class of the population most exposed to want, which subsists on small patches of potato ground.

Two months later he acknowledged a problem inherent in this

approach, namely the tenacious grip of the Highlanders on their land: 'But the desperate attachment of the people to the patches on which they are annually half-starved is something so wonderful that emigration to any place is still their last resource'.

That this last resort might be turned to fairly soon was indicated in the report of a Free Church deputation who visited Coll, Tiree, Ulva, Iona and Mull in January 1847:

> Nowhere did this section see more evident and manifest tokens of real want than in the island of Iona and on the opposite coast of the island of Mull, in the district of Ross. . . . The visiting members remarked here, as elsewhere, what, though apparently or comparatively trivial, is serious to the poor – their pigs and poultry gone. The former, without their wonted food, have literally disappeared in Mull, Tyree, Ulva and Iona; . . . and as for the latter species of property and profit to the humble cottager, the people of Iona told them, that being without feed ing at home, their poultry wandered and that eagles, ravens and carrion crow fell upon them and devoured them. In Iona and the Ross of Mull they found more sickness prevailing than else-where.[10]

By this time Iona had a Free Church minister as well as one for the Church of Scotland (or Established Church), since the Rev. Donald McVean had joined the new denomination in 1843. The Free Church had circulated a schedule of queries to the distressed areas and in his return dated 6 January 1847 Mr McVean stated that eighty-two families were now destitute of food throughout his parish of Iona and part of the Ross of Mull. He thought that the corn crop would only support rent-paying families for another four months. The Committee noted that most of the returns warned of future distress arising out of the immediate crisis.

The Established Church minister, the Rev. Alexander MacGregor, was one of those who replied to a plea from the Rev. Dr Norman MacLeod for information about the famine.[11] 'All the little shifts the poor could make' to extricate themselves from their difficulties were now exhausted, he wrote from Iona, and they were now in danger of being not only undernourished but also ill-clad: 'as this year they had to appropriate for food their little harvest earnings, which in favourable seasons they used to apply in the purchase of wool for clothing'. Most of the cottars had sold their only cow and the crofters were rapidly being reduced to the same level.

The 1846 rental for Iona listed thirty-seven tenants, providing the estate with an income in total of £290.7.6. The average rent was thus just under £8. Nearly a third of the tenants had shared holdings and

D

paid only £3–£5. In addition, there were the cottars and tradesmen, living mostly in the village with a small potato patch attached to their house. Over the whole of the Argyll insular estates there were at this time 567 small tenants and 563 cottar families paying no rent, roughly equal proportions. In Iona the proportion of rent-paying households was slightly higher – it had been forty-one to thirty-six at the 1841 Census. Their family size was also slightly larger and they thus had more mouths to feed. The crofters had traditionally provided some support to the poorer members of the community. Lorne's concern, as expressed in a letter to the Treasury in January 1847, was that although the cottars were the class sooner reached by the famine, 'both are now in distress'. For the small tenants to be so seriously reduced, as well as the landless, was a warning sign of problems ahead.

On 5 February 1847 the Central Board of Management (hereinafter referred to as the Central Board) was formed from the three existing relief committees – that of the Free Church and the two General Committees which had been nominated by public meetings in Edinburgh on 18 December 1846 and in Glasgow on 6 January 1847.[12] The Central Board consisted of a Glasgow and Edinburgh section, each with local committees for the receipt and administration of supplies. Iona fell into the Glasgow section and the convener of the local committee was first of all crofter Angus Lamont and then the Rev. Alexander MacGregor.

Depot ships were moored at Portree and Tobermory for the sorting of provisions. On 18 February 1847 twenty-five bolls each of oatmeal and wheatmeal were delivered to Iona with further supplies approximately monthly thereafter. The Central Board Inspector, on 16 July 1847, considered an allowance of eight bolls per week to 185 recipients in Iona too much. On his visit of 31 August he was satisfied to find a reduction to six bolls per week to 107 people. There is no indication as to who they were but a list in the Argyll Estate papers, undated but prior to 1849, shows those receiving aid from the relief fund to be more or less divided between crofters and cottars – ten crofter households representing fifty-two people and twelve cottars equivalent to forty-one people.

The Central Board report of July also noted that 'The population which some time ago was 420 is now reduced to 320 in consequence of removal by emigration'. The accuracy of these figures is suspect. They imply a sharp drop from 487 in 1845, in the two years before the full effects of the crisis took hold, and the population would have had to rise again to reach the 1851 Census total of 337. Another Central Board report, in October 1849, gives a figure of 405 which fits in better with the steady trend downward during those years. The importance of the observation in July 1847, however, is that some noticeable drop in the population *had* occurred. It was this year that was to lodge itself in island memory. Nearly forty years later, in reply to a question put by the Napier Commission as to what had happened to the previous large population, the Iona delegate said: 'They all emigrated in 1847'. The Census returns, shipping lists and other evidence show that this was a simplification, but the exodus that took place over the two decades between 1841 and 1861 did find a new and more desperate impetus in the events of 1847.

On 29 January the Rev. Alexander MacGregor convened a meeting of his parishioners in Iona and Ross when he read out a letter from the Duke of Argyll. From the reaction he reported, this letter seems to have expressed the Duke's view that some of the population would have to remove before a long-term solution could be found. The meeting was clearly designed to encourage people to consider emigration and the tenor of Mr MacGregor's subsequent report to the Duke was that he had felt duty-bound to warn them of continuing hardship at home and to present the alternative in a positive light. He had also read out a circular from Dr Lang, promoter of assisted schemes to Australia, and noted that 'many regard the offer of a free passage as a strong inducement'.

Those most affected by the crisis were least able to afford the means of going elsewhere, having no assets such as crop or stock to sell. This key problem was stressed by the Free Church minister also, Mr McVean, in various letters to the Duke around this time: 'But without obtaining a free passage there is certainly hardly a family among them who would be able to go'. And he added: 'But I cannot suppress the painful impression I have that those who will be the first to show a willingness to move are the very persons that I am sure Your Lordship would wish to be the last'. That the better-off and more industrious should stay, and the more dependent be encouraged to leave, was to be an increasingly clearer theme in Estate policy over the following years.

Both ministers were aware of the dilemma their flocks were in – facing the real possibility of starvation, hearing hints of assistance to leave, receiving letters of strong encouragement from those already overseas, yet remaining deeply attached to their native soil. The prevailing mood was described by Mr McVean in March of 1847:

> A good many of the Ross people I understand have thoroughly made up their minds for America and I make no doubt a considerable portion of the poor crofters of Iona will do so

also in a very short time though they manifest at present a great deal of perplexity and want of determination.

One outcome of the January meeting was the drawing up of a list of those willing to emigrate. An analysis of the list, dated 23 March, showed that 149 families (representing 963 people) had given in their names and twenty-four of them (185 people) were from Iona. The majority of these, nineteen, were cottars or tradesmen and seventeen of them were described as destitute. Only one of the five crofters was able to pay the cost of passage in full, the others being able to pay in part or only a little.

Where did the responsibility lie for the assistance which was so obviously needed, if the generally agreed aim of increased emigration was to be achieved? The role of the Central Board in relation to emigration was the subject of much discussion, both inside and outside of it. Some within Government circles felt that it should remain the proprietors', rather than the Board's, responsibility to promote and support emigration, especially as the public money raised had not been for that purpose but expressly for emergency food supplies.[13] The Marquis of Lorne had succeeded as eighth Duke of Argyll on 26 April 1847. He had obtained copy of a letter on the subject from Sir Charles Trevelyan, Assistant Secretary to the Treasury, to Sir John McNeill and he sent the former a lengthy response to its contents on 24 June 1847.

Argyll did agree with the validity of one objection raised, namely that North America had received as many settlers as it could then absorb in reasonable conditions and that adding uncontrolled numbers too soon might produce more distress. He did not however agree that using the Board's funds to aid voluntary emigration was a breach of faith with the subscribers. The Board's Committees had the trust of those subscribers to make their best judgement about how to achieve the object of relieving the destitution. Nor did Argyll feel that the policy of removing surplus population, through aiding emigration, should be seen as a separate plan from that of increasing industrial resources and the productivity of the land for the population as it stood. It was not, in his view, a case of one course or the other. According to local conditions either approach might be suitable or some improvement might be blended with some reduction in numbers. Throughout his detailed argument on this point, he remained cautious as to whether the theory of increasing productivity to support current levels of population could really be put effectively into practice. Even though this might work in some areas, a degree of emigration must at first accompany such change. On the other option he expressed himself more confidently : 'But I am quite as certain that in others, probably many others, the land never can be properly occupied either by landlords or tenants without a considerable increase in the size of the holdings and a consequent reduction in the numbers of the people'. He concluded by stating that the burden of emigration should not lie solely on the proprietor but that it was the moral obligation of all to relieve famine 'in the wisest and most provident way for the permanent interests of the distressed'.

This declared twin aim, of reducing populations and enlarging holdings, was methodically pursued in Iona as in other parts of the Argyll Estate. On the question of assisted emigration, a statement of sums paid by the Duke of Argyll through his Greenock bank is revealing. £10 paid for passage money in 1846 leapt to £1587.12.1 for the same purpose in 1847. The Estate accounts for 1846/7 show a sum of £1741.14.6 spent on stock, crops and allowances to tenants and cottars emigrating from Ross and Iona. On the charge side, there was £1493.18.10 income from the sale of this stock and crop.

There was a flurry of activity in the spring and summer of 1847. Alexander Thomson, the Duke's banker in Greenock, engaged ships, supervised boarding arrangements and attended to the emigrants' needs, including advancing money when necessary. He was clearly an energetic and considerate agent for the Estate. In one case he arranged for Iona emigrants to live on board ship until the sailing date, to avoid the fever common in Greenock's poor lodging houses and he also reported : 'I am happy to say that the Tiree and Iona people have all been so well and warmly clothed in home-made grey woollen, that we have had no occasion to open the Duchess's charitable bale of clothing sent from Roseneath', The people had to be conveyed from the islands to the Clyde and at one point the Duke tried to enlist the help of the Commissary General in Oban to provide a boat : '. . . as the arrangements I have made are essential for removing some portion of the redundant population of these estates, I think the purpose 'is one which the Government would readily aid in'.[14] The Treasury was not so ready to agree, however, fearing that it would set a precedent. Other correspondence indicates that in the end an Admiralty steamer, probably the *Porcupine*, was sent to Tiree, Ross and Iona on 7 June to bring people to the *Jamaica*, due to sail two days later. As the people travelled together on this first stage, it is not always possible to single out the numbers from Iona itself. For example, one note from the Factor simply stated : '. . . all who have been paid are off, 250 souls between Ross and Iona'.

John Lamont, a lawyer in Glasgow and very possibly from Iona himself, also acted for the Duke in dealing with departing tenants, including the two Iona families who boarded the *Ann-Harley* in July

1847. One of them, Malcolm MacInnes, petitioned the Duke through Lamont for passage money, pointing out that he had not been able to plant seed on his croft the previous year and so had not received compensation. The other, John MacFarlane, had been grateful for a £10 donation already received from the Duke but had now found that the £4.10.0 per head needed for the fare to New York was beyond his means. Lamont was trying to negotiate a reduced fare berth but expressed a general concern about the situation in a letter to Inveraray: 'I know not what is to become of some of these poor people on arrival in America. In consequence of the present high rates of passage money, after paying freight, most of them seem to be left pennyless'.

Lack of means was consistently highlighted as a basic problem. And a corresponding attitude on the part of the people was also emerging, that they had a right to some measure of support for this option being presented so vigorously to them. On a visit to the island estates in April 1847, John Stewart the Duke's Chamberlain found 'great numbers' willing to emigrate provided there was assistance. He cited in particular a deputation of two people from Iona who came to see him at Bunessan to ask what was being done for them. One tried to drive a bargain of 50/- for each member of his family, lowering this gradually to 30/- 'which last he appeared certain he was to get as a right'. Stewart's conclusion was that if 30/- per head was all that was preventing many from leaving, then this should just be paid.

A slight tone of irritation can be detected on the Estate's side at the dependence this was risking. After a trip to Iona to value emigrants' stock, Factor John Campbell wrote on 13 June 1847: 'The people have formed such an idea that they must have assistance to emigrate whether they require it or not that it is in vain to attempt doing anything in the meantime'.

Of the twenty-four Iona heads of households who signed the emigration petition in March 1847, all but two (representing eight people) did disappear from the population records. But six of them did not do so until after the 1851 Census. A further five are known to have gone in 1849 as their names appear on the passenger list of the *Barlow* that year. Only half of the petitioners, therefore, left in the immediate wake of the 1847 crisis and they included all but one of those who indicated they could at least pay something. Of the seventeen listed as destitute, ten definitely did not leave until two or five years later. Continuing support, either directly through food aid or indirectly through forms of employment, was therefore to become necessary.

It has been argued in a recent study of the Highland famine that many landowners did not suffer as dramatically as might have been expected from the sudden destitution, and consequent inability of their small-holders to pay rent, because that class of tenantry was no longer of central significance to the overall income of the estates.[15] The conversion into sheepwalks of land formerly held by small tenants was widespread by the 1840s, particularly in the north-west but also in much of Mull. By the end of that decade, seventy-four per cent, on average, of the total estate rental in fifteen of those areas was being met by tenants paying over £20 per year. An upward trend in sheep prices helped these larger farmers weather the 1840s storm and so provide some degree of financial stability for many landlords.

This pattern was not, however, universal. The Argyll insular estates were among those which still had very large numbers of small tenants paying under £20. In Iona this was entirely the case in 1846 when no one paid more than £13 and the average was less than £8. Even by 1850, after a rent rise and a start to the creation of bigger units, only thirty per cent of the rental came from tenants valued at over twenty pounds. Over the whole Kilfinichen parish, at the same period, this proportion was sixty-eight per cent. As a corollary to the reduction in numbers, therefore, consolidation of holdings and increased income became more visible objectives in the Estate's policy from 1847 onwards.

In 1847 the Iona rents were raised fifty per cent across the board, the sole exception being the Free Church minister. The average rent was now £12. This, rather than the potato famine itself, was the event to remain marked in people's memory. It formed the first complaint to the Napier Commission in 1883. And a hundred years after that a Ross of Mull tradition-bearer, Donald Morrison, readily recalled what he had always heard from his older generation : 'One bad thing happened in Iona. The rents were raised fifty per cent in one swoop in 1847, the year of the potato famine – a year of penury'.

The Factor, John Campbell, was later to justify the rise on the grounds that the island's good land had been undervalued and that higher rents would lead to greater efforts to make the crofts pay. This was not the first assertion that rents were lower than elsewhere. In 1841, for example, in evidence to the Select Committee on Emigration it was claimed that 'on the Duke of Argyll's estate in Mull they [the rents] are not too high ; they were about twenty per cent less than the general rate of letting in Mull and the condition of them was better'.

The immediate effect of the rent rise in Iona, however, was simply that most tenants could not meet the increase. The income from rents in 1846 had been £290.7.6. That anticipated for 1847 was £400 plus £5 drainage interest but the crofters' arrears amounted to £173.0.6. Arrears were not unknown. In 1840 £478 was owed between Ross and Iona although the Iona sum amounted only to £26, five per cent of the total. In 1845 the combined arrears were nearly £485 but in 1847 this shot up to £1063.11.0 owed, out of the joint rental of £2932.15.11. By 1849 arrears for the two places totalled £1653.0.7. The severe reduction in tenants' circumstances on both sides of the Sound, plus the extra demand laid on the Iona crofters, produced this further crisis of escalating debt. The arrears were not to drop substantially, nor finally to disappear, until the mid-1850s.

The consolidation of holdings also began in 1847. Up until 1846 five tenants were listed as crofting at Cùlbhuirg in the East End of Iona. By the following year two of them had moved to other crofts on the island and three had gone, presumably emigrated as their names were included on the March petition. The accounts noted that their crofts were resumed by the proprietor at an aggregate rental of thirty-nine pounds. In 1848 they were let as one holding to Duncan Mac-Phail of Torosay in Mull at a rent of sixty pounds. This signalled the start of a new category of landholding in Iona. These larger units were henceforward classified as 'farms' rather than 'crofts' and Macphail was thus the island's first farmer.

7

Continuing Crisis
1848–1855

Previous crop failures, although serious in their immediate impact, had not generally occurred more than one year in succession. The 1846 crisis, by contrast, did not end after one season. Blight continued to affect the potato crop in varying degrees of severity throughout the following years. Real economic recovery cannot be said to have taken solid root until after 1855.

In the course of 1847 a huge amount of money was raised for the relief efforts, including some from Canada where subscription lists were opened in Toronto and Montreal in aid of the destitute Highlands and Islands. In late 1847 supplies of 1000 barrels of flour, six of oatmeal, four of beef and 250 bushels of pease were sent from Canada, plus the offer of £750 surplus cash.[1] This generous response, and the efficient distribution, are factors generally recognised as having helped prevent outright starvation on the scale of the Irish disaster. The Highland emergency was contained, although it was not over. There was also considerable pressure not to create a further problem of over-dependence on outside resources. The Secretary of the Glasgow Section of the Central Board wrote in July 1847:

> . . . I think it is not only 'extremely desirable' but even *absolutely necessary* for the ultimate benefit of the people themselves that the two Committees should bring their operations to a close at harvest as completely as if it were certain that they would never have to commence them again. . . . the more that is given the more is demanded and that the people have already become too dependent on the fund.

A note from the Treasury concerning the final closure of the relief services in Scotland was dated 2 October 1847.[2]

The Central Board did however continue, with changes in both administration and policy. The system of distribution was handed over from the local committees to paid inspectors and distributors. Charles MacQuarrie, merchant in Bunessan, was inspector for Ross and Iona while Donald MacPhail, crofter and innkeeper, was made distributor for Iona. The policy was now to demand a return in work for the relief provided. The various employment schemes which emerged were also designed to reinject some cash into the local economy and to broaden available food resources.

Vegetables, seeds and plants were handed out, in an effort to extend gardens. Fishing stations were established, for example at Carsaig, Uisken and Bunessan in Mull and in the Sound of Iona. Crews from the east coast were engaged to work the boats and to instruct the locals in the arts of catching and curing fish. In particular it was hoped this might provide a future livelihood for cottars as '. . . no regular remunerative employment has ever been found in this place since the discontinuance of the kelp manufacture, the whole of this class of people have been, and are continually, in a state of destitution and idleness.

Reports from all stations were initially successful. On 3 April 1848 the Sound of Iona crew had a catch of 2000 fish salted and ready for market, in addition to having supplied hundreds of people locally. But by the end of 1850 profits were down. There had been bad weather and some of the better fishermen had moved away. It is not clear how long the stations continued but it is likely that the lack of any nearby market, as noted in the Board's 10th Report, precluded their permanent establishment. As far as direct employment in Iona went, they did not produce the desired results. In the 1851 Census no householder gave 'fisherman' as his occupation.

The great expansion in railway building in the Lowlands through the mid-nineteenth century had already provided some work for the able-bodied willing to migrate temporarily. In January 1847 100 labourers from the Ross area were due to go south for this purpose. A more localised programme of public works, to build or improve roads, bridges, quays and harbours throughout the distressed areas, was established by the Central Board from 1848. In Iona two roads were made, one from the village to the Cathedral and another from the village across to the west side of the island, making easier the carting of peat and produce. Two years later, in 1850, a slip pier was built, replacing the string of large boulders – the Carraig Fhada (long rock) – which had served as a rough landing place up until then.

Knitting, spinning and net-making were introduced, in an attempt to find occupations for women and infirm men. Results proved disappointing, however, judging from the report in November 1848 that the value of cloth and socks made in Bunessan and Iona fetched only two-thirds the price of the raw material.

By 1849 the average weekly distribution of meal to Iona was 4 bolls 28 lbs, to a number which varied between 111 and 175. But a deputation from the Board was not satisfied that this relief was properly compensated for, despite the range of employment activities described above. They reported: '. . . and it was in the Island of Iona alone that we met with the complaint of lax and improper distribution, inasmuch as parties there had received relief without being obliged to perform adequate work in return'. Yet conditions were difficult. If their own estimate of the population was correct, at 405, then between twenty-five and forty per cent were in need of assistance, and local inspector Charles MacQuarrie spelled out the persisting hardship:

> The poor people here are in a fearful state of destitution at present. Turnips and fish are all they have to subsist upon, except what little meal they get from those who can spare any. The Parochial Board have a few on their lists but not the twentieth that need assistance so that those who had a little are obliged to give rather than see our fellow creatures starve.

Argyll Estate papers also reflect a concern for increased industry and continuing support for the population, both on the Estate's own account and in interaction with the charitable effort. In January 1848 payments in connection with the Relief Committee were recorded, including wages to two Superintendents of labourers, one in Creich in the Ross of Mull and one in Iona. Outlay on drainage work went on until the mid-1850s, although this was almost all in Ross where there was a bigger proportion of boggy ground. The main expenditure in Iona, as already noted, had been in 1847 and was reflected in drainage interest added to some East End crofts at that time. Further small drainage charges were added to the East End in 1853 and 1854 and West End rents were also augmented in 1854 for this reason, mostly by just 1/-. That the object of improving the land was achieved may be judged by a brief but expressive reference to the East End's main wet area, once a peat bog, behind Clachanach croft. In a letter in 1860, to an uncle by then in Australia for over twenty years, Dugald MacArthur wrote: 'Dear uncle, you will be much surprised that there is a great improvement at Clachanach since you went away, Lochan More where you used to float your little boats is now a dry spot and gives a fine crop of potatoes and corn yearly'.

The Estate took up the knitting trial tried out by the Central Board and made a one-year contract with a hosier Donald Cameron, in June 1850, to deliver yarn and then collect finished articles from women in Tiree, Ross and Iona. One hundred and ninety-four women were employed, thirty of them in Iona but the payment was not large, about 15/- to £1 each over the year. By 1852 income from the hosiery sold was noted as £63.3.7 but payments to Cameron totalled £475. The experiment was not repeated.

A substantial section of the Estate accounts over these few years was still directly concerned with assisted emigration. Disbursements covered passage money, smacks to convey people to the Clyde, straw for berths on board, clothing and shoes for emigrants, the buying of stock and crops and wages for valuers, auctioneers and messengers. From Whitsunday 1848 until Whitsunday 1849 this amounted to £2441.18.5. In June 1849 two ships sailed for Canada with emigrants assisted by the Duke. The *Charlotte* took 339 from Mull and Tiree and the *Barlow* took 254, including fifty-two from Iona. The latter were all landless agricultural workers or villagers. The rates they paid ranged from £3.10.0 for a single man to £35.5.0 for the largest family of ten.

By this time it was the cottars, and not the crofting tenantry, who were the main target of the emigration programme. Correspondence between the island estates and Inveraray through the early 1850s reveals desperately poor conditions, especially for the landless. Entries in the accounts include meal and flannel for the destitute in Ross and Iona and a soup kitchen was opened at the Factor's house, Ardfenaig, from February 1852. Writing to the Duchess a week later about new cases of fever at Iona, Campbell added:

> They have all got flesh meat and those of them who are now able to work are receiving a daily supply of broth together with all the poor people at draining and trenching. I thought it was best to assist them in this way as they were not able to feed themselves from the weather being so bad than given them meal or augment their wages.

Although work was still being demanded in return for relief, it was clear that the burden on the Estate of providing food was not lessening. Already, after receiving another letter from Campbell describing the near-starvation of many, the Duke had decided what his main course of action should be:

> ... I think I must proceed with the emigration and wish to send a man to Ardfenaig to tell him to make out a list of the poorest and who are *able bodied* who will be prepared at any moment. I wish to send out those whom we should be obliged to feed if they stay at home, to get rid of that class is *the object*. ... I have written Mr. Thomson to look out for ships.[3]

Income from the sale of effects and expenditure on fares and sundry assistance continued to feature in the accounts until 1853 and in declining amounts till 1855. Six Iona families went to Australia in 1852, five of them under the assistance scheme operated by the Highland and Island Emigration Society, who asked proprietors to contribute one-third of the costs.[4] Those five families sailed on the

Marmion and two, described as 'eligible' young couples, needed no aid. The others, who had large families, received loans which they were bound to repay once settled. Clothing for these emigrants had also been sent round to Iona prior to their departure. The Society selected people on the basis of need but also with a view to their suitability as colonists. Thus, the fact that three of Colin Campbell's daughters had been working as dairy maids or house servants, and two sons had been in service in the Lowlands and Glasgow, will have contributed to the assessment of the family as 'excellent'. Similarly, widow Mary MacFarlane's daughter had been a farm servant for twelve months, three of her sons had been in service in Paisley or Arran and she herself was considered a 'strong, healthy woman'. All the families known to have left in 1852 were either cottars, the younger sons of tenants or had shared a crofting holding.

Of the thirty-seven holdings in Iona in 1846, six had disappeared by the following year – five in the consolidation of the Culbhuirg crofts into one farm and one half-croft in the West End. This had been worked by Malcolm MacInnes Jr, who went to Canada, and his co-tenant Donald MacDonald took over the holding. A descendant still has the receipt, showing £59.3.7 paid in cash on 21 June 1847 for stock, the value of half the crop and a share of the bull. By 1848 another West End crofter disappeared from the rental and in 1849 there was one fewer in the East End. Thus, by 1849, nineteen crofters still worked the West End and ten, plus one farmer, the East End: thirty tenants paying rent.

Although there was now less pressure on the land than in the first year of the potato failure, the tenants continued to experience economic difficulty, Almost all of them, including the farmer, were in arrears. In December 1849 twenty-one crofters petitioned the Factor in protest at 'the enormity of the present rent payable by us'. In an accompanying letter to the Duke, John Campbell acknowledged the low cattle prices which were exacerbating problems in the Highlands at that time: 'I am aware it is impossible for many of them to pay rents this year on account of their not getting their stock sold . . . The Iona crofters are not the worst off in this respect although the foremost to complain'.

Campbell advised that it might be politic to offer some abatement, at least to the larger crofters who did not qualify for relief, in order to keep them in the habit of paying something. Arrears did not therefore seem to be used as an excuse for getting rid of crofters, at least not in every instance. In 1850 a list of 'warnings of removal' due to arrears had eleven names from Iona.[5] Five of these did eventually disappear from the island but not immediately. The other six remained. There

Table 3.

	Iona rent (including drainage interest)	Arrears
1847	£405. 0. 0	£173. 0. 6
1848	£428. 5. 0	£263.10.11
1849	£430. 7. 0	£331.12. 5
1850	£430. 9. 0	£459.13. 7
1851	£404. 8. 0	£459. 2. 3
1852	£430.11. 6	£612.14. 7

were some fluctuations in the rents. In 1850 six shillings was added to all the West End crofts for enlarged common pasture from a vacated croft. Reductions of a few pounds were made on some crofts the next year, to rise slightly in 1852 and drop again overall in 1853.

But the significant new scale of arrears which had followed the 1847 rent rise was an accumulating problem, as Table 3 illustrates. By 1852 everyone was in debt. But in 1853 the arrears almost entirely disappeared. For three years only one tenant was in default and from 1856 until 1860 inclusive there were no arrears at all. They were not entered in the Estate Accounts as 'irrecoverable'. Thirty years later a summary of rents and arrears from 1847 was drawn up for the eighth Duke and the writer made a specific note that the arrears disappeared in 1853 and had not been written off, 'leaving it to be inferred that they had been paid'. It is a little hard to believe that such high amounts could have been cleared in a single year from the crofters' own and still very stretched resources. Perhaps the Factor recognised that they were now in a position where they *could* pay the annual rent without too much difficulty, but were never likely to catch up with the accumulated arrears owed. The discreet removal of this burden might have been seen as an encouragement to maintain prompt rent payments.

On the other hand, the reduction in arrears coincided with a definite upturn in cattle prices from 1852. Incomes may also have been steadily recovering with the help of savings from seasonal earnings. It has been shown that temporary migration from High-lands to Lowlands not only continued but increased during the desti-tution years and included more heads of crofter, along with cottar, households.[6] In 1851 it was noted of the parish that contained Iona: 'Of the inhabitants in this parish a considerable number go annually to seek employment in the south but nearly all return for the winter'.[7]

Emigration in the early 1850s reduced the tenantry further, to twenty-five households, but by 1855 this core had survived the worst of the famine years and dealt, albeit reluctantly, with the rising rents. Moreover, the rent they brought in was also stable and, at around £425, was forty-seven per cent more than the income produced by the thirty-seven tenants of 1846.

Some of this increase was due to the process of amalgamation begun in 1847. Cùlbhuirg farm, formed that year, continued to command a rent, after adjustments, of about £50. Also in the East End, the Established Church minister took over land worth £27, part or all of the area between the Cathedral and Clachanach where three families had been listed in 1841. In the West End, the highest-paying croft in 1846 had been near to the village and worked by the inn-keeper or spirit-dealer. After a couple of years in the Estate's hands, after the last occupier left, it was combined with the croft at Maol and let in 1853 at £25.10.0 to Duncan MacPhail, son of the farmer at Cùlbhuirg.

The expansion of such larger units was still at the heart of Estate policy. Writing to the Duke in February 1853, with another rent complaint from West End crofters (which he dismissed as local agitation), John Campbell stated: 'I had a man from Islay looking at these crofts and would take the half or the whole of the West End if it could be arranged'. It seems clear that Campbell was working towards the partition of the island into only two farms. This idea was favoured by one visitor in 1857, W. Maxwell, who was not impressed by what he regarded as old-fashioned agricultural methods and believed that '... no improvement can be looked for; but were the island only divided into two farms, with enterprising tenants, then old things would pass away'. His views may well have been influenced by the fact that he also visited Ardfenaig where he saw 'the great improvement and excellent farming carried out by Mr Campbell'.[8]

The picture of the island drawn from the 1851 Census and an 1855 unofficial census shows a distinct redistribution of the population.[9] Extra households clustered on crofts were generally gone and the cottar/tradesman group was, by 1855, almost entirely in the village. (The only exceptions were the West End herding family of Campbells at Cùldamph and James MacArthur, a merchant still living on his brother's East End croft, but who obtained a holding of his own by 1859.)

The greater loss through out-migration had initially been borne by the rent-paying families, who dropped by 106 individuals over the 1841–51 decade as opposed to a fall of sixty-two among the landless families. But between 1851 and 1855 the first group only lost a further twenty-eight people while the cottars fell by another thirty-one, half as many again. This bears out the view expressed by several witnesses to the McNeill Report in 1851 that those who left Iona and Ross around 1847 were relatively better off and that the more recent waves of emigration had taken away those of a poorer class.

The 'Report to the Board of Supervision by Sir John McNeill on the Western Highlands and Islands', 1851 (the McNeill Report) was an inquiry to ascertain the extent of poverty in that area and to remind Parochial Boards of their obligations to provide adequate relief for the disabled and destitute and to plan for future emergencies. Sir John met with the Parochial Board of Kilfinichen and Kilviceuen on 18 February in Bunessan and took evidence from the parish ministers, local tenants and the Estate Factor and Ground Officer.[10] On 12 February one of the Board of Supervision's officers had visited several croft houses in Iona. The Parochial Board's response echoed the evidence that destitution was still rife and likely to increase. Charles MacQuarrie had as many as 1500 on his list in April 1850 and the average for the rest of the year had been 1180, or nearly half the total district population of 2577.

Several witnesses believed that material conditions had in fact deteriorated since 1846 as, in addition to the continuing potato blight, grain yields were lower, many had had to sell off stock to buy food and had begun to incur arrears of rent or debt. All concurred in the view that the regular receipt of relief, although averting the worst consequences of the famine, had had a bad effect on the character of the people, inducing dependence and indolence. It led them, again unanimously, to suggest further emigration as the only solution. Indeed, the poorer people were represented as seeking that solution themselves : 'The cottars and small crofters are now most desirous to emigrate and regret that they did not do so when the opportunity was formerly offered to them. I have applications daily from persons desirous to emigrate'. The size of holdings considered viable was a key factor, now that the potato could not be depended upon to produce basic food from even the smallest plot. Witnesses generally agreed that crofters paying under £15 rent would continue to find themselves in a spiral of diminishing returns. A croft of this size in Iona supported eight cows and two followers and produced four to five bolls of grain from one boll sown. This corresponded more or less with the capacity of the three crofts visited and described by Mr Peterkin, the Board's officer. The rental of each was £15 and they were all in arrears. He remarked, however, that they did not appear to him to be poor.

John Campbell put the minimum value of a croft where the family might be brought up in tolerable circumstances higher, at £20 a year. It was at this level he hoped to grant leases, as an inducement to industry. His evidence was consistent with the views he expressed elsewhere, that the days of the tiny plots yielding a subsistence living were over and that there should be fewer people : 'I am satisfied that the population on the Duke's property in this parish cannot be made self sustaining unless it is reduced by at least one half'.

The Duke's Ground Officer, Alexander MacDonald, supported Campbell's opinion that the Iona crofts could bear the higher rents he had imposed :

> I am of opinion that, at the advanced rents, the crofts in Iona for a man with a family, are perhaps more desirable than a croft at the same rent in Ross. It will not keep so many cattle, but it will produce more food. Two cows for milk in Iona will give as much as three in the Ross.

His next point, however, underlined the uneasy transition for the crofters, from a largely subsistence economy to one where cash played a bigger part :

> I am quite sure that the crofters in Iona (prices and rents remaining the same) cannot long keep their lands. The crofters are falling into arrear of rent and some have been forced to sell stock, to pay their rents. Two of the Iona tenants were, at Whitsunday, under the necessity of giving up their crofts from inability to pay and maintain themselves.

The Board's officer had noted that '. . . as the cottars live in the midst of them [the crofters] there is no danger of their suffering from want'. But if crofters were feeling the pinch, as MacDonald was suggesting, then this might not have applied for much longer. It was the Rev. Alexander MacGregor's feeling that '. . . a larger proportion of the cottars are tradesmen' in Iona, giving them the advantage of a skill or product to sell or barter. As we have seen, however, those without land were badly off during this period and they too had problems of rent. The Iona villagers had long paid a nominal sum of 5/- for their houses and nothing at all for the strip of garden behind. But in 1853 they were obliged to pay 10/- as rent for the eighth of an acre they occupied and, two years later, an additional £1 for their house. A meal distribution book used in Tobermory during the relief operations had ten names from Iona for the first serious years up to 1849.[11] They were mostly widows or single women plus two cottar families. But five more names were added for 1850–2, four cottars and one elderly crofter.

Guidebooks of this period, or the few extant travellers' accounts, do not add substantially to our understanding of how the people lived through these difficult times. Two valuable first-hand impressions have survived, however, contained in two sets of letters.[12] One was published as a small book in 1849 by the Rev. J. C. Richmond, an American who spent a week in Iona in July 1849. The other is the unpublished correspondence between Henry Davenport Graham and his family. After some years at sea, Graham was sent to Iona on health grounds to stay as a guest of the McVeans from 1848 until about 1854. During these years he made the drawings and notes for which he became famous, published in *Antiquities of Iona* (1850) and *The Birds of Iona and Mull* (1890). The writers made each other's acquaintance, as Richmond was befriended by Mr McVean during his stay and, indeed, invited to preach to the Free Church congregation.

Both observers found the people very poor, their food supplies meagre and their dwellings wretched. 'The houses which all the people live in are such miserable hovels that an English pig would not live in' wrote Graham. And Richmond remarked that although the schoolmaster's cabin was one of the best in the island, having the unusual feature of floorboards and lit by means of a primitive fish-oil lamp, most of his readers would think it impossible for anyone to exist there a week. He understood that only the charitable relief supplies had prevented many from perishing. Poultry and cattle had suffered too from the loss of the potato and he reported the excitement aroused by news of a pig brought into the Ross of Mull, the first seen since the destitution began. Graham had arrived in Iona in February 1848 and in August that year he wrote: 'We have begun eating our potatoes which is very agreeable as I have not seen a potato since I came here, in fact we had no vegetables except dried beans. The blight is making fearful ravages among them here, some fields are quite black with it'.

In one of his first letters Graham mentioned the 'great source of revenue to the islanders' of the flocks of visitors, many of whom distributed money and clothes. The lack of hard cash, a critical factor in the people's ability to extricate themselves from their predicament, was noticed by Richmond:

> The currency of Iona, for the people have scarcely any money, may be said to consist of eggs which are exceedingly cheap . . . Those who have time to examine the manner in which commercial affairs are conducted in Iona might seek out the merchant's abode where they may see an ounce of that new luxury tea, the like amount of that Highland necessity of life, tobacco, sold for so many eggs, which are laid down in the same manner as halfpence except that being formerly estimated at a farthing each the standard is now raised and their value is a third of a penny.

Trading had not entirely ceased but Graham complained of the slowness of the commercial smacks between the islands and Glasgow and of spoilt or underweight cargo due to carelessness or exploitation by the traders. He added that the islanders made as much use of another, free, source: 'There have been at least four or five wrecks this winter close to the island . . . Yesterday a poor man picked up a cask of pork. . . . The people of this island gain at least half their living by the wrecks, a great many valuable things are picked up which are never heard of as they conceal it, for fear of having to give them up'.

The observations of both men were not entirely negative, however. Despite misgivings about poor accommodation in the cottage which served as an inn, Richmond was pleasantly surprised:

> Three rooms! This was already a great deal where we had reason to expect only one. In the kitchen the peat upon the hearth-stane sent forth volumes of fragrant smoke that penetrated into and filled the room for the guests which contained two narrow beds. The floor was of the original soil; but a grate had been set and a good peat fire prevented it from being so damp and cold as it might otherwise have been; for it was a November day in July and summer seems just thinking of coming here. The landlord and his wife were most respectful, attentive and kind; and it was remarkable, under circumstances so outwardly unfavourable, that everything was scrupulously neat.

Later he reported a 'delicious meal' of a few small fish, fresh eggs, oatmeal cakes baked with a girdle, a little tea and milk. He also made specific mention of the important contribution of fish: '. . . codfish, flounders and ling and sometimes large numbers of gurnet, which assists them in sustaining life'.

Richmond was deeply impressed by an incident which he considered 'remarkable, when the extreme poverty of the people is remembered'. A Frenchman tried to hire a boat for Staffa on a Sunday and despite raising his offered fare to three guineas, the equivalent of sixty days wages, he was unsuccessful. Two boys were tempted and even put their boat out, but a relative on the shore and, according to Richmond the voice of their own conscience, persuaded them to return. More than once Graham mentioned the spirit of kinship and mutual support: 'It is very pleasing to see how very anxious the poor people of this place are for one another's safety, all the inhabitants of the island live together in such harmony that it is like a large family . . . Most of the islanders are related to one another and they carry out their claims of connexion to the utmost extent; a second cousin is considered a very near relation'.

The social bonds that held the community together, and traditional values such as Sabbath observance, had clearly not been undermined by the disruptive effects of destitution and emigration. Graham's letters, which number twenty-seven from February 1848 until May 1850, contain relatively few references to the potato famine and its consequences, aside from the extracts quoted above. Many of them, of course, were concerned with his own activities, the preparation of his book on the antiquities and his growing interest in ornithology. Yet his writing was lively and observant and contained many details about ordinary events in island life – ploughing and sowing, postal and steamer services, boat outings and picnics with locals, the weather, Communion Day, having cloth made by the weaver, the antics of a less than docile bull. He appeared to believe that the root of the islanders' poverty lay in their tendency to idleness, but this was a frequent misjudgement by outsiders of the crofting lifestyle. Had the way of life in Iona been thoroughly destroyed by the events of the late 1840s, then this would surely have featured more strongly in the observations of a visitor who clearly acquired a great affection for the place and its people. The overall impression conveyed by his correspondence during these key years of change was that, despite the very real problems, many aspects of life went on as before.

Graham's interest in bird life prompted an observation on the changing balance in livestock, published in *The Birds of Iona* from a note written in 1853 :

> Since the ports were open to the importation of foreign cattle, the rearing of black cattle has been almost abandoned in these parts of the Highlands ; consequently sheep have taken their place and in Iona, where two years ago, you would hardly find a sheep, now you will see scores of them ; and when, two years ago, not a Rook ever came to the island, now the hill pastures are black with them.[13]

This was a slight exaggeration, as the rearing of cattle did continue to play an important part in the island's economy. Another visitor in 1853, who spent a week in a crofter's house, commented on the 'excellent mountain pasture to numerous herds of cattle'.[14] The movement toward a higher proportion of sheep had indeed begun but it was to be a gradual process.

8

Adjustment at Home and Abroad

Boosted by the Royal Tour of 1847, the tourist route to the Western Isles flourished and grew, as the population in these parts suffered and diminished. In 1851 Messrs Hutcheson took over from G. & J. Burns their West Highland fleet including the *Dolphin*, which had been Burns' first iron steamer launched in 1844. She sailed from Oban to Staffa and Iona on a popular day trip three times a week.[1]

Despite the problems being posed by his impoverished tenants on all his island estates, the Duke of Argyll did not neglect the needs of visitors to his most famous property. Various items in the Estate Accounts refer to improvements in this regard. In 1854 a house in Iona village was restored and whitewashed for the reception of travellers. A landing place for tourists was made in 1858 and repaired at regular intervals thereafter. In the same year a joiner was paid for 'forms for pebble sellers at Iona'. The 1860 edition of Oliver and Boyd's guidebook commented favourably on these benches set up in the Nunnery for this popular tourist trade, formerly the sole preserve of troops of clamouring children. Repairs were made to the Cathedral ruins and rubbish cleared from the road leading to them. Gates were placed at the burial ground of the kings.

In 1851 Archibald MacDonald, weaver, was appointed Postmaster and a receiving house for mail was established in the village street.[2] From that date until the 1870s mail was collected and delivered on foot by Donald MacInnes, from Bunessan to Fionnphort and across the Iona ferry. His wages were three shillings a week and from 1854 the Estate paid him an extra pound per year to make a special call at Ardfenaig House for the Factor's mail. Crossing the mile of water between Iona and the Ross of Mull will have posed little problem, weather permitting, for a population where so many had a small boat. Hiring anyone available for passage to the other side was the usual practice, as implied by William Reeves writing in 1857:

> In calm weather a strong voice may be heard across the strait, which is about an English mile wide. The only mode, however, now in use of making a signal for a boat is to raise a smoke by burning a bundle of heather: and as each owner of a boat has a

particular signal spot, it is at once known on this island whose services are required.[3]

Two men in particular, a MacGilvray and a MacDougall, both from Ross, began to be named as 'ferrymen' from the 1850s and in the Estate Accounts there are regular references to allowances for them, to the purchase of a skiff from Tiree for the Iona ferry and to carpenter's repairs to it.

Communications with the outside world were thus improving. On the less public side of the island's life, however, hardship still threatened during the second half of the decade. In 1855 'meal given as assistance to Dugald McColl and family, Iona' was entered in the accounts for the Estate. The Factor's correspondence with the Duke in December 1856 mentions that he was obliged to find work for five more people who were actually starving. A list of crofts dated the same month had three names from Iona, who had been 'supplied with meal by the Chamberlain and who must diminish their stock to maintain themselves during the current year'. It also noted that a good many other crofters had asked for meal, but been refused as they were in arrears of rent. This must have applied to Ross, as the accounts show virtually no arrears in Iona from the crop of 1853 to 1860. Despite this slightly healthier situation on the Iona side of the Sound, two young crofting families from the West End were given individual assistance by the Duke in 1859 to emigrate: £16.16.0 to Peter MacArthur to go to North America and £12 to Alexander Black to go to New Zealand. Larger landholders also encountered problems, for example following the suspension of the Western Bank in 1857: 'Some of the drovers have lost severely . . . One of the Mac-Phails of Iona had 27 head which he could not dispose of . . . went somewhere else to try and sell them . . . He will suffer severely but I hope he will be able to stand his ground as he is a most useful man on the property'.[4] As the decade ended, the weather was still not on the side of those scraping a living from the soil. Duncan Ferguson, an elder of the Baptist Church in the Ross of Mull who regularly visited all parts of the parish to preach, wrote in April 1859: 'I send the contributions from friends. I thought more would have been got but the people are much straitened by reason of the severity of this long winter and the little increase of the last harvest. They have been buying Indian meal for their cattle. I have not seen such scarcity of provender within my recollection'.[5]

One responsibility of the Parochial Board, set up in 1845, was to ensure medical attendance for the poor and to appoint Medical Officers for the parish. From the late 1840s until the mid-1850s they carried out instructions from the Board of Supervision for the prevention of cholera, which involved the improvement of ventilation and cleanliness in the houses. Two committees were appointed in Iona to oversee these sanitary measures, the Rev. A. MacGregor and Colin Campbell for the East End and the Rev. D. McVean and Angus Lamont for the West End.[6] Widespread vaccination for smallpox had helped reduce the mortality rate earlier in the century and Mr McVean reported in 1843 that he had vaccinated a number of children himself, the nearest doctor at that time being at Torloisk in the west end of Mull.[7] By the 1850s however, a Medical Officer was based in Bunessan, serving Ross and Iona. There were regular allowances from the Argyll Estate accounts to this doctor, for attending the poor who were not paupers. And the Estate also gave small allowances to individual tenants who had a disabled or mentally ill member of the family to look after.[8]

By the Census of 1861 fourteen tenants in the West End and eight in the East End, plus the two ministers, were working the land on a pattern that was to remain set through to the end of the century and beyond. The average croft size was given as twelve to fourteen acres and only two holdings were now shared. Apart from the herd's family at the West End, no landless people lived outside the village.

There had been little mobility between the occupiers of crofts or farms and the villagers. In the 1840s three tenants moved *to* the village. One was a weaver, John MacInnes, whose brother continued to croft at the West End. Another, Dugald MacColl, moved just after the big rent rise in 1847 and was listed as 'farm labourer' by 1851. The third, Donald MacInnes, had been one of three families living at Mùr, one of the crofts just north of the Cathedral which became absorbed into a single holding, and he was absent as 'railway labourer' by 1851. In the 1850s Archibald Black became a fisherman in the village, leaving his East End croft to the husband and sons of his eldest sister, as his own only son had become a doctor. There is evidence of only one family moving in the opposite direction, *from* the village. This was Donald MacDonald, who first shared a West End croft with Malcolm MacInnes, then took over the whole holding when Mac-Innes emigrated. MacDonald's descendants say that a condition of his moving to a croft was that he give up his previous trade as a boat-builder.

By 1861 it was an ageing population, those over 50 years now representing twenty-two per cent of the total, as contrasted with the twelve per·cent they comprised in 1841. Not only had more young families left, but younger people in the remaining families were continuing to go away for seasonal and, increasingly, permanent work. In the 1855 list ten women and four men aged between eighteen and thirty were absent in service or as apprentices to trade or at sea. In 1858 the numbers were fifteen women and ten men. From the subsequent Census returns it is clear that most of them did not come back to live in Iona.

In a search of the 1851 and 1871 Census records of all Greenock parishes, and a sample of Glasgow and Paisley parishes, a few young single men and women belonging to Iona have been traced. They were listed, for example, as 'shipwright' or 'housemaid'. At 1871 the wives in five households were noted as born in Iona, implying that they had met their husbands while working away from home. In only two young families, both in Greenock in 1851 and 1871, was the husband from Iona: Donald MacCormick, shoemaker and John MacFarlane, ship's carpenter. In each case, from the date of birth of the eldest child, it is clear that they were already settled in Greenock before 1846.

This fits in with evidence, noted earlier, of a small amount of migration from the Ross of Mull and Iona to the Lowlands, partly through the long tradition of seasonal movement for harvest and other work and partly due to the direct sea link with the Clydeside towns. No trace was found, however, of any of the families who disappeared from Iona between 1846 and 1861. These totalled forty-nine, thirty of whom are known to have gone overseas either from shipping lists, Estate papers or the testimony of descendants. There was only one definite case during this period of a move to the Scottish mainland, when Malcolm MacLucas was given £1.10.0 by the Estate in 1856 'to remove himself and family from Iona to Lorne'. He worked first in a cordite factory south of Oban and then set up a boat-hiring business in that town.

Studies of Highland–Lowland migration have shown that it began as early as the late seventeenth century and increased steadily through the eighteenth, with the expansion of trading links and the herring fishery out of the Clyde. By the mid-nineteenth century one in nine of Greenock's population had been born in the Highlands and that town's biggest catchment area was southern Argyll. It may well be that some families from Iona settled in the urban lowlands in the wake of the 1840s destitution crisis. Yet the stronger thesis is that the great majority of them emigrated.

The existence already, in Canada and south Australia, of small pockets of Iona, Mull and Tiree settlers was mentioned regularly as an incentive during the debate over emigration. Farming was more attractive to a rural people than unfamiliar factory work in the city and in the sparsely populated territories overseas it was possible to recreate, to some degree, the social and cultural cohesion of the townships they were leaving behind. Links of kinship were a strong draw. James MacQuarrie and Catherine MacInnes left Iona in 1852 to settle in Eldon Township, Victoria County in Upper Canada, or Canada West, as Ontario was then known.[9] James's two sisters, both married to men from Mull, had been there since the 1830s. In 1855 Catherine's sister, Janet MacInnes, joined them. Also in that township were MacEacherns, MacFarlanes and MacDonalds from Iona.

Grey and Bruce Counties in the western part of the province had similar concentrations of Iona and Mull settlers during this period. There are indications that some emigrants stopped first of all in Peel County, much nearer to Toronto. John Cameron went to a place called Thistletown to stay with another MacFarlane family from Iona, who had left before 1841. He in fact became established in that area, but Archibald MacArthur and two sisters, Ann and Elizabeth, were only a short time in Caledon, Peel County before moving to take up their own land further north. Once settled in Glenelg, Grey County, Archibald married Mary MacArthur, the daughter of emigrants from Bunessan in the Ross of Mull. Here were MacInneses, MacDonalds, and MacFarlanes, all from Iona and there were further examples of intermarriage between the emigrant families. The daughters of two of Archibald MacArthur's brothers were to marry two MacInnes brothers.[10]

An extensive study of Tiree settlers in Canada in the mid-nineteenth century has revealed this pattern in even greater detail.[11] Many of them used the stepping-stone of an earlier emigrant community in Brock County, on their way to permanent homesteads farther north and west. The large settlements of Tiree people which developed there maintained a distinctive and close-knit identity. Oral tradition collected from descendants of these pioneers stresses the importance in the early days of communal work and mutual help, plus the carrying on of customs, skills and crafts brought from their crofting way of life at home. There is no reason to doubt that the emigrants from Iona, Mull and other parts of the Highlands underwent the same experience.

Support for new arrivals was necessary, as the Estate assistance had been for the passage and did not include the costs of settlement although Alexander Thomson in Greenock did make arrangements with a contact in Montreal to give Argyll Estate arrivals directions, and if necessary the means, to reach their friends and kindred farther inland. A *History of Glenelg Township* notes that character references were required to qualify for free land grants. Descendants of James and Catherine MacArthur, who left Iona in June 1847 and settled in Greenock township, have preserved the letter written by

the Rev. Alexander MacGregor. In it he attested that the couple had
always conducted themselves 'honestly, soberly and industriously'
and expressed the hope that they might be 'received into any Christian community where God in his providence may be pleased to order
their lot'.

There were daunting difficulties for emigrants to overcome. Contemporary newspapers, personal letters and Government reports tell
of many dying from epidemics of disease on board ship or of hardships due to the unaccustomed cold and inadequate provision for new
settlers. In November 1847 the *Quebec Chronicle* noted that deaths
from cholera at Grosse Isle, the quarantine point for arrivals, plus the
deaths on passage, had totalled for the season 'the fearful number' of
9634. Cholera had reached Britain in 1831 and from 1832 the disease
broke out at intervals in British North America, usually brought by
immigrants despite the quarantine arrangements which had been
swiftly set up. There was a major outbreak in 1849 and several
sources reported that the Ross and Iona people who left in June of
that year suffered considerable illness and privation on arrival.

One reason this became known was through a story of courage and
initiative on the part of nineteen-year-old Malcolm MacLucas from
Iona, who had accompanied a MacEachern family on the *Barlow*.
Alarmed by the cholera raging in Ontario when they reached Hamilton, he made his way back to Quebec and asked to work his passage
home again on the same ship. On his return the Duke's banker in
Greenock, Mr Thomson, questioned the boy in Gaelic and was
satisfied he was telling the truth. He now wished to stay in Glasgow
and apprentice himself to a blacksmith.[12] Another version of this
incident relates that the boy was in fact the sole survivor of the
family.[13] In another tale of individual tragedy, a MacInnes family
from Iona lost sight of one of their children in the bustle and confusion of the Canadian entry port. The father stayed behind to look for
him but the boy was never found.[14]

Yet, despite the hazards of a long voyage and a strange country,
many settlers did well. A letter from Alan Lamont to his son-in-law
Angus MacPhail in Iona, written in 1853, stressed the attractions of
plenty and independence in the new life:

    ... This will give you some idea of the climate and soil of Canada
    West. Whenever a person gets the wood burnt and the ground
    cleared he has nothing more to do farther than throwing the seed
    into the ground any time he thinks proper, then harrow it and
    fence it and he may depend upon good crop. .... All vegetables
    and fruits grow here to perfection and your mother made a good
    deal of jelly and jam on the produce of this garden and she made

100 lbs of sugar on the sap of the Maple tree. . . . I see you want my opinion about such a person as yourself with your family to come to this country. In reply, my opinion is that every person who is under a burden not easy carried to throw it off as soon as possible and emigrate to this quarter. I regret very much that I have spent the most of my days under so many masters – Landlords, Writers, Chamberlains, Factors etc. . . .

And from the other side of the world Iona emigrant James Campbell wrote to Dugald MacArthur: 'But with all its faults Australia is better than the old country, there being always plenty to eat and drink and a little spare cash into the bargain'.

Colin McVean, a son of the Free Church minster in Iona, had personal experience of how the emigrants had prospered when he visited Canada in 1876 and again in 1884.[15] His father had kept in touch with many former parishioners from Ross and Iona, now settled mostly in Grey and Bruce Counties in Ontario, and they gave Colin a warm welcome. The impression that he was visiting an extension of his home parish was reinforced by the common use of Gaelic, in conversation and at church, and by the further chance encounters he had. At a hotel in Toronto the head waiter turned out to have been a boyhood playmate in Iona. On the coach northward two passengers were from Ross and the driver was the son of an old servant of Colin's grandmother at Ardfenaig. Indeed, nearly everyone they met on the road had a connection with his area and 'at a stopping place, a small village where we changed horses, I was soon discovered by a knot of Mull and Iona men'.

Colin was pleased to find his old friends thriving in their new communities with well-cultivated farms and comfortable dwellings. They were clearly satisfied with their own achievement: 'They have proved themselves capable and enterprising settlers and worthy citizens of the Dominion . . . With very natural and proper pride many of them showed me their title deeds to their farms with the remark, accompanied by a smile and twinkle of humour in the eye "We are our own lairds here"'.

Although the departure of one, or a few, families at a time will have occurred throughout the period as money or assistance became available, nearly two-thirds of the total who left Iona between 1841 and 1861 did so in three blocks. The last of these was in the summer of 1852 when thirty-nine people travelled to Liverpool to embark on two ships for Australia. In 1849 fifty-two had gone with the *Barlow* to Canada. And a precise memory has been passed down in oral tradition that at some point 'ninety-eight people left Iona in one day'.[16]

These last two departures are corroborated by Richmond in 1849 who noted : '. . . fifty lately emigrated in one body and not two years ago one hundred left their homes, those poor cottages which now stand melancholy and deserted'. This indicates the year of the larger exodus as 1847, the beginning of the period when emigration was most actively promoted and assisted by the Estate. The impact of this event was not just because of its scale but also, as Colin McVean recalled many years later, because the parting was to be permanent. He had been nine years old when these hundred or so people left, most of them he believed for Canada :

> The scene on Port Rònain Iona at their departure was one to impress itself vividly on the mind and it did so on mine, young as I then was. The ship, which had previously embarked the emigrants from Mull, lay at anchor in the bay and the boats waiting those from Iona were at the Carraig Fhada while collected on the beach were most of our islanders. The grief at parting of relatives and friends under the full belief they were never again to meet one another in this world was heartrending and most pathetic.

How people felt about the unexpected turn of events which uprooted so many of them from a long-established home and way of life is not clear-cut. The contemporary records have indicated that significant numbers opted for emigration and indeed pressed for the help to make it possible. They were able to recognise that a move out of their stricken circumstances could only be of benefit. This rational decision, however, could coexist with the very genuine emotional wrench of leaving their birthplace and kindred. An islander writing in the 1880s said : 'Many of the inhabitants still remember those who left falling down and kissing the ground of their dear native land ere they embarked for a land which many of them never reached'.[17] And a song fragment collected in Canada reflects nostalgia :

> 'S fad' tha mi bho I mo chàirdean,
> Far 'n d 'rinn mi a fàgail uile,
> O tha mise fo ghruaimean.

> (I am far from Iona, land of my kin,
> where I left them all,
> O I am melancholy.)[18]

Even once well-settled, the effects of their experience on the emigrants was complex. For some, despite the undeniable improvement in their material conditions, the close bonds with what they had left behind were never severed. On his second trip to Canada, Colin McVean was even more impressed. He visited one very fine property of 360 acres where a spacious stone and lime house had replaced the earlier log cabin. The owner was from the Ross of Mull and his wife from Iona. McVean recalled that on taking leave of his hostess he remarked : ' "Is this not better than the street of Iona ?" In a burst of energetic Gaelic she replied : "I would rather be on the street of Iona on shellfish than here" '.

By 1861 the population of Iona was just over half of what it had been twenty years before. The Census records show a fall in the number of inhabitants from 496 to 263. But natural increase had mitigated the effects of this sharp decline. The real level of out-migration during these two decades was 299, a figure which represented sixty per cent of the 1841 total. The most substantial movement of people – 168 – had occurred between 1845 and 1851. In the span of those six years the islanders had seen one-third of their neighbours and relatives leave.

There was a small measure of movement in the opposite direction, bringing new families into the island. Although the same processes of change had been at work in neighbouring islands, resulting in similar high levels of emigration, some mobility within the district was still evident during the 1840s and 1850s. In addition to the MacPhail father and son from Mull who took over the new farming units in Iona, incomers included a fisherman and his wife from Gometra and four men from Mull – one crofter, a crofter/innkeeper, an agricultural labourer and a merchant.

Migration was, however, overwhelmingly outward. Such a rapid reduction must have had a social, as well as an economic impact on a small, close-knit community. It was not in itself a new experience to take leave of their fellows but this had always been in the context of temporary passage to the Lowlands or, in the case of permanent departure, at intervals and in small numbers. Now, within a few years, the people had been separated – to all intents and purposes for ever – from a significant section of their kindred.

Early reports of the potato failure had stressed an increased incidence in Iona and Ross of sickness, such as influenza, dysentery and typhus fever, and of deaths.[19] The evidence does not, however, point to higher mortality in Iona, either directly through starvation or indirectly through lowered resistance to disease due to malnutrition. Deaths registered in the OPR for the island in 1847 totalled five, no more than the average over the five years between 1841 and 1845. From 1846 to 1850 the average dropped to 2.8 per year. The winter of 1846/7 would have been the most critical time, before the benefit of the main relief effort was felt. Several observers claimed that the imported grain did avert starvation and loss of life.[20]

The usefulness of the OPR is limited by the probability that all deaths were not recorded, by the fact that few entries included cause of death or age, and by the interruption in 1843 of the Disruption. That year, when the Established Church minister for Iona left his charge, there were no death entries at all and there may have been under-registration during the following few years. The highest number of deaths recorded was from 1837 to 1840, perhaps inferring that the earlier crop crisis of 1836/7 led to increased disease and mortality. It is as likely, however, that the higher numbers were due simply to the much higher population level at that point.

A further demographic consequence of the famine decade was a discernible fall in the number of marriages and baptisms on Iona. There was a much sharper drop in the latter but assessment of this must be qualified by evidence that the baptism register became less reliable in the 1840s. The fertility rate of the remaining population remained high through until the 1880s. The fewer marriage and baptism entries from the mid-1840s may simply be a reflection of the fact that the bulk of emigrants from the island were young couples and families with grown-up children.

It was undoubtedly a period of great hardship and uncertainty. Since the great crises of famine and disease of the late seventeenth century, subsequent periods of critical food shortage had been endured but also survived. Highly self-sufficient societies, used to seasonal fluctuations in food supply, were able to cope. They proved unable to cope, however, with the severity and suddenness of the 1846 potato blight or, crucially, with its recurrence over several years. During the early part of the nineteenth century their economy had gradually been steered from a subsistence to a commercial footing, but the activities needed to generate the money for this were not yet either sufficiently healthy or numerous. The destitution crisis accelerated this process. Among those who saw leaving as the less unhappy alternative were many who had been living at the most marginal level. Those who remained met with continuing privation and had to face up to the new realities of rising rents and mounting arrears. Their only recourse was to create more wealth from within their own resources, either by increasing the productivity of their holdings or contributing their labour to the Estate. John Campbell made this crystal clear in December 1850:

> I have daily numerous applications for food but I distinctly tell them that not one pound of meal is in future to be given to anyone able to work save as he or she work for it first and unless they work they must just starve, having had the offer to emigrate those not taking advantage of it had no further claim upon proprietors for relief.

There is no evidence that the Duke of Argyll planned to clear Iona and turn it into a sheepwalk, although he was subject to pressure to follow this general path. A letter from one R. MacLachlan in January 1850 praised the grazing value of his island estates and strongly urged the Duke to consider '. . . that your crofters are the cheapest rented persons of their class in the British Empire and that crofting is the *worst* mode of occupancy for you. . . . At the present rent you *cannot lose* by getting rid of all the crofters or any portion of them at any time'.

It *was* however the Duke's intention to maximise the agricultural potential of the island through larger units which would be worked by fewer people and bring in a higher return. He pursued this aim consistently and provided the means for many to leave at a moment when circumstances combined to make staying an increasingly harsh alternative. He did not abandon his tenants to the consequences of the famine and acted swiftly to supply emergency meal and then emigration assistance, albeit accompanied by a strong measure of self-interest. He was certainly aware of the Government's view that the landed classes should bear some responsibility for alleviating the plight of their people. And it would not have benefitted his own long-term plan if the tenantry were too weakened in body, spirit or resources either to remove or to better their own conditions at home. Furthermore, reforms of the Poor Law meant that he might be legally obliged to provide for the able-bodied poor remaining on his Estate. As John Campbell bluntly put it: 'The more that are sent off the better, when once off all expense is at an end with them but while here it is a never ending drag on the property'. From 1846 until 1852, the years of worst crisis, the accounts for the Argyll Insular Estates show totals of £6679.17.4 spent on emigration costs and £1756.9.10 for payments in connection with the Relief Committee and for direct assistance such as meal, seed or medical aid for the poor. The proportions of those totals that may be directly attributed to Mull and Iona are £2970.9.2 and £776.7.4 for emigration and relief, respectively.[21]

As the repercussions of the potato blight became clear in 1847, the Rev. Donald McVean had referred to the 'perplexity and want of determination' among the people of Ross and Iona. To whom did they look for leadership in such insecure times? Both ministers were definitely influential. Mr MacGregor of the Established Church organised the meeting to discuss emigration in February 1847 and acted as a channel for information on assisted passage from the Duke and other sources, such as Dr Lang's Australia scheme. The Established Church was identified with the landlords' interests and its Highland ministers, with one or two notable exceptions, have been criticised for doing little or nothing to advocate the crofters' cause during the years of the clearances and the later land agitation. An abstract of denominations at the end of the local 1855 census for Iona shows a perceptibly greater drop in the number of adherents to the Established Church than to the Free Church since 1845. Whether this reflected a change of allegiance by a number of church-goers, or the fact that more of the Established Church congregation were willing to emigrate, can only be speculation.

The Free Church, on the other hand, had been associated with anti-landlordism from the outset and might have been expected to defend the people's right to stay. The swift and generous fundraising by its Lowland membership to alleviate the Highlanders' distress was a significant part of the relief effort. In Iona it is evident that Mr McVean formed strong and affectionate bonds with his parishioners. A writer to *The Witness* in 1850 described a group of emigrants with whom he had spoken the previous June and who had 'expressed deep sorrow at leaving their native land and particularly the gospel. This led me to ask what minister they heard at home. They replied Mr. McVean of the Free Church in Iona'. This was the time when the *Charlotte* and the *Barlow* left and McVean went to Greenock himself to distribute one hundred bibles to those on board. He also kept closely in touch for many years with those who settled in Canada.

Some of his congregation may have been reluctant to leave their church and home, but from Mr McVean's correspondence with the Duke it is clear that he agreed with the policy that considerable numbers would have to emigrate. There is also the slightly surprising fact that he appears to have had a close friendship with the family of John Campbell, the Duke's highly unpopular Factor. Campbell's wife was certainly a member of the Free Church and she made arrangements on one occasion for the special presentation of a bible to Mr McVean.[22] It has already been noted that the only holding to escape the 1847 rent rise of fifty per cent was that worked by Mr McVean although, at twelve pounds per year, it was already one of the more substantially rented crofts. Relations between McVean and the Factor were complicated further by the fact that the former had married a Susan Maclean, whose family had been tenants at Ardfenaig in the Ross of Mull for generations until Campbell had taken it over for his own use. The conflicting emotions this situation aroused are illustrated in an incident recounted by H. D. Graham, while at the Free Church manse in 1848:

> A short time ago a Miss Maclean a niece of Mrs. McVean's was staying in the house, a very charitable young lady of strict religious principles; on hearing one day that Mr. McVean stopped at

the Factor's (Mr. Campbell's) house and had lunched there, she burst out most vehemently 'How could you do such a thing! I wonder the first mouthful did not choke you!'

The Factor himself, of course, took the lead within the community in carrying out the Estate's policy. He oversaw the distribution of meal, the employment of men at drainage work, the sale of emigrants' stock and crops, the redistribution of vacated crofts into larger holdings and, in the Ross of Mull, their allocation to families such as MacNiven or MacDiarmid whom he had brought with him from Islay. All these activities were highly visible and widely disliked. It will be argued in the following section that Campbell may have drawn to himself a disproportionate amount of hatred and blame for the hardships attending the post-famine years. He was undoubtedly unflinching in seeing through tasks which he regarded as necessary evils in a time of inevitable change. The coincidence of his arrival at the very point when the blight struck ensured that his reputation would be irrevocably linked to the disaster that ensued.

By 1861 the crowded population of Iona had been shaken up and thinned out but it had not been decimated. The crisis they had experienced had been severe but, as has been argued in relation to the evidence from H. D. Graham, many aspects of daily life followed their ordinary course. Large numbers of people had gone and others had come in, yet over sixty per cent of households bore a surname that had been present on the island since at least 1779.

A sense of this continuity, despite the unsettled period, comes through in a letter written in 1860 by Dugald MacArthur to his uncle Neil who had gone to Australia before 1841. Much had changed, but other things remained the same and new circumstances were bringing their own pattern, as for example in his reference to the Disruption. He himself was to continue as precentor for more than fifty years. This letter is the only available example of a direct voice from within the crofting community of Iona at the close of these two pivotal decades. It is therefore worth quoting at length. It reflects, too, the close ties of family and friends despite barriers of time and distance. Neil MacArthur had lost touch with Iona since his departure but word of his address had reached home through another emigrant, Donald Maclean from Mull, who was a brother of Mrs Susan McVean.

Iona
30th January 1860

My dear Uncle,

I have not heard from you since you went there, I thought it my duty to write you the following lines in order to let you know how we are in Iona. We are situated at Clachanach as we were when you left us. Your old worthy mother is still going about in middling good health. My father is not getting his health as he would wish but he is, thank God, able to move about.

My mother died long ago and there is not one of the family living except myself and my two sisters . . . My uncle Charles went to America and died on the passage. My aunt Catherine went to America also and both her and her family are well. . . . I have often thought of going to Australia myself but was kept back as there is not one that would keep up the farm. But if I was so careless about my grandmother as you were I think I might have gone away long before now. My grandmother and Mary were just making for me every thing as lovely as my mother would do. I was but very young when my mother died . . .

I have to tell you that I received two letters from Neil Cameron your cousin in New Zealand. He is in good health and is very well off. He has a great farm. I have written to him in order that he might find you . . . A great number of the Iona people have emigrated both to America and Australia and there is not the third part of those you knew here now but there are others in their place from other places . . .

I am waiting from getting married till I hear how you are placed, whether you are working at your trade or at a farm. We have two Ministers in this parish now after the church reformed . . . I am a Precentor in the established church during the last eight years.

I have no more to say in this letter till I received one from you. But my dear Uncle I will conclude with my kind love to yourself and wife. My father and the rest also join with me, your mother especially sends her best love to you.

> I remain
> Dear Uncle
> Dugald MacArthur

Section IV

1860–1890

9

The Broadening of Horizons

The period following the potato famine decade was less traumatic throughout the Highlands. Tensions between landlords and tenants lowered as economic difficulties reduced, the number of evictions declined, and the great waves of emigration ceased. Rising cattle prices brought in a steadier income, backed up by some earnings from fishing and from temporary work in the Lowlands. The basis of the crofting system, however, was still very insecure. No local industry emerged to generate cash on the scale that kelp had done and declining self-sufficiency in food and material goods meant that little money could be saved for improvements to land or housing.

The population of the Highlands and Islands continued to fall at a rate that was overall much less steep than that during the 1840s and 1850s, although there were regional variations. The numbers in Iona remained fairly stable. In fact they rose slightly in the 1870s and dropped by only six per cent between the 1861 and the 1891 Census. This followed the trend of the whole Highlands area and contrasted with the neighbouring island of Mull, where the introduction of sheep farms took a heavier toll (see Table 4).

A breakdown of Census statistics for Iona shows that between 1861 and 1891 the number of crofter and farmer households was virtually static and the individuals they represented increased. The size of these families had not diminished greatly from the preceding period. Their households comprised a mean of six children plus farm servants and, in the later decades, boarded-out children from Glasgow. The number of village households, however, decreased and the total number of individuals they contained did so even more markedly. Although those who had families matched the crofters' average of six children, and although several households also took in city boarders, there was a higher proportion of elderly couples and widows living in the village.

The trend set in the 1850s thus continued. Then, the landless population in Iona had dropped by thirty-five per cent and between 1861 and 1891 it fell by a further thirty per cent. The crofting and farming tenantry, on the other hand, had dropped by only five per cent between 1851 and 1861 and in the following thirty years it rose by the same amount.

The larger farming units in Iona, formed by the amalgamation of

Table 4.

	Iona	Kilfinichen & Kilviceuen	Mull	Highlands & Islands
1861	263	2497	7240	174,983
1891	247	1745	5029	164,281
	−6%	−30%	−30%	−6%

(Source: F. Fraser Darling, *West Highland Survey*, 1955.)

crofts from the 1840s onward, became fully established during this period. By 1871 Maol farm had approximately doubled in size. There appeared to be no question of vacant crofts being added to other crofters' holdings. When Archibald MacDonald emigrated from Martyrs Bay in 1858, the croft was let to farmer Angus MacPhail of Cùlbhuirg until his death in 1862. For the next two years it was rented by absentees: first by Walter Elliott, who already held substantial lands from the Duke at Scoor and Shiaba in the Ross and at Glens and Knock in Torosay parish; the second year by Mrs Campbell Paterson who also rented part of Glens and Knock. (In 1864 Mrs Paterson bought Lochaline Estate in Morvern and during her ownership there ordered some deeply resented clearances.) From 1864 this holding was added to Maol and in 1866 the neighbouring croft at Martyrs Bay made up the last portion of the farm, when Mary Lamont retired leaving no heir.

A cousin of hers, also a Mary Lamont from Ulva, had married into a family who were to become prominent in Iona life. In 1868, by then Mrs George Ritchie, she signed the lease for the Columba Hotel which had been adapted by the Duke from the former Free Church manse. Captain George Ritchie had moved from Ayrshire to Tobermory where he operated coastal smacks and ran the Mishnish Hotel. Along with the new Iona hotel came a holding now named the Columba farm. Most of this had once been croft land, some of it rented latterly by the Established Church minister, and it also included fields worked by the Free Church minister, adjacent to the village. From Whitsun 1874 Ritchie also took over Cùlbhuirg farm. Map 4 illustrates the development of these holdings.

The three decades between 1860 and 1890 were to bring the Iona tenants into a series of disputes with the Estate over rents and conditions. Elsewhere in the Highlands, widespread land agitation was to lead in the 1880s to a Royal Commission and an Act of Parliament. The Iona crofters kept abreast of such current affairs. Before resuming the account of their economic difficulties, we will look at

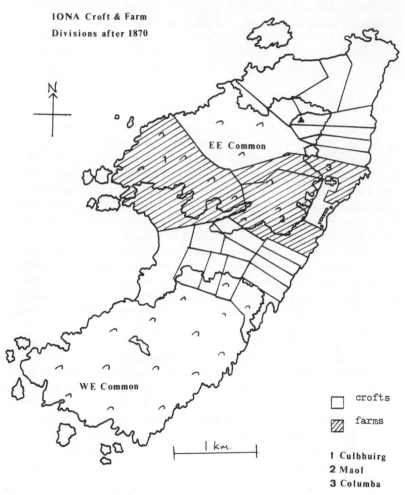

IONA Croft & Farm
Divisions after 1870

N

EE Common

WE Common

1 km.

☐ crofts

▨ farms

1 Culbhuirg
2 Maol
3 Columba

Map 4. Iona – 1870 croft/farm divisions.

the ways in which opportunities for trade, travel and education were opening up for the island during these years, and at some of the events and personalities of their lively cultural and community life.

In 1861 the screw steamer the *Islesman* inaugurated a passenger service from Glasgow which included Bunessan among several west coast stops on its way to the Outer Hebrides. This route became a vital link for the islands, bringing in goods, shipping out livestock and produce, providing a swifter means of travelling directly to the Clyde and the industrial Lowlands beyond. By the early 1870s the *Dunvegan Castle* from the Martin Orme fleet, occasionally replaced by the *Talisman*, was calling at Iona every week with cargo and passengers. In July 1875 the *Dunara Castle* took over the run, establishing a connection with the inner and outer isles that was to become particularly identified with this sturdy vessel for over seventy years.

The service for tourists also expanded from the 1850s, after the firm of G. & J. Burns handed over their fleet of West Highland paddle steamers to David and Alexander Hutcheson. The *Pioneer* and the *Mountaineer*, joined after 1866 by the *Chevalier*, sailed from Oban to Staffa and Iona three days a week (later five) during the summer season. The Iona correspondents to the *Oban Times* and the *North British Daily Mail* regularly reported the first and last appearances of these ships each year, in early June and early October. They had become a signal for the turn of the seasons.

These improvements in communication increased the possibilities for trade and the 1867 entry in Slater's Directory[1] shows the establishment of merchants in a variety of goods, alongside those still practising traditional crafts:

Post Office, Island of Iona: Archibald
           MacDonald, Post Master
           Letters are despatched to Oban on
           the mornings of Tuesday, Thursday
           and Saturday and arrive therefrom
           on the evening of the same day.
Parliamentary School, Iona: Angus McInnes,
           Master
Boot and Shoe Makers: Archibald MacPhail, Hugh
           Stewart
Smiths: Peter MacInnes
Grocers and Dealers in Sundries: John
           McCormick, Lachlan Maclean
Innkeepers and Vintners: Lachlan Maclean
Linen and Woollen Drapers: John McCormick
Tailors: William MacFarlane, Neil MacKay

Weavers: Alexander MacDonald, John MacDonald,
                John MacInnes, Archibald
                MacDonald (also Guide to the
                ruins)
Cattle Dealer: Duncan MacPhail
Conveyance by Water – to Staffa and Iona, a
                steamer, three times a week
                during the summer.

Basic foods were still provided from the island's own produce and
natural resources, as listed by the Duke of Argyll in his own book on
Iona in 1870:

> The island now supports upwards of 200 cows and heifers, 140
> younger beasts, about 600 sheep and lambs, 25 horses and some
> three-score of the pachyderms so dear to all the children of Erin.
> It grows also a considerable quantity of grain. . . . The large
> flounders of the Sound of Iona are still an important item in the
> diet of its people.[2]

The convoluted and slightly sarcastic reference to sixty pigs may have
reflected some disdain on the part of the Duke for this livestock.
There was certainly a well-known prejudice against keeping pigs in
many parts of the Highlands. Iona had been noted as an exception to
this by James MacDonald in 1808, and an analysis of the Poor Law
Inquiry Commission returns for 1843 reveal that only in Orkney and
Iona were pigs found in the homes of the poor.[3] Stocks had clearly
built up again since the virtual disappearance of this animal during the
potato blight years. When livestock returns were made for the 1883
Royal Commission the total number of pigs kept by crofters was by
then forty-nine, an average of three each. Most villagers also kept
one.

Latterly, pigs were regularly slaughtered and consumed locally but
up until the late nineteenth century references imply they were
articles for export rather than a source of food. This was W. Maxwell's information in 1857: 'Of late years as the demand in the low
country for pork increases, the people, when they can manage it
generally fatten one or more pigs, not however for their own consumption pork being in their eyes unclean! and therefore forbidden,
consequently they go to pay the rent'. And in December 1877 an Iona
correspondent reported to the *Oban Times*: 'Descendants of Ham.
There will be a scarcity of grunters in the island for some time owing
to the large shipment which took place last Tuesday per *Dunara
Castle*'.

W. Maxwell also noticed a few small patches of turnips 'which,
judging from their luxuriant appearance, thrive well'. A Ross of Mull

tenant had stated to the 1851 McNeill Report that this was a new crop in the district: 'Most of the larger crofters now grow some turnip, which they never attempted while the potato succeeded'. Another item mentioned for the first time in 1868 by a writer for the *Journal of Agriculture* was fruit: 'In the gardens are excellent potatoes and in some of them gooseberry and currant bushes and, in one instance at least, some fair apple trees'.[4]

Constance Gordon Cumming, who visited Iona in 1876, praised 'the excellence and abundance of dairy produce, the bowls of creamy milk and snowy curds are an attraction in themselves. Such fresh floury scones too, baked by the most motherly of Highland land-ladies'.[5] Iona's reputation for plentiful milk and barley had clearly not diminished since Bishop Pococke's visit more than a hundred years before.

A visitor with a specialist interest has left a brief description of the old style of central hearth and of the crafting of a household artefact.[6] James Miln, an archaeologist, took shelter in a cottage on Iona in the summer of 1868 and his attention was caught by a small vase which resembled ancient pottery. He was surprised to learn that the old woman, who was originally from Tiree, had made it herself without the benefit of a furnace. She immediately fetched clay from her garden and neatly moulded three small vases. She then invited him to return once they had dried. Miln continued:

> At ten o'clock next morning I returned to the cottage. The only fireplace was a slab of stone in the centre of the room, on which a few pieces of turf were burning. The old woman placed the vases on the fire, poured milk into them and allowed them to remain until the milk had boiled for some time. When the operation, which did not much exceed half-an-hour, was concluded, the vases had acquired sufficient hardness and had all the appearance of the ancient pottery of the dolmens.

Tiree people were known to be skilled in the making of these little clay pitchers or 'crogain' and, perhaps under their influence, the art had obviously been alive in Iona also for a time. W. Keddie's guide-book of 1850 mentioned it: 'They have an ancient practice also of forming a milk jug, of antique appearance, out of clay found in the island'.[7]

By the 1870s gabled houses with chimneys were replacing the older style, where smoke had to find its way out through the thatch. The Sanitary Inspector for the parish was actively promoting the need for more ventilation and better drainage. In 1876 Constance Cumming befriended a family who invited her in to sit beside the peat fire in what she described as 'the only cottage still on the isle with the old fashioned fireplace hollowed in the centre of the earthen floor, and with no chimney except a hole in the middle of the roof'. The 1861 Census recorded four houses with only one windowed room and seventeen with three. By 1881 there were still five cottages with a single window but twenty-nine, or sixty-three per cent, had three. In the early 1860s, two-storied slated houses began to appear. The first on the island is said to have been Achabhaich croft house, whose number of rooms with a window jumped from three to six between 1861 and 1871. So did the house of shopkeeper John McCormick who rebuilt and heightened his dwelling to provide accommodation as an inn. This became the Argyll Hotel. In November 1879 a news report from Iona stated : 'A good double cottage has been erected this last summer in the village by the proprietor. It tends greatly to improve the appearance of the place. The old thatched houses are gradually giving way to the more substantial-built and slated houses.' These new semi-detached cottages were named 'Victoria' and 'Staffa' and stand at the north-east end of the village street.

One necessity which Iona had long been unable to provide in abundance was fuel. Men, women, horses and carts had to be ferried back and forth across the Sound for the digging of peat from part of the Creich moss in the Ross of Mull. Once dried, the peats were carted to the shore at Deargphort to be stacked, each household's supply in an allocated spot, ready for calm seas for the last stage to Iona. High wind and waves could jeopardise the whole undertaking, as happened in November 1877 :

> Owing to the very wet season and generally stormy weather, it was impossible for the people to get their peats ferried across the Sound. Most of the people are, in consequence, out of fuel and in the present prevailing state of the weather must remain so. Those who are entirely out of fuel have to go to the moor and pull heather, which makes but a very poor substitute. Every available piece of wood is readily burned. The shores are well scanned morning and evening for anything that could help the fire.[8]

The next month the *Oban Times* reported that the smack *Jane* of Tiree arrived in Iona from Ardrossan with a full cargo of coals, presumably in response to the particular scarcity of the normal fuel source that year. But the days of peat burning were numbered. Another hazard was the sweeping away of entire peat stacks by storms and high tides, both on the Mull shore and in front of houses in Iona village or along Sligineach. This was what happened in the severe winter gale of 1880 and in even worse conditions in autumn 1881, as described by one correspondent :

> This month has been one of the stormiest we remember. . . . We

have never seen such heavy seas as swept through the Sound on
Tuesday. . . . Large pits of potatoes are washed away and many
peat stacks on the Ross side belonging to Iona. A great number
of people have thus lost their winter fuel. Such heavy losses
falling upon poor people at this time of year must be severely
felt.'

The Estate decided to take action. In 1882 the peat rights in Ross
were withdrawn from the Iona people and a rent reduction of two
pounds allowed in lieu, for the purchase of coal from the mainland.
Some accounts indicate that the moss was in any case becoming exhausted and that there had been complaints by Mull crofters of damage by Iona horses to their neighbouring pasture. It may be that the
horses themselves were not unhappy to see an end to the peat cutting.
The story goes that a horse belonging to Calum Bàn (Iona crofter
Malcolm Ferguson) went missing from the moss. It was found back
at the landing place and already standing in Calum's boat, as if ready
and anxious to go home. The people agreed that if a rent decrease
allowed them to buy coal, 'they would not for the future run the risk
of losing their boats or injuring their horses crossing the Sound'.[10]
But they were not happy at the size of the reduction, which they
considered to be insufficient. Their complaint was to feature in the
evidence to the Napier Commission of 1883 : 'I would say that they
would require £5 for coals in the year . . . They were saving that price,
because they were carting and ferrying them with their own boats.
. . .The money was of more consideration to them than the time
wasted.' This claim is borne out by the coal bills of one crofter, John
MacMillan. Using five or six tons each year, he paid £3.10.4 in 1883,
£3.8.6 in 1884 and £4.8.0 in 1889. This price, from 11/6 to 14/6 per
ton, was calculated on the basis of the bulk price as the island's whole
supply was imported in two or three loads each summer. Captain
Ritchie of the Columba Hotel acted as purchasing agent, ordering
from coal merchants on the Ayr or Clyde coast and collecting payments from the islanders.

The contributor to the *Journal of Agriculture* of 1868 commented
of Iona : 'there is no special appearance of poverty on the island'. the
Parochial Board minutes from the 1860s onward record only three or
four names from Iona as regularly on the poor roll. They were all
cottars, usually widows and elderly. They received sums ranging
from 2/6 to 8/- per month in addition to clothing, boots, blankets and
fuel as required. Special allowances were sometimes made to parishioners for the support of a chronically ill or disabled relative and
arrears of poor and school rates were occasionally struck off as
'irrecoverable on grounds of poverty'. Three crofters in Iona came

into this category in 1882 and one in 1887. The existence of the landless cottars remained the most precarious, as in the example provided by an unseasonal storm in May 1872 : 'When day broke the full extent of the disaster was seen. A boat belonging to a very poor but respectable old man was broken into fragments. With it he lost his all as it was his only means of support'.[11]

Two cases of petty crime in 1868 involved the theft of a barrel of potatoes from a barn and oatmeal and butter from a house.[12] The mother-in-law of the suspect gave evidence which implied that the woman in question was not in fact destitute. Perhaps her regular source of income had been delayed and this may have led her to steal as a last resort: 'My son is married and working as a carpenter in Greenock. His wife with her family live in this village. So far as I am aware she is not ill off. He sends supplies to her from Greenock ever since he went which is now about two or three months ago'.

As the need to earn or save cash within the local economy in-creased, such contributions of money or goods from relatives work-ing or settled elsewhere continued to be important. The recollections of Iona natives today make clear that this was common practice by the late nineteenth and early twentieth centuries. But there is no reason to doubt that it had long been the norm before then. One example from the 1860s was Charles MacArthur who by this period was training for foreign mission work with the Church and who, throughout his life, sent part of his earnings to help his family at Achabhaich.

Another factor, of special relevance to a famous place such as Iona, was the interest of 'benevolent gentlemen' among the regular visitors to the island. The latter part of the century saw a steady stream of donations and support of various kinds, particularly for the poorer people. Principal among these benefactors was Thomas Cook, pion-eer of the package tour business, who conducted his first excursion to Glasgow, Edinburgh and Loch Lomond in 1846. The next year he 'followed the Queen and Prince Albert over the route which they made royal'.[13] The Scottish tours were the staple of Cook's enter-prise in the early days and he accompanied his clients personally, several times each season. Thus by 1858 he could refer to his fortieth visit to Iona when, on landing from the *Pioneer*, he was greeted by the ministers Mr MacGregor and Mr McVean and all the islanders.

On all his excursions, Thomas Cook encouraged his customers – a captive audience aboard the steamship – to contribute to collections for the welfare of those living amid the historic sites of Iona which they had just visited. The particular object of these appeals was to provide fishing boats and to this end Cook enlisted the support of Dr

Alexander Fletcher, already active in the Skye Improvement Society for the same purpose. Dr Fletcher was present on the 1858 trip, to deliver the newest boat named the *Duke of Argyle*. Upon sight of her the crews of companion boats the *Legh Richmond* and the *Thomas Cook* hoisted their flags and cheered loudly. Since the scheme began in Skye in 1851 one hundred boats had been purchased, of which twenty-six had come since 1855 to Iona and Mull. The islanders were asked to repay the cost of the boats by instalments which, it was reported, they were rapidly doing.[14]

Thomas Cook continued his close association with Iona throughout his life. He donated a medicine chest to the school, for the use of the local people, and in August 1885 he presented 'a handsome bookcase filled with 250 volumes' as an addition to the existing library. The affection and respect in which he was held by the islanders is indicated in the report of that occasion, when a large number of them gathered in the schoolhouse.[15] Among the several speeches of thanks was one from John MacDonald, vice-president of the Library Committee, who said 'that his presence among them was always a pleasure, not only because of the gifts he brought but because of the kindness of spirit he showed . . . The full story of Mr. Cook's goodness to Iona would be a lengthy, though an interesting chapter'. In February 1890 the state of his health merited a news item in the *Oban Times*: 'Many of the islanders of Iona to whom Mr. Thomas Cook of Leicester has been a great friend will be glad to learn that that gentleman is recovering from his serious illness'.

Another 'great friend' of the island, who may very well have come to Scotland on a Cook's tour, was Mr Frederick Clapp of Exeter. From his first visit in 1857 he also raised money for fishing nets and boats, namely the *City of Exeter*, the *Tenax Exon*, the *Children's Friend* and the *Star of the West*. Only the last survived until the 1880s, the others being wrecked in stormy weather. Mr Clapp also sent a Christmas donation, with unfailing regularity, to be distributed among the needy. This was met with considerable appreciation as it was usually the only form of outside support, apart from that given by the Parochial Board. In 1873 it was: 'the only charitable gift which the poor of this place received this severe winter'. Even after he died in 1889, his widow sent the normal contribution in her husband's memory.

During his own visits to Iona, Mr Clapp clearly enjoyed entertaining the islanders. One such tea party for the children of the parish was also designed to set up a Penny Savings Bank in Iona and Creich and the host explained to his young guests the advantages of this new idea. On another occasion a hundred and fifty local people and visitors feasted on tea, bread, jam and sweets at the Columba Hotel, where Mr Clapp was staying. And on the event of his marriage in London, he even arranged for a 'soiree' for the children in Iona that same day.

The emergence of local newspapers in the latter part of the nineteenth century brought the islanders still further into contact with the outside world. Their own contributions to these papers also provide a new store of detail on the life of the community, particularly on learning and leisure activities. The *Oban Times* began in 1866, taking over the *Oban Monthly Pictorial Magazine* of five years' standing. The *Oban Telegraph* ran from 1876 and the *Oban Express* from 1888, these two amalgamating in 1902. One of the first reports in the *Oban Times* from Iona mentioned the Iona Mutual Improvement Society which, according to its secretary Dugald McVean, a son of the Free Church minister, 'was originated by young men of the island and has all along been sustained without extraneous aid by the subscriptions of its members and honorary members. Its object is simply the mental culture and improvement of its members in pursuance of which it has established a public reading room'. A series of lectures organised by the Society was also noted. Within a single week in 1867 the members heard Mr Kyle from Glasgow talk on 'Trades Unions', 'The Game Laws' and 'A Tour through Prussia during the late war', these 'admirable addresses' then rounded off by 'a very interesting lecture on Astronomy' from the Rev. Donald McVean.[16]

Debates were also a feature of the Society and two of its founders were men whose eloquence and wit became renowned in the island : Malcolm Ferguson and Neil MacKay. They were regularly in demand to take the chair, or deliver recitations or a vote of thanks, at meetings, concerts and presentations. Malcolm Ferguson was always known locally as Calum Bàn (fair-haired Malcolm) and in an appreciation written shortly after his death in December 1920, the minister noted that he had been a founder member of the Mull and Iona Association 'which had its origins in the Mutual Improvement Society which met from time to time in Bunessan and Iona'. The 'Mull and Iona' was one of the first Highland Associations in Glasgow, set up in 1866. This clue to a connection with the native intellectuals supports the view that the initial aim of these associations was less concerned with the Annual Gathering of music and dance, for which they later became known, and more with the promotion of welfare and education for Highlanders, both at home and exiled in the city.

Neil MacKay, a tailor to trade, came to Iona from Campbeltown in the early 1860s, married a young widow from a long-established local family and settled in the village. Taigh an Tàilleir (the tailor's house) quickly became established as a ceilidh house or meeting place for the exchange of news, views and stories. These were by no means restricted to local events. MacKay's obituary in the *Oban Times* of 11 January 1896 recalled these days:

> His keen memory and originality of speech made him one of the most competent men in a company . . . An advanced liberal in politics, his pen was always fearlessly used on behalf of the oppressed. His house was the place of rendezvous for old and young and he was seldom applied to in vain for news of a far away ship or the gist of a political speech.

During the 1870s and 1880s Neil MacKay was the Iona correspondent for the *North British Daily Mail (NBDM)*, a Glasgow-based paper which gave good coverage to rural affairs by devoting several columns each day to 'Local Notes' from around the country. There is no doubt that this and other newspapers were read, passed round and discussed by crofters and villagers in Iona.

Horizons were widening, both geographically and educationally. The *Oban Times* obituary of Dr Duncan MacArthur on 20 May 1905, a native of Iona, referred to him as 'one of a band of young men who in the sixties and seventies left this far famed island to pursue their studies at the University . . . and almost all of them became afterwards men of influence and prominence in their different spheres'. Duncan practised as a doctor in Wakefield but kept closely in touch with Iona through annual visits home. He too was a founder member of the Mull and Iona Association in Glasgow. A contribution to his medical studies came from his elder brother Charles MacArthur, born at Achabhaich in 1831, whose story was among the more unusual of those who made a career far from the island.

When a young man, Charles acted as Cathedral guide and his intelligence caught the attention of a visitor from the Anglican Church, Bishop Chapman of Ceylon. He offered Charles a missionary college education. After ordination by the Bishop of London in 1857 Charles was sent to Ceylon, where he became a priest and lived for nearly twenty years. During this time he translated the Pentateuch into Tamil, which he had learned. Invalided back to Britain, he ended his days as the parish clergyman of Burlingham in Norfolk.

Other Iona-born ministers from this period included the Rev. Donald Alexander MacDonald, born at Calva in 1847, who studied at Glasgow University and the Free Church College. He served for many years as Convenor of Inverness County Education Authority, for which he was awarded the Honorary degree of DD by Glasgow University. The Rev. John Peter Campbell was born at Lagandòrain in 1846 and, towards the end of the century, two MacDonald brothers from Machir – Angus and Coll Archibald – both entered the ministry. Coll A. also received an Honorary degree from Glasgow University for his service as Convenor of Perth County Education Committee.

Dr Donald Black was born at Cnoc Cùl Phàil in 1839 and became Medical Officer for the parish, based in Bunessan, before moving to South Uist in 1877. In gratitude to him, his patients there paid for the erection of a headstone over his grave in the Rèilig Orain upon his death in 1885. Alexander and Donald MacArthur, two brothers from Achabhaich, entered the clothing trade in Birmingham and later brought in Charles and Neil MacDonald, their nephews from Ardionra.

Charles MacArthur, born at Clachanach in 1864, worked on the West Highland steamers of David MacBrayne as a teenager and at the age of twenty spent his first full season at sea, as his father wrote to relatives in 1884: 'Charles left me for the first winter, he used to be away in the summers. He is wishing to pass for Mate and he must serve 4 years before the mast . . . that is the way'. Later he became a trawler skipper out of Leith. A spell as ordinary seaman with the local shipping line was a common start for the very many young Hebridean men who went to sea. It was the required apprenticeship before an intensive course at navigation school. Reaching the level of captain was a desirable aim as it was more stable. Only he and the Chief Engineer were automatically kept on a ship, the rest of the crew being signed up for each voyage. Perfect colour vision was one natural attribute that was mandatory and the time then taken to gain a captain's ticket depended on the opportunities that arose. Donald MacMillan from Lagnagiogan became captain of the *Dunara Castle* around 1912 and later of the *Hebrides*. Colin Cameron from Traighmòr also became a sea captain as did Gregor, Hugh and Dugald MacDonald from Machir and their brother John was a chief officer. There were a number of others from Iona over the years. The aptitude of island boys in handling boats from an early age, and their familiarity with nautical terms, was undoubtedly a great advantage for those drawn to make a career at sea.

The annual Inspection now required by Government gave consistently favourable reports of Iona School (see Chapter 14). But it was not only formal learning that shaped the minds and fostered the abilities of the young people of the island. Observers writing of those who made a successful career away from Iona, and of those who made a mark in local life, stressed the degree to which many were self-educated. The Mutual Improvement Society, begun on their own initiative, was one example. Great pride too was taken in the library and good use made of it. An encyclopaedia, for example, became known as 'leabhar Chaluim' (Calum's book) as Calum Bàn took each volume home in turn and read it right through. Books came from other sources also, as a friend of the popular romantic novelist William Black recalled: 'Once, at Iona, I saw him carrying a box of books to a crofter's cottage, a gift for one or two struggling lads on the isolated island who were striving to add to their store of knowledge even amid the hard surroundings of their daily life'.[17]

Another who benefitted from the library was Alexander Mac-Donald, born in 1819 into one of the two branches of weaver Mac-Donalds in the village. Known by the nickname 'The Mathematical Weaver', he fascinated local children and astonished visiting academics by working out complex problems of trigonometry and algebra by his own original method. Angus MacKay recalled hearing that he wrote them on his weaver's apron. He frequently sent solutions to the *Oban Times*, under the pen-name of 'Retsila' which was 'Alister' in reverse. George Ritchie, who as a boy often watched the weaver at work, later remembered the experience:

> While weaving he studied deeply and seemed to do the weaving automatically. He would suddenly get up from the form, and on a piece of slate that was always at hand commence figuring. He thought audibly and always in Gaelic. Squares and cubes and powers and the wily X and unknown quantities were then subjected to the keen scrutiny of an alert scientific brain. . . . There was quite a good library in Iona in those days . . . so that with the dim light of the 'cruisgen' Retsila would be found engrossed with Josephus, Gibbons, etc.[18]

Alexander attracted nicknames. He was also known as 'The Duchess's Weaver', as the Duchess of Argyll supplied him with an extra large loom to weave special webs from his own designs. And as 'an t-Each Donn' (the brown horse) he is said to have run an unofficial school in his house for a time. His brother Allan Macdonald was in fact the official schoolmaster from 1871 to 1876 and on two occasions at least, when that post was vacant, Alexander was asked to teach on an interim basis. He did so to the satisfaction of parents, Inspectors and the Factor John Campbell who even recommended to the Duke that Alexander be given a small salary, to avoid closing the school when he took up his normal summer job of landing passengers from Hutcheson's steamer.[19]

On 15 and 16 October 1878 a Regatta and Games were held in Iona and reported with great detail and colour by Neil MacKay in his *NBDM* column. He stated that it was 'the first attempt to have a regatta here since 1834' and his account of the opening race captured the atmosphere of the day :

> The course was from the anchorage Iona, round the Lianaich at the mouth of the Bunessan harbour and back, a distance of about ten miles. At the start of the races it was just such a day as the lovers of racing would be jubilant over, every boat starting under reefed sails, fully expecting it would blow great guns. When about half distance the wind took off a little, then every reef was shaken out for the final run homeward. The races were well contested by both classes.

The Games included amusements such as the sack and three-legged races, as well as throwing the hammer, tossing the caber and putting the shot. The climax was a fiercely contested tug-of-war between Iona and Ross. The Regatta and Games became regular events for three years at least.

Another sporting fixture was the shinty match on New Year's Day, a tradition widely observed as F. Marian McNeill noted :

> In the Highlands the great New Year game is camanachd or shinty, which is played with a ball and a curved stick called a caman. The whole community – men, women and children in their best attire, with a piper at their head – used to turn out to see the Iomain Mhòr, the great shinty match.[20]

The Iona men went to the wood at Loch Pot I, just beyond Fionnphort, to cut branches to make their camans. In 1883 the older game gave way to a football match for the first time when captains Neil MacCormick, Sìthean and Coll MacDonald, Post Office led their teams to a one-all draw. Football remained the preferred New Year match in Iona although in many places, including on Fionnphort beach across the Sound, shinty continued to be the custom until early this century. Hugh MacKinnon from Eigg remembered the annual New Year shinty there up until 1925.[21]

Until late in the nineteenth century New Year was celebrated 'old style' on 12 January in line with the Julian calendar, which was in force until the calculation of dates was adjusted by Pope Gregory XIII in 1582 and eventually introduced in Britain in 1751. On the last day but one of 1878 an attempt was made in Iona to move to the 'new style' of recognising 1 January. It was another sign of wider communication with the outside world but, as the *NBDM* wryly recorded, changes to one of the year's major social events was not to be considered lightly :

> A good deal was said both for and against. It was quite apparent that a majority were in favour of the new style but objections were urged against the untimely notice of only one day to

consider and make the necessary arrangements and that such a time-honoured custom ought not to be so lightly departed from on so trivial a notice. One reason given, perhaps characteristic of highlandmen, was that the principle element conducive to highland philosophy at New Year was still on board the *Dunara Castle* and if the next day was stormy no liquor could be landed (which was the case) . . . Our absent friends will no doubt be glad to hear that the New Year was held again on the 12th as usual by the other half . . .

The following year, everyone celebrated on 12 January without a murmur.

Postal services improved swiftly during this period, in step with the expansion in steamship communications. By 1877 a new route to Oban via Dalmally speeded up the transfer of mail to Mull and in addition the *Pioneer* began to carry a mail bag directly to Iona every weekday of her summer sailings. Around 1873 there began the long association of a Maclean family with the ferry service by sailing skiff between Fionnphort and Iona. Allan Maclean from Deargphort in the Ross of Mull became ferryman but, due to his sudden death after only a few years, his young son Coll took over in the late 1870s. Colla Mòr, as he was always known locally, was to be a familiar figure to islanders and visitors alike for over fifty years.

In winter the mail service reverted to three times a week, but it still made an important contribution to island life as an article describing Iona in the 1880s made clear:

The post is eagerly looked for by most of the people who are now as well posted up in the Afghan difficulty, the Soudanese war and in fact in almost all our foreign political controversies as they are in the naval and military expedition to Skye. The newspapers are now eagerly read regarding all Highland matters and affairs of the nation generally.[22]

By this time there was much news, highly pertinent to their condition, for any informed crofting community to discuss. Disturbances in Skye, Tiree and Lewis had spilled over into riots until public and political pressure forced the Government to appoint a Royal Commission headed by Lord Napier and Ettrick in 1883. Two years later five representatives of the Crofter's Party captured Highland constituencies in the General Election, among them Mr D. H. MacFarlane in Argyll. A recognised influence in this wave of agitation was John Murdoch, editor of *The Highlander* magazine. He gave a well-attended talk in Iona schoolroom in 1876, another in 1883, and in 1884 someone from every household turned out to hear him again, this time as a delegate from the new Highland Land Law Reform

Association (HLLRA). A branch was formed in Iona shortly after that meeting with Malcolm Ferguson as Chairman, David Kirkpatrick (Schoolmaster) as Secretary, Alexander MacDonald as Treasurer and members Alexander MacInnes, Donald MacDonald and Lachlan Maclean from the West End, Archibald MacPhail and Donald Mac-Donald from the East End.[23]

Coll A. MacDonald, who was born in 1873, used to run with other small boys after school to Peter MacInnes's smiddy in the village – 'oir bha Pàrlamaid nan seann daoine an sin' (for that was the old folk's Parliament). A lively debate would be going on about the crofters' question then facing the country. They had all read MacFarlane's speeches in the newspaper and everyone had his own cure for the problem. Coll compared the sparks of the discussion with the sparks of fire as the bellows fanned the flames and as each point was punctuated by the clash of Pàraig Gobha's hammer on the anvil.[24]

Long accustomed to reading, talking and exchanging views, the people of Iona were well prepared when the 1883 Commission, commonly known as the Napier Commission after its chairman, gave them an opportunity to present their case.

The Napier Commission and the Crofters' Act

Central to the Iona crofters' list of grievances, as laid before the Napier Commission, was the high rent they had to pay. By the end of their tour the Commissioners had held seventy-one meetings, received testimony from 775 people and their report noted that the principal cause of dissatisfaction was restriction on land. In only six places did the question of rent play a more prominent role than that of land – Kilmuir in Skye, the Orkney island of Rousay, Clyth in Caithness, Tiree, the Ross of Mull and Iona. Three were the insular estates of the Duke of Argyll. In the Abstract of Returns to the Commission, the average acreage of arable land in an Iona croft was entered as 8.1 and the average rent, including common pasture, £20.9.6. This compared with averages of £2.18.1 for 8.7 acres in Barra, £5.8.1 for 13.4 acres in North Uist and £7.14.4 for 7 acres in Kilmuir. The Iona rents were the highest listed.

Before examining why the rents had reached these levels, we should consider what economic resources were available to the crofters to meet them. The basic means of payment was still the sale of livestock:

> Large shipments of cattle, pigs, sheep and potatoes left here last week by the steamers *Dunara Castle* and *St. Clair* for Glasgow. We are sorry to hear that the prices realised for the livestock were very low, which must affect the crofters much, as they depend wholly upon the livestock for the payment of their rents.

That was reported in the *NBDM* in November 1879. Saleable stock needed good crops for feed and many of the newspaper reports through the 1870s and 1880s reflected anxiety about the damage done by wet summers or stormy autumns and recurring sign of blight in the potato, as in October 1876 for example:

> The past fortnight has been very stormy and wet and a considerable quantity of crop is still exposed in stack on the fields . . . The crops this year are inferior; fodder for cattle will, in consequence, be very scarce. Potatoes are much under the average owing to the continuous heavy rains; disease is spreading among them very fast.

Fishing continued to be a part-time occupation, providing a useful supplement to the diet, rather than developing into a commercial enterprise. There were regular newspaper reports of good local catches of cod, ling, herring and lobster and east coast luggers were in the area in pursuit of the same species, plus eel and skate. But there is no indication that any, other than a few cottars, depended on fishing as a main source of income. In the view of Neil MacKay, writing to the *NBDM* in April 1875, this was a pity : 'Unfortunately, there are not many fishermen in this district. If there were a few good persevering crews, with suitable boats, a good thing could be made of it'.

The period when kelp manufacture was a highly profitable business had long passed, but as late as 1878 there was a reference to 'the house situated near to the Free Church and formerly used as a kelp house'.[1] In October 1873 an unusually high tide swept away a pile of collected seaweed plus a quantity of made kelp and the Argyll Estate Chamberlain reported to the Duke that £29.10.2 had been realised from kelp manufactured in Iona in 1872. These references all probably relate to efforts by the Duke to revive the kelp industry in parts of his Estate in the early 1860s. A report from Kintyre suggested a three- or four-month trial there and 'at the end of that time . . . permanent works might be established in Iona or elsewhere'. The British Seaweed Company judged an experiment at Tiree to be premature but made an interim proposal for Iona : 'Our probable plan in Iona would be to stack the tangle in winter and ship it in summer and to make kelp with the remainder'.

By 1868 there was a kelp contractor temporarily resident in the village'.[2] (John Campbell was still mindful of his long-term plan to reduce the island's population. He told the Duke that if the Seaweed Company wished to send anyone there to instruct the cottars, 'it would be better to send a single man as Iona is already overpopulous'.) This renewed burst of kelping activity did not appear to benefit the people to any significant extent. It was the Factor, rather than they themselves, who was now selling the product and some of the promised wages for labouring and carting were never paid.

Caring for boarded-out children from Glasgow was one new and undoubtedly welcome source of additional income for some Iona households during this period. The placing of orphans and deprived urban children with guardians, in preference to institutional care, was a distinctive feature of social welfare administration in Scotland from the late eighteenth century.[3] As far as possible, rural districts were chosen and homes were carefully selected by the city Parochial Boards. A few shillings per week was paid for each child's keep and some clothing was provided. In a survey of the system for the Board of Supervision in 1873, Inspectors of Poor found it to be working, on

Table 5.

For boarding 18 children	£121. 9. 6
To shoemakers	£ 7. 1. 3
To tailors	£ 4.17.11
To schoolmaster	£ 14.19. 0
plus	
Medical attendance	£ 1. 0. 0 (one visit)
Clothing material to value of	£ 15.12.10

the whole, very successfully. Between 1860 and 1868 up to eighteen children were placed in Iona by the City of Glasgow parish. Inspectors were well satisfied. The island was considered a healthy spot and far enough away to deter drunken or violent relatives from pestering the children. The guardians formed affectionate ties with their charges and were eager to adopt them as their own at twelve years old, this being the general practice.

But in 1868 Factor John Campbell issued a peremptory order for the immediate removal of all the children from Iona, drawing a scathing attack from Mr Kyle of Glasgow's Parochial Board. He demolished the Factor's argument that the boarded-out children were responsible for the nuisance of pebble-selling to visitors, since the siege of every arriving boat had been made by the native youth long before their city companions arrived and 'since their removal the trade is carried out as brisk as ever'. He denied that the children were paupers: 'Does he know that all of them had two suits of clothes, each one for work days and another for Sabbath with good stout shoes and stockings . . . and it was a pleasant sight to see them all going to church on Sunday in charge of their teacher'. And he refuted the allegation that the children brought no advantage to the people of the island. On the contrary, 'they have stated to us over and over again that they did not know how they could have made up the high rents of their crofts had it not been for the children's money'. He calculated that over the previous twelve months £148.7.8 in hard cash had been sent to the island (see Table 5).

The Duke did not have prior knowledge of his Factor's action and questioned him closely on it when the row over the removal became public. Campbell was forced to admit that the children were in good health, nearly all lodged with people who had no family of their own and were usefully employed at harvest, herding or other light work. He insisted, however, on his favourite theme that once the teenagers were legally adopted these extra inhabitants would be an unnecessary burden on an already sufficient population.

The children were removed, but the objections had not originated with the Duke and from 1882 through to the First World War the practice was resumed, this time from Barony Parish in Glasgow. In the Ross of Mull, where children were also placed, they became known by the nickname of 'Barneys'. By 1886 Barony had 427 children in fifty-four locations. Iona was one of eight places where there were more than twenty children. The numbers in Iona rose to over thirty, in the homes of both crofters and villagers, and the annual inspections by Barony Parochial Board consistently found that the children were healthy and happy, their lodgings clean and comfortable and their progress at school good. By 1891 fifteen households, out of a total of forty, were receiving an allowance for their boarded-out children.

Both the *Oban Times* and the *North British Daily Mail* reports of the 1870s and 1880s are full of references to tourism and comparisons of the state of the trade from one season to the next. For example, in August 1872: 'Seldom has the Sound of Iona presented such an animated appearance as it did last week. Yachts of every description arrived daily'. And two months later: 'We have had more strangers staying on the island than on any previous year'. In August 1873: '... from fifty to sixty tourists make their appearance here daily, so that the hotel-keepers, guides, boatmen etc. are making a fair harvest. Like other watering places we have had our share of the Glasgow folks as a number now, instead of going "down the water", venture "round the Mull" ...' (In 1851 Hutchesons had begun to aim for the Glasgow Fair market, advertising cheap excursions of three days from Oban to Staffa and Iona at 10/- or 12/6 for a married couple.)

An item in August 1881 read: 'It is seldom we have had so many visitors residing on the island as this year, particularly in private lodgings. The demand for private lodgings is every year on the increase'. This particular point was raised during the inquiry by the Napier Commission who asked the Iona delegate: 'Those who come to Iona seem to prefer living in private cottages? And you think, if you had a good lease of the place, the tenants would be encouraged to build such houses as would let?' The answer was unequivocal: 'Yes; I think it is the best way the place would pay, in my opinion'.

In 1885 the graceful paddle steamer the *Grenadier* was commissioned by David MacBrayne and she plied the Staffa and Iona route through most of her long career, which ended tragically in a fire while berthed at Oban's North Pier in 1927. Her first visit of the summer in 1889 was hailed by one correspondent as 'bringing with her light and sunshine'. More prosaically, she also brought income as this report the same September indicated: 'For the last three months nearly, Iona has been literally "flooded" with tourists and all the letable

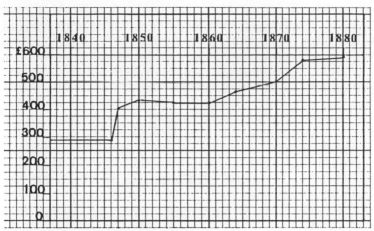

Figure 5. Estate income from Iona rents.

houses on the island have been let, some for long periods'.

The summer season was, however, short and all families could not move out of their houses to make way for paying guests. The principal source of economic support remained the land, and what could be grown and raised on it. Margins were very slim. Mary MacMillan, whose father John took over his uncle's holding in 1879, recalled his frequent remark that in the early days all money had to be set aside for the rent and there was virtually nothing to spare at the end of the year. The extracts from his income and expenditure notebook in Appendix 3 bear this out. The first year quoted, 1883, had a high expenditure which was only balanced by donations from his brother, who was at sea, and from an uncle, who had emigrated to Australia. In the case of another crofter an Estate report dated February 1882 stated : 'Has 5 of a family all young. Brother in America assists, could not carry on otherwise'. The delegate to the Napier Commission in October 1883 said : 'For the last fourteen or fifteen years I did not put a shoe on my foot, a shirt on my back or a bonnet on my head with any profit I derived from the croft'. And Dugald MacArthur wrote in 1884 to an emigrant relative :

Clachanach was only paying £10 at your time and on the same ground I am paying £21 and about £2 between poor money and road money. So you may guess that it is not very easy to pay everything . . . from day to day we are struggling the best way we can.

Figure 5 shows the fluctuation of rents over the period and the points when they rose most sharply. When considering the Estate's attitude to its crofting land and the income to be derived from it, we must return to the events of 1846 – the disastrous potato famine and the arrival of John Campbell, known in Iona and Mull as the Factor Mòr (big factor). Campbell was himself a farmer of note. His farm at Ardfenaig extended to over 1300 acres and was highly commended in the *Journal of Agriculture* of 1868 for its mixed husbandry, new strains of livestock and modern labour-saving implements. He was ambitious for the holdings under his care, doubtless calculating that their improvement would likewise enhance his own reputation. The crisis of 1846 and the following years strengthened the view which he consistently put forward, that larger farming units with fewer inhabitants would be a more efficient way of working the land. This would bring a better return and provide a higher standard of living for the people.

Some of the smaller rises arose from one or two shillings being added to rents overall, or from farms' income – for example, from the creation of Cùlbhuirg farm in 1848, the Columba farm in 1870, and the extension of Maol around the same time. It was the crofting tenantry, however, who bore the brunt of the three main increases. The first and steepest was the addition of fifty per cent laid on every croft but one in 1847. (The exception was land adjacent to the Free Church manse and worked by the minister. It eventually became part of the Columba farm.) As has been noted in Chapter 7, despite protests and persistent arrears at first, most crofters did remain on their holdings and did succeed in meeting the higher sums.

The second surge in the rents came in 1864 when the West End crofters were asked for an extra 16/- each in return for the common pasturage of a vacated croft which they would not, however, be allowed to stock. They petitioned the Duke with their objections to this and the result was an even worse imposition. They had to sign a paper agreeing not only to the 16/- but also a further £4.4.0, or lose their holdings. Setting out this incident in a later statement, John MacMillan added : '. . . and this latter sum I have repeatedly heard my relatives assert was laid on the rent in order to show them, that the factor etc must be obeyed without being questioned, or any attempt being made to find out whether his commands were in keeping with reason, justice or truth'. Indeed, the extra four guineas was referred to bluntly as a 'fine for making demur to the factor's arrangements' when these crofters were to bring their rent complaints to the Crofters' Commission in 1890.[4]

The East End received similarly arbitrary treatment in 1872. In March they were served with a notice of removal 'from house, crop, garden and everything in possession at Whitsunday next' and shortly afterwards they were summoned to the Factor's office to sign another paper making them liable 'to any rent he would think fit to impose'.[5] The story that Dugald and Neil MacArthur remember hearing was that the Factor decided to put an extra fifty pounds on the total East End rent and the crofters were to work out for themselves how to divide it. The feeling was that, as he knew they would find it hard to agree, he could then impose the rise and evict them if they were unable to pay. He would then make the East End into one farm.

A reprieve came when the Factor Mòr died in late summer 1872. The following spring the new Chamberlain, James Wyllie, asked the Mull Ground Officer to report on the size and quality of the East End crofters' land and stock. This was to be done without their know-ledge. The Ground Officer's assessment was careful and sympathetic. He considered that an increase of no more than twenty-five pounds overall would be fair, particularly in view of current circumstances : 'I can assure you they are ill off this year. Some of them, their crop of potatoes failed and their other crop was not very good, and they will require to buy meal, seed corn and seed potatoes'. But despite this recommendation, the full fifty pounds was added to East End rents in 1874. By this time, therefore, nine holdings were rented at twenty pounds or over, and ten at between fourteen and nineteen pounds per year.

That the Factor Mòr consciously sought to force the Iona rents upward is undeniable. But the experience of the East End crofters suggests that to place responsibility for such a policy exclusively at his door would be unfair. There were undoubtedly occasions when he followed no counsel but his own – as in the case of the boarded-out children in 1868 – but as far as rents were concerned his strategy appeared to be in line with that of the Estate. In his many statements on the subject, the eighth Duke of Argyll defended the sound prin-ciples on which his island estates had been managed over the years.[6] The people were better off on holdings of a viable size and only outright bankruptcy was a reason to evict them : 'I am opposed to the system of very small crofts as I am equally opposed to the system of farms enormously large. My aim has been to consolidate the small crofts gradually, as the vacancies by death and insolvency arose, . . . into farms of a variety of sizes'. He was not averse to incomers, who brought new skills and knowledge, 'yet, as a matter of fact, all my farms in Mull and Iona, with only two exceptions, are held by Highlanders'.

In the Duke's view, accusations of unjust management against factors were ill-founded. They were even more so, and more hurtful, in the particular case of John Campbell who was no longer alive and able to answer the charges. Referring to Campbell's widow and her charitable works the Duke went on : 'Within the last few weeks I have heard her name – and her husband's name too – mentioned with grateful remembrance among the really poor on the Ross of Mull'.

The picture of John Campbell and his reputation is complex. No Estate figure looms larger in the history of Iona, the Ross of Mull and Tiree, both for the significance of his actions as Factor and for the subsequent tradition that surrounds him to this day. His death became a special focus for pent-up bitterness. A common version, as told by another John Campbell, born in Iona and brought up in the Ross, is of a very gruesome end : 'He came alive like a maggoty sheep. A curse came on him . . . hens were put under his arms to see if it would draw out the maggots, hens – yes, it was a curse, a man that would put a match to your house to put you out of it'.

A song made by a Ross of Mull crofter Uisdean Ross talks of rejoicing at news of the Factor Mòr's death and the bonfires lit in celebration in the exile settlements of Canada.[7] Dugald MacArthur remembers listening to his father talk about this song with a Captain MacFarlane at Cùlbhalla in Mull. One line says : 'S 'n uair a thèid iad do'n bhàta nì sinn gàir a bhios èibhinn' (when they go to the boat we will laugh with glee), an allusion to the taking of the body by sea to Campbell's native Islay for burial. Yet an eyewitness account of the funeral conveys a very different impression. As this came from the Factor Mòr's own brother it was understandably loyal to the deceased's memory, but there would have been no reason entirely to invent all of the details in the scene he described :

> . . . the Bier, with the longest coffin I ever saw, being carried shoulder high by twelve of the tenants who were relieved by others at short intervals . . . these rough looking men on shouldering the Bier sobbed and cried like children and all who understood Gaelic – which embraced all present – could hear them muttering regrets for the loss of their best friend ; and all agreeing that they should never see his like again. At nine we reached the new pier at Bunessan . . . The whole throng pressed us to take them to Islay which we could not but we did take about sixty and, at ten in the most brilliant sunshine and on a smooth sea we started on our mournful errand.[8]

It has been argued by scholars of oral tradition that factors, rather than landlords, unwittingly drew to themselves the blame for traumatic events affecting a community.[9] It was they who were more visible, personally issuing orders and collecting rents, and they inspired none of the ties of traditional allegiance which may have still lingered around the landlord. It is noteworthy that remarkably few songs and stories relating directly to the potato famine and its dire consequences have come down by word of mouth in any part of the Highlands. The emotions aroused by these events have either been consciously suppressed or diverted elsewhere – into, for example in respect of the Argyll Estate islands, the opprobrium heaped on the Factor Mòr. The polarity of local views on this subject is illustrated in an exchange of correspondence in the *Oban Times* in 1887. The first writer held the Duke of Argyll directly responsible for high rents and harsh treatment of tenants in Ross and Iona. Another claimed, however, that 'the Duke was unaware of the doings of his late factor and his underlings' and added: 'It is well known that there was no tenantry better off and better treated than the Duke's in Ross before Campbell and MacNiven came from Islay'.

For six years following the first big rent increase of 1847 the Iona crofters fell badly into arrears. From 1853 until 1856, however, there were few arrears and from 1856 to 1860 there were none. In 1861 they reappeared when the West End tenants owed £61.3.0 and the East End £35.12.6. Although these sums fell substantially by 1864 to under ten pounds in total, arrears continued to feature in the Estate accounts to a greater or lesser degree through to the end of the 1880s. From evidence to the Napier Commission it seems that the Iona people preferred to borrow money rather than be in arrears; in answer to the question 'Is it the fact that they are obliged to borrow money very often to pay their rents?' the delegate stated 'Yes, I know that of my own personal knowledge'.

In the early 1880s seventeen Iona crofters petitioned for a reduction in rent as they had failed to sell sufficient stock at the last Bunessan market.[10] Only nine or ten head of cattle had been sold from Iona and the Ross and at only a third of the former price. This problem must have been compounded by the particularly severe weather of 1880 and 1881. The storm of January 1880, during which the Tay Bridge disaster happened, was reported in the *OT* to have 'left its mark with more or less effect on every homestead on the island'. Even it was almost eclipsed by the series of furious gales in the autumn of 1881, when thatch and slates were blown off and hay-stacks, corn stooks, carts of peat, barrels of potatoes, and boats were seriously damaged or swept clean away. A list of losses suffered by crofters in Iona was drawn up by the Estate, on the basis of which some compensation was paid and seed potatoes, oats and barley supplied.

These storms, plus some recurrence of the potato blight and the low cattle prices, led to the worst scarcity since the late 1840s in the Highlands and Islands. Sparks of defiance over lost grazings in Skye spread to Tiree, Barra, Lewis and the mainland and fuelled the general atmosphere of unrest in crofting communities. In March 1883 the Government responded, by appointing the Napier Commission 'to inquire into the condition of the crofters and cottars in the Highlands and Islands of Scotland and all matters affecting the same'.

A letter dated 11 July 1883, signed by twenty-five crofters and villagers in Iona, earnestly requested the Napier Commission to visit their island to hear their grievances. The Free Church was booked for the occasion. But after the hearing at Bunessan the Commissioners were forced by bad weather to return to the mainland. East End crofter Malcolm Ferguson (Calum Bàn) was delegated to go to one of the final sessions in Glasgow on 19 October, to represent the three groups of islanders who had submitted written statements – the crofters of the East and West Ends and the villagers.[11]   The Iona crofters' basic request was for 'fair rent, security of tenure and compensation for improvement'. At the heart of their complaints were the increased rents which they considered to be fully double what the holdings were worth. Calum Bàn asserted several times in his evidence that returns from the land itself were much diminished from the time when these rents were set. He attributed this partly to soil erosion, from persistent rain and storms, and partly to soil exhaustion, from the vicious circle of constant cropping and over-stocking in an effort to meet the higher rents:

> I have seen in wet weather, particularly in winter time, the sea quite dark for fifty or sixty yards round the coast, with the substance of the soil washed away altogether with the floods that were coming. . . . The soil is less productive. It does not yield any returns. . . . it would be far better to have less stock and to have them always in good order.

Although he did admit under questioning that the island had to support only half the population of the 1840s, and that one family now held the same area of land previously cultivated by three or four, Calum Bàn maintained firmly that they were if anything worse off:

> They are not so poor as they were in 1847 and 1849 and perhaps 1850 but in my younger days the people were better off than they are now. . . . I remember thirty years ago when they would put six or seven quarters of barley and bere and oats and rye to the mill to make into meal, and perhaps would sell in the market three or four quarters besides; but now, supposing they would thresh every sheaf they have in their ground, in some years they would not take more than two or three quarters off it altogether.

The same problem was highlighted by crofter John MacMillan in a later statement for the Crofters Commission in 1890: 'Previous to my predecessor's death it was quite a common thing with him to sail in company with others in a boat to Bunessan loaded with grain to be ground into meal but nowadays it is an utter impossibility to do so'.

The souming for an Iona croft was given as eight cows and one horse. Calum Bàn added that everyone now also kept between six and ten sheep although these had not been allowed at one time : 'The late factor made us put away our sheep'. The over-grazing which Calum Bàn believed was destructive may well have related to the growing numbers of sheep and, indeed, a specific complaint about their overstocking on Calva croft had been investigated by the Chamberlain in 1879. The crofter claimed that the forty extra wintering hoggs he had taken on were kept within his own boundaries and seldom grazed on the common, and that his reason for keeping so many sheep that year was because his stock of cattle was so much reduced. All the East End crofters at that time 'admitted that unless some sheep were kept they could not carry on profitably'.[12]

A range of other complaints added to the crofters' sense of grievance against the Estate and the late Factor in particular. These included the removal in 1860 from the West End common pasture of Cnoc Mòr, a hill above the village where tenants were used to grazing their horses and where it was relatively easy to catch them for crossing the Sound to the peat cutting or for routine farm work. The tenants had also suffered from the spread of foot and mouth disease in their stock, which had allegedly been infected from a bull bought by the Factor Mòr in 1849 and deliberately landed in Iona to avoid the contamination of his own animals in Mull.

There was also the much disliked practice of 'mòrlanachd' or compulsory, unpaid labour for the Estate. The Napier Commission return noted under 'obligations incumbent on the tenant' : 'Six days annually of their servants, horses and carts in repairing roads, watercourses etc', although the evidence revealed that this had not been enforced for a number of years. This suggests that the Factor Mòr was the last to exact it. The resentment felt by tenants at this extra burden has come down in oral tradition. Iona people sometimes had to cross to the Factor's farm at Fidden in Mull to dig potatoes or build walls and they had to take their food with them, as neither it nor money were given in return. Another well-known story is that of Iain Phàraig (John MacInnes of An Os) who was delayed trying to catch a horse in the West End hills before going to cart stones for the Factor Mòr. When he was reprimanded for being late, his ironic retort was : 'Nach cum sibh as mo thuarasdal e ?' (Won't you just take it off my wages ?). It was considered a rash remark to one who commanded such authority.

Four villagers signed a separate statement to the Commission which began : 'We are crofters by rights not cottars. We pay our rent to Mr. Wyllie the Duke's factor. We cannot keep any stock because our crofts are limited to one eighth of an acre'. Their payment since the mid-1850s of thirty shillings for house and garden had, in their view, altered their status. They were aggrieved, however, that the Estate did not recognise this and did not grant to them, as to the crofters, the same compensation for storm losses, nor seed and potatoes in a bad year, nor a reduction in rent to purchase coal. They also claimed that a summons of removal was served on them by the Factor in 1859.

For the purposes of the Napier Commission, however, most of them came into the category of cottars, defined as occupants of houses whose annual rent did not exceed two pounds and who held no land or pastoral privileges directly from the landlord. The rents of several villagers did rise to two pounds or more in 1859, the year of the removal notice, which may therefore have been used as a scare tactic. They were from the trade and commercial class – the postmaster, the postman, the weaver-cum-boatman and the two shopkeepers.

In November 1883 the *Celtic Magazine*, founded by Alexander MacKenzie who was a well-known campaigner for the crofters' cause, noted the end of the Napier Commission's tour :

> Whatever may be the outcome of its labours . . . the Commission has already done unspeakable good by exposing the evils of Highland estate management to the world. The report will be looked forward to with great interest but whatever it may recommend public opinion will assuredly force a very great and early change in the relationship between landlord and tenant in the Highlands, to the advantage of both.

When the Commission did report, however, neither landlords nor land reformers were entirely happy. Napier wished to set a minimum size for a croft, effectively excluding the numerous small tenants, and to revive a system of townships with responsibility for working and managing the land. In the event, the Gladstone Government by-passed these proposals and used the Irish Land Act as the basis for the Crofters Holdings (Scotland) Act of 1886. This provided crofters with security of tenure as long as the rent was paid, with the right to compensation for improvements and the right to bequeath the tenancy, and a Crofters Commission was set up with the power to determine 'fair' rents up to a limit of thirty pounds. (This maximum became fifty pounds under later legislation in 1911.) But the Crofters Act did nothing to extend the areas of land available for crofting and this was a major disappointment to those active in the reform movement. Land raids and public protest continued until a further Royal Commission set up in 1892 went some way toward allocating land from deer forests and grouse moors back into cultivation.

Although restrictions on the amount of crofting land did not feature as largely as elsewhere in the Iona tenants' evidence to the Napier Commission, they remained alert to opportunities for re-claiming it. In 1884 they wrote to the Duke suggesting that, on the forthcoming expiry of its lease, Maol farm be 'made into two competent holdings of two crofts each'. This would be the necessary inducement to attract a working blacksmith, which the island currently lacked, and they had a suitable candidate in mind. This fairly bold step may have originated in prejudice against the farmer who took over the lease of Maol in 1878. He was Richard Sinclair, born in Mull and closely related to the MacNivens, one of the families brought in from Islay to Mull and Tiree by the Factor Mòr. The request appears to have been ignored by the Estate.

A newspaper item in December 1884 indicates that, when the Duke's Chamberlain came to collect the rents, a reduction of ten per cent was made in Iona and seventeen per cent in the Ross. Just under two years later, however, the Iona crofters again petitioned the Duke (Fig. 6). They expressed gratitude for the recent generous reduction but, despite this, 'we find ourselves even more deeply embarrassed than last year. That the continuance of low markets and the extra expense of obtaining coals we find that the rents drawn during 1846 would be as much as we could honestly pay'. The Duke replied: 'I have come to the conclusion that the only satisfactory way of settling the question of rents will be to apply to the new Commission to put a valuation upon your crofts'. Similarly, he felt unable to agree to several recent requests for improvements since, under the Crofters Act, he could not be sure that the rents fixed would be sufficient to bring back interest on his outlay.

The Duke agreed that improved fences and houses would be of benefit. He chided them gently on their 'old fashioned' agriculture and cited the kitchen garden lately established on one small farm – for which he had offered prizes of five and ten pounds – as a fine example of increased produce. He concluded: 'I would be very glad to see the crofts on Iona *models* for all others. The soil is excellent and you have easy access to markets. But your husbandry, tho' far better than your neighbours, is still far behind the times'.

The Duke of Argyll was clearly not opposed to the existence of crofts and crofters and he was accepting the inevitability of the new legal situation, whereby his tenants could have recourse to an independent body to set the rents he would receive. He had, however,

F

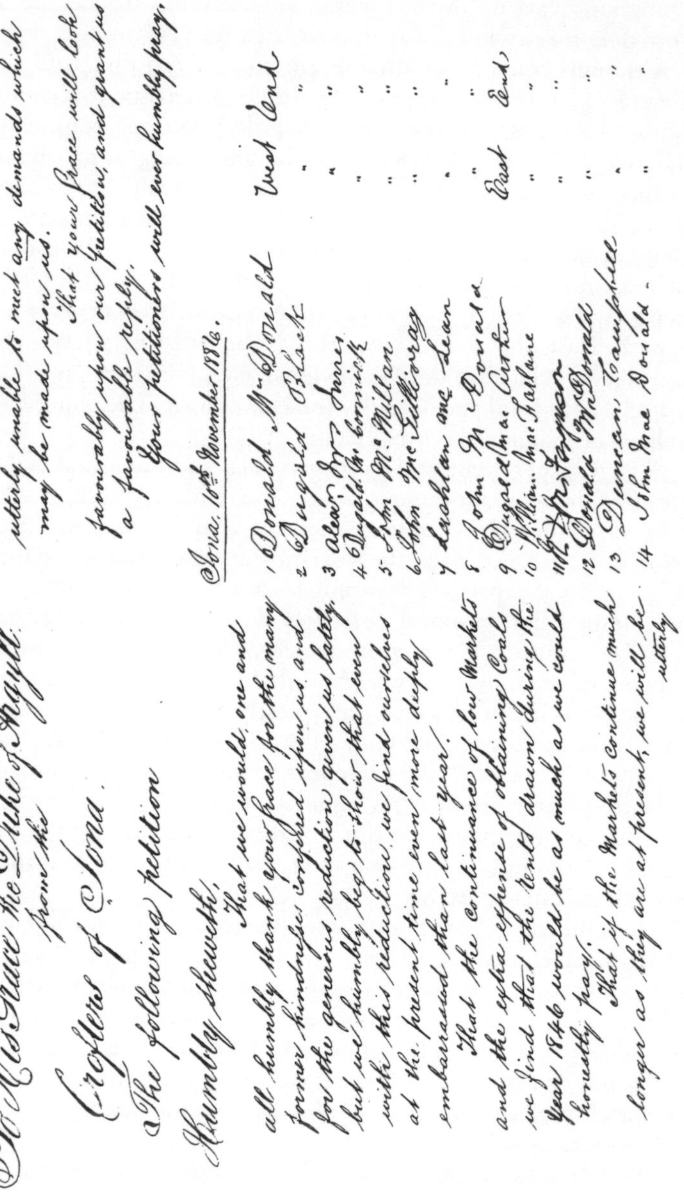

To His Grace the Duke of Argyll
from the
Crofters of Iona.

The following petition
Humbly sheweth:

That we would, one and all humbly thank your Grace for the many former kindnesses conferred upon us and for the general reduction given us lately, but we humbly beg to show that even with this reduction, we find ourselves at the present time even more deeply embarrassed than last year.

That the continuance of our Market and the extra expense of obtaining Coal, we find that the rents drawn during the year 1846 would be as much as we could honestly pay.

That if the Markets continue much longer as they are at present, we will be utterly

utterly unable to meet any demands which may be made upon us.

That your Grace will look favourably upon our petition and grant us a favourable reply.

Your petitioners will ever humbly pray.

Iona, 16th November 1886.

1 Donald McDonald   West End
2 Dugald Black   "
3 Allan ... Ross   "
4 Dugald McCormick   "
5 John McMillan   "
6 John McGillivray   "
7 Archibald McLean   "
8 John Gn Donald   East End
9 Archibald Curtin   "
10 William McFarlane   "
11 ... Ferguson   "
12 Donald McDonald   "
13 Duncan Campbell   "
14 John Shaw Donald   "

Figure 6. Copy of 1886 petition to Duke.

been vociferously opposed both to the Napier Commission and to the Act that followed it. He had become the most articulate and best-known defender of the principle of private land ownership and had resigned his post of Lord Privy Seal in Gladstone's Government over the Irish Land Bill of 1881. The Duke's own response to the Napier Commission was to publish a pamphlet on the management of the Tiree and Mull estates for over a century, in which he set out the reasons for his firm belief that 'every single step towards improvement which has been taken during the last 130 years has been taken by the proprietor and not by the people'.[13] He was convinced that his achievements rested on the ability to amalgamate crofts as they fell vacant and so create units of viable size, and on the direct contractual relationship between him and the tenants. He argued that the Act would put an absolute stop to such advances.

Although the Duke was right to recognise the undoubted progress in the Highland smallholders' standards of living since the mid eighteenth century, and although he was more realistic than some observers of the time about the impact of an inexorably rising population, he did underestimate the fundamental flaw in his system – its inherent insecurity. Arbitrary eviction and the imposition of higher rents without means of recourse had long represented twin threats to the crofter's basic livelihood. Their removal provided the crucial incentive needed to improve land, working methods and housing.

The Duke's views on land reform were voiced forcefully and publically but the counter-arguments were put equally strongly. John Murdoch gave the Commissioners additional evidence on behalf of several crofting communities, including the Ross of Mull, and in it he stated:

> There have been extensive and elaborate statements laid before the Commission in regard to the expenditure of large sums of money by proprietors in improving their estates . . . [this] expenditure in Sutherland, in Lewis, in the Long Island, in Ross of Mull, Iona and Tiree, cannot be shown to have done any good to the crofters. On the contrary it has done them harm in many cases in that it has helped others to add their crofts to their own farms. . . . The outlay of the Duke of Argyll is credited with a large increase of rent but the great cloud of witnesses, the greater number of the population, complain of this as one of the causes of their sorrows.[14]

An item in the *Oban Times* of 18 December 1886 reported from Iona: 'A meeting of crofters was held in the schoolroom on Wednesday night when they decided to ask the Crofters Commission to visit the island'. The people may have been anxious to test out the new system but it was not until April 1890 that the Commission was able to sit in Bunessan, where it received evidence from fifty-four crofters in the Ross. On 16 and 17 April the Commissioners crossed to Iona to hear sixteen crofters from the West End and four from the East End.[15] A Mr John Campbell from Oban acted as agent for the applicants and Dr Alexander McKechnie of Bunessan as Gaelic interpreter. The outcome was a reduction of between ten and thirty-five per cent on the rents and the partial or total cancellation of the arrears which every applicant had accumulated. Two East End crofters who had not applied were subsequently put on the same footing as the rest through a reduction in both rent and arrears by the Estate. Taking into account the ten per cent abatement granted in 1884, all Iona crofters were now paying an average rent of £10.10.0 – between thirty-five and fifty per cent less for their holdings than when the Napier Commission met.

For them, then, the Crofters' Act had settled their major grievance. The *Oban Times* reporter expressed satisfaction with the proceedings of the Crofters Commission on 26 April 1890:

> On the whole the evidence adduced was very favourable from crofters' point of view and there were some extraordinary cases of rack-renting. The bulk of the evidence was given with an intelligence rarely to be met with in Highlands or Lowlands and on this fact alone the Ross of Mull and Iona crofters deserve to be congratulated. Even those who lived in Factor Campbell's days and who experienced the full force of his high-handed management, seem to be gradually awakening to the fact that the Earth is the Lord's and not the Laird's and given for the good of man and not for the good merely of a few individuals.

Over the next twenty-five years little was to change in the basic crofting and farming economy of Iona. The Brand Commission, set up to examine the potential for extending crofting land, met in Bunessan in 1894 and investigated several cases justifying additional grazing in the Ross of Mull but there was no representation from Iona. The natural limitations of a small island meant that the encroachment of large sheep farms or sporting estates did not apply. The absence of this particular Highland problem here was not universally understood, as novelist William Black observed drily in an article on romantic misrepresentation of the Hebrides:

> This reminds one of the member of the House of Commons who got up in his place and declared that even the sacred soil of Iona was given over to grouse and deer; and no one thought it worthwhile to tell him that all the deer and grouse in Iona might be put in a single pie and nothing be found below the crust.[16]

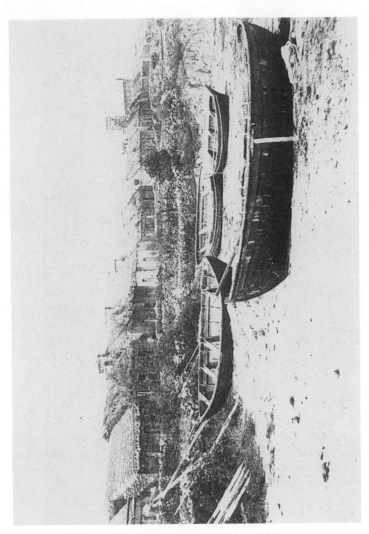

Plate 9. Iona village photographed in September 1856 by Thomas Keith. All the houses are of one storey and thatched.

Plate 10. Visitors embarking at Iona slipway for the paddle-steamer *The Grenadier* c.1890.

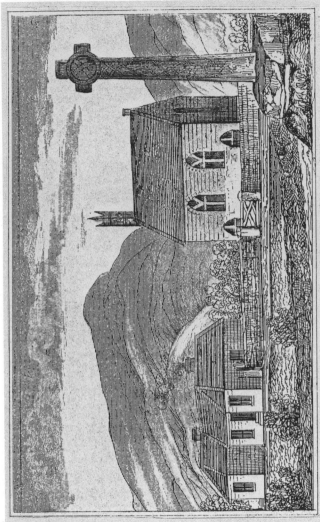

PARISH CHURCH & MANSE
IONA.

Plate 11. Sketch of Parish Church and Manse by Colin A. McVean, a son of the Reverend Donald McVean. Published in *Iona and the Ionians* by W. Maxwell in 1857.

Plate 12. The ruins of Iona Cathedral, as seen by visitors up until 1902.
Photographed by George Washington Wilson, probably in the late 1860s.

Plate 13. Rev. Archibald MacMillan (centre), parish minister Iona, along with visiting ministers and three elders of the Kirk Session on 14 July 1905. The occasion was the opening of the Cathedral for worship after the first phase of restoration.

Plate 14. Schoolchildren gathered for their annual picnic, c.1910, with teacher Mr James Wood. The flags were presented by the Duke of Argyll.

Plate 15. Transporting livestock. (a) Swimming two horses, one either side of the boat's stern, from Mull to Iona in the 1920s. (b) Sheep taken one by one down the jetty, to be ferried out to the cargo steamer, *Dunara Castle*. 1908.

Plate 16a. Haymaking c.1912. Hector MacNiven, Maol, is in the centre with his mother, Mary, to the left.

Plate 16b. Loading stirks at Iona jetty for ferrying to Mull, c.1910. Their heads are being tied to the thwarts.

Section V

1890–1914

11

Social Life
and Traditional Skills

At the Census of 1891 there were 247 people in Iona, only two fewer than the number listed in 1779 by the Duke of Argyll's Chamberlain. Over these hundred and twelve years the population curve had swept back down to almost exactly the same point. In some respects the structure too was similar. The farming and crofting tenants of 1891, with their families, represented seventy-three per cent of the population compared with seventy-six per cent in 1779. The gender division was reversed but still roughly equivalent: fifty-two per cent of the 1891 total were male, fifty-two per cent in 1779 were female. By 1891, however, the trend of the second half of the century toward an ageing population was well established. Those over fifty years comprised twenty-three per cent of the total, whereas in 1779 (males only) and in 1791 (males and females) they had represented only ten per cent.

The social and economic context in which these 247 inhabitants now lived was of course significantly altered from that of a century before. The crofters' fight for a fair rent had been won, but along with security of tenure came the limitations on the size of smallholdings. If higher incomes became necessary, crofters had to seek the assignation of another croft or turn to additional cash-earning activities, such as working at roads or occasional building, acting as boatmen for the summer steamers and letting out houses to visitors. Two crofts were vacated entirely during this period, both through emigration to Canada. In 1889 the MacDonalds left the double holding at Calva, which was then let jointly to the East End tenants for grazing until 1904 when it was assigned to Archibald MacArthur of Clachanach. In 1902 another MacDonald family departed from Sandbank, which passed to John MacInnes at neighbouring Greenbank in 1904. In 1895 the shared croft at Machir became a single holding when one of the tenants, Neil MacCormick, died. The nineteen tenants working eighteen crofts at the time of the Napier Commission thus dropped slightly by the turn of the century to sixteen, six in the East End and ten in the West End.

The years at the close of the nineteenth century and up to the start of the First World War represent, in many ways, a transition period between an old world and a new. Further improvements in communications and in the standard of living, which were to accelerate throughout the twentieth century, began to appear. On the other hand, many agricultural practices, social customs and traditional crafts, with roots in long usage over many generations, were still very much alive. These did not by any means all die off overnight. But the old society to which they belonged did change rapidly and permanently after the watershed of the 1914–1918 War. The present older generation of Iona natives provide a link to this period, through their own memories or those of their parents, thus reinforcing some of the lines of continuity which run through the history of the island's crofting community.

In 1893 a travel writer named Malcolm Ferguson spent a week on Iona and in the preface of his account of this visit he acknowledged his debt to the local crofter of the same name – but better known as Calum Bàn – who had acted as guide and informant: 'My namesake of Iona, I daresay, is one of the most intelligent and best read natives of the place. I was much surprised to find him so thoroughly posted up in everything of importance going on in the outside world, and especially in the adjacent islands of Mull, Great Britain and Ireland'.[1]. The zeal for self-education had by no means diminished. In 1897 the Debating and Mutual Improvement Association was revived by the younger men and the opening paper given by the minister, Rev. Archibald MacMillan, was on 'The reading of books and how to set about it'. Subjects local and national, historical and topical were all tackled. Neil MacKay, the tailor and newspaper correspondent, once corrected a visiting speaker on a detail referring to the Crimean War – he had not been there, but he had read about it. Among other topics, the debaters agreed that 'enlarging the present boatslip is preferable to building a new one at Port na Frang' and that 'intermediate holdings are the best'. In 1904 the prized collection of library books finally gained their own home when a building gifted by Andrew Carnegie was opened by Lady Victoria Campbell, daughter of the eighth Duke of Argyll. The library became a regular gathering place on Friday evenings and after the business of returning and issuing books, the young folk were sent home and the men would stay for a ceilidh round the fire.

Many of the young people, whether boarded-out or native, were increasingly seeking opportunities for employment away from the island. Ferguson commented on this growing mobility:

Comparatively few of either young men or women remain on the island. . . . A goodly number of the young men follow a seafaring life, engineering, shipbuilding, etc. Not a few hold responsible positions in Mr. MacBrayne's widely-famed fleet of steamers. Many of the young women leave their native homes to be engaged in domestic service. At the end of last year there were not more than ten native girls above sixteen years of age on the island and still fewer young men.

The local impact was noticeable, as a newspaper item on the opening of the Iona singing class in the winter of 1884 had noted: 'The attendance is not so large this season as last, as a great many of the youths, male and female, have gone south in search of employment'. An Iona native recalls that her grandmother, bringing up a family on a croft in the 1890s, insisted that they all go to learn a trade or skill, the boys to become a blacksmith and ship's engineer, the girls to dressmaking and nursing.[2]

The appointment of a Medical Officer of Health for Argyll from 1891 strengthened the efforts of the Mull district Sanitary Inspector to improve water supplies, sanitation and the control of infectious diseases. His first report, which was a general overview of the county, commented that in many parts 'there appears to be a morbid dread of infectious disease'.[3] This no doubt had its roots in the high rate of mortality, particularly among children, when epidemics struck earlier in the century. Isolation was often the only available counter-weapon. The MacArthurs at Clachanach had lost three young sons around 1840. One, five years old, had been sent to stay with an aunt at Calva, the most remote croft, when smallpox broke out; but he was homesick, made his own way home over the hills and caught a chill which proved fatal. A descendant of that family recalls a fear of second-hand clothes, due to the risk of tuberculosis, and when her grandfather died in 1909 the bed was taken outside and burned.

Children were kept at home by parents, or the school was closed, at the first sign of disease spreading, as in the case of whooping cough in 1903, influenza in 1908 and scarlet fever in 1912. Much needed work was also carried out on new drains and dry closets for the school and provision was made for the regular cleaning and disinfecting of the classrooms.[4]

All crofts and farms had at least one well within fairly easy reach and a barrel to collect rain water was also common. A good water supply for all the people of the village caused concern to the County authorities during the 1890s but by 1904 the Sanitary Inspector reported: 'In the village of Iona there are now two sources from which the people get their water and they have had a supply all the year round though rather short in very dry weather in Summer'.[5] Clothes and blankets were often taken to the well for washing, until piped water began to become available from the 1920s. An old firegrate might be set up at the well so that a pot of water could be kept boiling. The cottage at Burnside stands near enough to the stream for a pot to be hung on a swee, or right-angled iron bar, formerly fixed to the gable wall above an open-air fire. The women would spread the washing out on the grass to dry, while the children herded the cattle out of curiosity's reach.

The doctor for the area continued to be based at Bunessan, a fact attributed – perhaps mischievously – to the good health and long life of the Iona people by two visitors in the early 1890s. William Winter wrote: 'No doctor dwells in the place and no resident of it is ever sick. Death may come by drowning or other accident but as a rule, the people live until they are worn out and so expire naturally, from extreme age'.[6] Malcolm Ferguson believed that the bracing fresh air was one reason for the local longevity and added: 'But possibly another cause may be owing to the fact that there are no doctors of any sort on the island, not even a single quack of the noble profession'.

Such universal immunity to illness is unlikely to be based on fact. It is true, however, that a good proportion of people lived to an old age; sixty per cent of those whose deaths were noted between 1870s and 1890s had reached seventy-five years or over. The community probably numbered a few who developed special skills in diagnosing sickness and preparing natural remedies from plants. Ann Black, who lived at the East End from 1852 until 1926, was known as a good 'muime' or midwife.

The security of tenure afforded by the 1886 Crofters' Act led to widespread improvement in housing. Malcolm Ferguson observed in 1893 that Iona had eighteen slated houses and thirty-one thatched cottages, six and twenty of which respectively belonged to crofters. He was impressed with their appearance:

> The three farmers' houses are substantially built with stone and lime and slated. The crofters' dwellings are all pretty much alike in style and size, with a good roomy kitchen at the one end and a good sized room or parlour in the other, with either one or two other small places used as sleeping apartments, and a loft above for storing odds and ends. The houses are all well thatched with bere or rye straw and elaborately secured with a network of ropes of various sorts . . .

Specialist building skills were generally imported. Alistair MacArthur, the 'Clachair Mòr Tirisdeach' (big Tiree stonemason), built several houses in Iona and two MacCallum cousins from Kintra – Iain and Dòmhnall Phàraig – are particularly remembered for their expertise in splitting and dressing the red Ross of Mull granite.[7] It was said that Dòmhnall Phàraig could cut the stone as if it was cheese.

He would study it first, to see which way the grain was running and chisel several holes along the line, turning the chisel by sixty degrees as his two sons hammered it alternately. Then he inserted small pieces of metal with a wedge between. The wedges were hit in turn until the granite split clean apart. This was a very helpful skill as it rendered usable – for walls, houses and barns – the many boulders scattered along the eastern shoreline of the island.

Thatching was a communal task although only three or four would work on the roof itself, as Willie MacDonald explains:

> Only those that were known to be good thatchers got to do it – Johnnie Campbell East End, John MacMillan, Duncan MacGill-vray – others would help by handing up the thatch. When they put out word that a house was to be thatched and it was a good day, then they all came round. They could take off the roof and re-do it in a summer's day, though they would sometimes take off the old thatch the night before.

'Muran' or bent grass was sometimes used to thatch byres but it was never so plentiful in Iona as in other Hebridean islands. Peter Mac-Innes remembers the main material as being 'seagal gallda' (lowland rye), straw grown from rye seed brought in from the mainland:

> They found it was stronger. After threshing they combed it with a wooden comb with spiked nails through it and tied the thatch into very small sheaves, not big bundles. You laid the sheaves as if you were slating a roof, you worked up the way . . . It was held down by wire netting in my day, in the old days it was 'sìoman', rope made of heather – that was big labour to gather the heather and twist it.

The lattice-work of ropes, or netting, was tied to pegs fixed in the wall below. It was common in Iona houses for one or two lengths of wood or iron to be laid along the foot of the thatch, possibly to prevent the net cutting into the straw.

Coal had been established from 1882 as the major fuel for domestic use, along with oil lamps and candles for lighting. For exactly one hundred years the arrival of the coal puffer was to be an event of importance in island life. It was greeted with excitement by the children, who raced out of school at the end of the day to watch the unloading. Everyone who had a horse and cart collected their own load and often that of a villager who had no means of transport. Calum Bàn, for example, always delivered coal to Mrs Catherine MacDonald at the house in the village called Knock na Cross. Her father had been Archibald Black, Calum's uncle. This assistance to neighbours and kindred was a continuation of the earlier custom of ferrying peats for those who had no boat. Those who did not live nearby left their coal piled on the bank above the beach and took only the last cartful home, fetching the rest at a later date.

Several of the tasks involved in working the land and sea required collective effort and were regulated by customary practice. They were also very labour intensive and the school log book contains regular references to the absence of children due to croft work as, for example, on 8 November 1907: 'Attendance good but a few of the older scholars have been engaged at potato-lifting' or, on 9 October 1908: 'Attendance rather lower owing to harvest work'. Outside of school hours there were daily chores for young folk, such as going to the hill pasture to check the sheep, herding cattle in the days before fences afforded the crops protection, or exercising the horses as the late Angus MacKay recalled while talking to the author: 'I was with your grandfather at the time and I had to take the two horses out every day to the burn for a drink. I used to jump on one's back and the other would come behind me'.

At the first ploughing of the spring the 'deireidh bhuain' or last sheaf from the previous autumn's harvest was taken down from its place on the kitchen wall and fed to the horse. At Clachanach it was usually a single narrow sheaf, about one to one and a half inches in diameter and decorated with ribbon. It was never forgotten. This custom was widespread throughout the farming areas of Scotland at one time, under various names. The two most common terms in the Highlands referred originally to two different practices. The 'maighdean' (or maiden) had a decorative function at the celebration of bringing home the harvest, while the 'cailleach' (or old woman) was thrown into the field of whoever was last with their harvest as a sign of derision. 'A'Mhaighdean', 'A'Chailleach' and simply, 'Deireidh Bhuain' are all names recalled in Iona. In an article on these traditions Calum Maclean surmised that as their origins faded from memory the terms merged or were confused.[8] He saw the last sheaf in a house in Craignish, Argyll as late as 1958. But the custom is not extinct even today. Jeannie Gibson, a crofter at Knockan in the Ross of Mull, had an oat sheaf plaited into a circle hanging above her fireplace in September 1989. Her name for it is 'A'Mhaighdean Bhuana' and she replaces it at the end of each harvest.

Most crofters had only one horse, which was therefore shared with their neighbour as each holding was ploughed. Mutual dependency of this kind can provide clues to kinship, for example: 'One year Archie MacFarlane fell out with his neighbours and needed help with ploughing. He got use of a horse from Hector Maclean and I remember the old folk saying that it was because there was a connection'.[9] There was indeed a distant relationship through their grandmothers, both from branches of the Lamont family.

Each croft also had an allocation of the shoreline where wrack could be collected as fertiliser for the fields. The crofters bordering on the beaches along Sligineach at the West End had a system of casting lots for the total gathered, as a dispute in the early 1860s revealed when one was accused of filling his cart before the others : 'It is a rule among us that we all go together to collect the seaweed so that everyone will get his equal share . . . there are eight of us about the seaweed cast ashore on said beach'.[10] Disagreement over seaweed rights was by no means new. It had been the subject of a satirical poem by Angus Lamont much earlier in the century. This is included in Appendix IV.

The preparation of the land for sowing seems to have been interwoven with deep sea fishing, at the time when there were big expeditions to the 'cuan' (ocean) for cod and ling. Calum Cameron's father Donald was growing up in the 1860s and 1870s :

> You can see at Beul Mòr yet where they had the fishing boats on that side of the island, going out to the cuan . . . They went well out, I heard my father saying that they never took food, just water.
>
> He would go out as a boy, it was an awful long day – oh, he said they would be so tired walking back from Beul Mòr carrying the fish.
>
> They ploughed the ground in the spring and left it like that. Then they fished out there until they saw the whole of Iona, the arable, yellow – they stopped the fishing then.
>
> And the job of the kids, they went along and pulled the mustard and threw it in the furrow – great manure. And to get a good germination – you know May and June are often the driest months of the year – they steeped the seed overnight . . .

When several men returned from fishing together, the catch was divided. Piles were laid out, beginning with the biggest fish, lots were drawn and a passer-by would be asked to turn his or her back and call out the lots.

Occasionally the sea provided a free bounty as, for example, when a huge shoal of saithe beached itself below Lagandòrain. Women filled their aprons and men their carts and the Cowley Fathers, resident at the Bishop's House, came in for their share of what they described as a 'draught of fishes quite beyond record'. Their journal pinpoints the date as November 1907.[11]

A recollection common to everyone brought up in Iona in the early part of this century is that of dried fish on rods or ropes, hung in the loft or above the kitchen fire or over dykes. Angus MacKay :

> Of course they ate a lot of salted and dried fish. You had to gut them and put them in salt, keep them there for a while and take them out two at a time. You put two together, tied them round like that and then one in between and then broke it and you could put them on the fence for a while to dry. Then you could take them in and put them on the pulleys. Then you had the herrings too, barrels of herring, a lot of it from Loch Fyne.

Some people developed particular skills. Hector MacNiven and Hector Maclean became well known for catching the flounders for which the Sound of Iona was renowned, but which required the preparation of digging bait then setting and lifting lines. The Mac-Donalds at Ardionra were good at finding the best rock pools for crabs. Knowledge of fishing marks was passed on. For example, Johnnie Campbell told Dugald MacArthur that when a boat was out to the west of the island and could see Cnoc an t-Suidhe aligned with a certain hill at Ardionra, that was a good place for cod. If fishing to the south-west, then the island of Rèidhlean should be lined up with the hill on Lunga.

A few seals were caught from time to time on the rocky islets such as Soa, and the fat boiled down to make a veterinary ointment for sheep or cattle flesh wounds. The sealskin might be cured. A news item in 1868 said that the skin of a seal caught on the Machair had been made into 'spleuchans', probably purses or tobacco pouches.

Communal tasks related to livestock included the dipping and clipping of sheep and putting them out to graze on the offshore islands of Soa, shared by the West End crofters, or Rèidhlean, which went with Calva. They also had to be ferried by small boat to the *Dunara* to be shipped for sale in Glasgow, although one or two might be sold to merchant Lachlan Maclean for local consumption. The notebook kept by John MacMillan of Lagnagiogan shows that Mac-lean was paying fourteen to sixteen shillings for a lamb carcase, twenty-four to thirty shillings for that of a sheep and ten shillings for a young pig for rearing. The prices obtained from MacPherson and Buchanan in Glasgow for livestock were generally a little higher but from them had to be deducted the cost of freight which amounted, for example, to three shillings for one sheep in 1890, five shillings for one pig plus seven and sixpence for three lambs and one sheep in 1895, and ten shillings for six lambs in 1898.

In the late nineteenth century it was common for all the crofters, and many of the village people, to keep a pig. They became less common for a time after most died of a disease which was blamed

indirectly on the wreck of a ship named the *Labrador* on 1 March
1899. The Machair shore was red with apples, part of her spilled
cargo, which washed ashore in such numbers that people ended up
feeding them to the pigs. This unusual item in their diet was thought
to have killed them.

Pigs which did not go for export were by this time slaughtered by
each household in turn and the meat shared among neighbours. It
was the accepted rule that the owner of the boar received one piglet
from each litter in payment.[12]

In the mid-1860s a MacGillvray family had come to Cnoc Orain
croft in Iona. They were always known locally as 'na dròbhairean' as
they were related to a famous Mull family of cattle drovers. Coll A.
MacDonald wrote of John MacGillvray's reminiscences of the droving days:

> The Iona folk complain that they have difficulty getting away
> their sheep and cattle. But is there not a fair in Bunessan in May
> and August and the *Dunara* to take sheep and lambs to Glas-
> gow? That is not the same as the wandering people used to have
> to do. I was but a boy when I went with my uncle Donald to
> Falkirk. We were driving a herd of black cattle . . . We got them
> through Glen Mòr but that was only the start of our problems.
> We ferried them from Grasspoint to Kerrera and over the strait
> to Lorne. We took shelter for the night at Taynuilt and were up
> on the move again with the blackbird . . . There was a pound or
> two of oatmeal in a fold of our plaid. Each man had a wooden
> cup and a horn spoon and I saw one make 'fuarag' in the heel of
> his boot and lick his lips afterwards . . . We made brose with
> water from the stream and took the road.[13]

John Cameron, settled in Iona by 1779, earned the nickname 'Iain
Ruadh Sasunnach' (Red John the Englishman) as he once drove his
cattle on beyond the Falkirk tryst as far as Carlisle, to obtain a better
price for them. He is supposed to have been the first person to bring
white flour back to Iona.[14]

The droving route described by John MacGillvray began, in Iona,
at Sgeir nam Mart (cattle rock) at the tip of Tràigh Bàn nam Manach
and crossed to Deargphort in the Ross of Mull. In early times the
cattle may have been swum over the mile of water at Bunessan market
times, but by the late nineteenth century they were always ferried in
open boats. Malcolm Ferguson recorded a vivid description of such a
scene in 1893: 'Two strong active men stand up to their middle in the
water; the one grasps the animal by the forelegs, the other by the
hindlegs and back to back pull with the hands and give a sudden
shove with their shoulders, and the animal is whummelled heels over

head into the boat'. Its four legs tied firmly together, it lay on a bed of
bracken on the floor of the boat for the short crossing. Two or three
cows or up to six stirks could be transported at once but, as Ferguson
also noted, a bull was usually made to swim behind the boat. Angus
MacKay helped with this on one occasion.

> I remember once swimming a bull. It was the bull from the
> North End, I remember fine . . . A few of us went down, it was
> from Port an Diseirt because of where the tide was. It was a
> good place to get to Fionnphort with the tide behind you. There
> was Johnnie Campbell, Duncan MacArthur, Archie MacFarlane
> and Hughie MacGillvray who was in for MacKenzie's share of
> it. Two or three of us went down for the sgoth mhòr and we took
> the wee boat with us too. I went in the wee boat. And we got the
> bull out. And if he was not swimming too well I would give him
> a wee dunt from behind with the wee boat. You needed a strong
> boat and rowers. The bull was going to Uisken.

Ferguson noticed that, apart from one dairy herd of Ayrshire cows
and a few odd animals of the same breed, all the cattle on the island
were Highland. And the proprietor had recently presented each
township with a 'splendid' Highland bull.

Horses were always swum to Fionnphort when destined for the
annual Salen horse fair each August, in the north-east part of Mull.
This was an event famous throughout the whole district. On the first
day hundreds of horses would be on show, brought from the Ross of
Mull, Iona, Coll, Tiree and Morvern. On the second day the Glasgow
dealers transacted their business. Iona was well known for the breed-
ing and training of horses and the islanders' skill in working with
them. Indeed the local nickname for Iona people was 'na h-eich' (the
horses). (Creich folk were known as calves, Kintra as stirks and
Ardtun as hoggs.) Among those often involved in the swimming of
horses were Angus MacKay, Willie MacDonald, Neil and Dugald
MacArthur.[15] It had to be timed for slack water, to avoid strong
currents in the middle of the Sound. The best and shortest swim was
with the ebb tide from Port an Diseirt but sometimes they took the
opposite direction, going with the last of the flood from one of the
creeks at Sligineach.

The horse's halter was passed to the boat and someone would
walk a little way with it into the water: '. . . and then the horse
would walk sideways and of course the boat kept the strain on it
and when it turned to go the other way it would gradually be going
in up to its knees, and then its belly, and finally it was waterborne.
The boat then eased so that it was close up and off they went'. The
owner, who knew the horse best, would be in the stern with the

halter, keeping it close and encouraging it. If the horse was not swimming well, easing the line enough for him to go under briefly and get a fright would make him kick out more strongly. And when he smelled the land he often gave a final spurt. He was then led back out of the water and galloped up and down the beach to dry off.

That the horses generally swam with confidence, and could do so over quite long distances, is indicated in a drawing of Staffa by the French engraver Panckoucke made in 1831. It clearly shows a rowing boat with four men and three horses close behind and the footnote states:

> As we moved away, we had a curious meeting with a boat from Iona, crewed by Hebrideans leading with a rope in the sea three small black Scottish horses, which were swimming around the boat, not like those in our climes – with that anxious agitation that accompanies fear – but with the calm of very skilful swimmers used to long crossings.[16]

Peter MacInnes, who was born in 1810, practised as the island blacksmith in addition to working his croft until the early 1880s. He had learned his trade in Uddingston with John Gray and Co., a well-known firm of the day. As a craftsman in ironwork, he also made the railing round the Ridge of the Kings in the Rèilig Orain. The smiddy stood in the village, at the head of the jetty. It was a communal resource and often used also as shelter, store and place to gather and talk. Archibald MacArthur had a small smiddy behind Clachanach, where he could shoe a horse occasionally and do light welding such as replacing a worn plough sock. John MacInnes, who apprenticed as a blacksmith, also had a smiddy below Sandbank. But the village smiddy was the main one and after Peter MacInnes retired it was used every month by a smith who came over from Mull.

Encouraged, perhaps, by the Duke's prizes for increased produce, the Iona gardens gained a good reputation. Gardens at Maol farm, at Calva and Achabhaich crofts were considered to be particularly fine. The following writer was describing Maol when he reported to the *Oban Times* on 5 January 1895: 'I see fir, beech, and other trees growing finely in a garden on the highest farm on the island, where there is also an excellent vegetable garden, with a fine bed of strawberries and some good flowers. In the village gardens vegetables and flowers grow remarkably well'. From his own childhood at Clachanach Dugald MacArthur remembers cabbage, turnip, beetroot, carrots, parsnips, greens, blackcurrants, redcurrants, logan berries and masses of rhubarb.

Butter was churned at home and stored after salting in big stone crocks. Making it was a task often assigned to young folk as the same informant recalls :

> . . . many a time. We did it mainly in the churn about three gallons, a circular thing that sat on two legs . . . inside it were a couple of big propellers and you just kept cawing the handle. . . . It would take about three-quarters of an hour sometimes to churn. . . . You put in a quart or so of cold water at a certain stage, when the butter was beginning to show up as little bits, that would mean it was separating off into buttermilk and butter. . . . then you gave it about twenty more turns.

The buttermilk, taken off by a tap at the bottom of the churn, was used in scones, or as a drink. The frothy cream taken off about half-way through the churning was mixed with oatmeal and sugar to make another refreshing drink called 'fuarag'. Some households made cheese but many people imported the big round cheeses from Coll.

With the coming of the cargo steamer groceries, wheat bread, barrels of apples and sacks of meal or flour could be purchased direct from Glasgow. The firm of Archibald Hamilton and Sons dealt with a number of Iona families and they would regularly take fresh eggs or potatoes as part payment of bills.

Despite the long-term effects of intensive working, as emphasised in the Napier Commission evidence, Iona's arable land continued to impress the visitor. Ferguson was surprised to see 'as heavy and luxuriant crops on some fields as I had seen last season in any part of Scotland. The principal crops raised are bere, rye, oats, potatoes and ryegrass hay. Not a boll of grain has been either imported or exported for the last forty years'. The lack of grain surpluses, as compared with former times, had in fact been one of the crofters' complaints in the 1880s. The situation was balanced by the decreasing dependency on home-produced grain for human consumption now that the range and availability of foodstuffs was greater. Crops were thus being grown primarily for animal fodder. The notebook extracts in Appendix III, kept by John MacMillan, indicate the pattern of sowing and harvesting on one typical croft and the stores gathered in for winter provision.

There is a particularly detailed account of potato production. As was common practice, one of the villagers (in this case Lachlan Maclean) had a few drills in one corner of the croft. Notes were made and plans drawn over several years to show how many potatoes of which variety were planted in different parts of the fields. For example :

> Garramore is pure Snowflakes. Head rig of Wellfield are first started with Porrims and the outer drills are Snowflakes.

Garrahennan is started with Bruces on each side and when these
are done Porrims are begun and when these are finished
Snowflakes are begun which finish the three rigs. In the headrig
are pure Champions, and so ends the mixture we have of
potatoes for the year 1895.

Champions had been a familiar and well-liked variety of potato in the
West Highlands since 1863. They were first grown in Iona when the
Duke of Argyll presented seed Champions in 1880. Other varieties
mentioned in the notebook are less well known, at least as specified
here. Prior to 1923 it was quite legal to give potatoes local or alternative names. One of the earliest potatoes listed in Britain is Village
Blacksmith, in 1836, and four drills of those were noted in Iona for
1893, given by the schoolmaster Mr Kirkpatrick. It is very likely that
varieties will have been experimented with and exchanged. The Lar-
ocheshells, which may have been a parochial name, were described as
'of a reddish colour' and 'supposed to be the best potato of 1893'.[17]

Mary MacMillan remembered the potato creels her father made
and whose dimensions were also detailed in his notebook. They were
squarish, to stand upright in the field, and they could then be carried
on a person's back.

The strengthening of links with the mainland and the growing
material prosperity are reflected in the declining internal commerce
of the island. Since the mid-nineteenth century no carpenter, boat-
builder or wheelwright had been listed in the Census returns and the
last shoemaker died in 1893. That same year, Ferguson commented
on the fact that fewer traditional crafts were now practised in Iona:

There are no tradesmen or mechanics on the island except one
tailor and one weaver, both of whom are frequently employed at
other work during the summer season. Thirty years ago there
were two tailors, two shoemakers, six weavers and one blacksmith. Formerly the natives used to manufacture their own wool
into tweeds, tartan plaids, plaidings, druggets etc but now they
are obliged to send their wool to Greenock, Galashiels, Selkirk
and other places to be manufactured. The old spinning-wheel
which had been much used on the island from time immemorial,
is now rapidly falling into disuse and evidently will soon be a
thing of the past.

The trade which continued over the longest period was weaving.
Willie MacDonald, the last of four generations of weaver Mac-
Donalds in Iona village, learned initially from his father Coll who, in
his youth, had gone to study the craft at Inveraray. Willie recalls that
many of the old folk did some spinning for the weaver and that
everyone kept one black sheep, so that wool did not have to be dyed

for black or dark brown shades. His sister Annie used to collect heather, flag iris roots, crotal from the rocks and, later, onion skins to produce the dyes. The wool was layered in a pot with the plants and boiled without stirring.

Coll also made up a tartan of his own. His father before him was given some practice in weaving tartans when H. D. Graham was staying at the Free Church Manse in the late 1840s. He commissioned cloth in the Graham and the Douglas patterns, having a suit made up in the latter, and he wrote enthusiastically about the quality of a web he was sending to his father: '. . . its having been dressed, dyed, spun and woven in Iona on Archy McDonald's loom under the superintendence of Mrs. McVean. The green is dyed from heather and never fades but will stand washing . . .'. The Free Church minister's wife clearly took a close interest in the weaving trade and around the same time had been bequeathed a sum of fifty pounds 'for the encouragement of Iona manufacture'.

The steady influx of summer visitors provided a market for new arts and crafts. One of these captured the attention of Malcolm Ferguson: 'The Iona Press is quite a unique and interesting little establishment, superintended personally by Miss Muir . . . assisted by a tall, handsome, dark-eyed native damsel hardly out of her teens, whom I have seen with her bare well-formed arms working hard at the press'. The founders of this initiative in 1887 had been Miss Muir's brother William Muir, former manager of the Tormor granite quarry, and John MacCormick, eldest son of the quarry foreman and grandson of a shoemaker who had moved from Iona to the Ross in the 1830s. Inspired by Iona's history as an ancient seat of monastic learning, their aim was to provide tourists with 'literary as well as geological mementoes of the sacred isle. Native labour is as far as possible employed – the books being illuminated in watercolours by the island girls'.[18]

Over the five or six years of its existence the Iona Press, housed in a former bothy behind the Columba Hotel, produced a dozen small pamphlets of which at least three ran to two editions. One of these, 'The Blessing of the Ship', sold four hundred copies of its first run. It contained, in Gaelic with English translation, 'a form of prayer used in olden times by the sailors of Iona and the isles on beginning a voyage' and reflected the keen interest of John MacCormick in the legends, lore and traditions of his native area. Other booklets included 'Ossian's Address to the Sun'; a version, with tune, of the epic ballad 'Bàs Fhraoich' (the Death of Fraoch); a prayer said to have been used by the Iona schoolchildren in 1832; and an example of the 'Rann Calluinn' or rhyme recited at New Year throughout the

Highlands. Drawings of local scenes or borders of Celtic design decorated the printed page. As these were hand-painted, the richness and variety of the colours used differed in individual copies, sometimes to spectacularly beautiful effect.

The Press never completed the full list of publications intended, which included a history of Iona, but a small range of postcards was printed under its name and sold, along with other souvenirs, in a small gift shop run by Miss Muir until the 1920s.

Flora Ritchie, who acted as housekeeper for her father at the Columba Hotel, assisted at the Iona Press for a few years and was herself widely read and intelligent. Several members of this remarkable family developed talents and interests that were to benefit the island and that have generated much affectionate reminiscence among those who knew them. Georgina Ritchie married the Rev. Archibald MacMillan, Iona's minister, in 1892. Another sister, Mary Lamont Ritchie, became governess to a Royal household in Russia and had to flee, penniless, at the time of the Revolution. Captain George Ritchie was an intrepid sailor from his first voyage across the Atlantic by clipper at the age of fourteen. He was among the crew who brought the famous US navy ship the *Constitution* on her last sail to Boston, he lived alone with Aborigines in the Australian bush, and he was a free citizen of Canton. Not many years before his death at the age of eighty-one he rowed and sailed a seven-foot punt single-handed from Greenock to Iona.[19]

This eccentric sea-dog also had his family's gift with words, to which is attributed the fact that Iona gained a library building in 1904. His brother Robert Lamont Ritchie was minister of Andrew Carnegie's parish of Creich in Sutherland and asked George to pilot Carnegie's yacht on a tour of the West coast. It was at the time when the millionaire was presenting libraries to towns and villages throughout Scotland, a fact which George artlessly raised with him, then adding pointedly: '. . . while we in Iona have books given by Legh Richmond, Thomas Cook and others and we have no building to house them'. The point was taken and four hundred pounds came Iona's way. The Rev. Robert Ritchie bequeathed his own collection of books to Iona Cathedral to form the basis of a small library there too.

Meanwhile another brother, Alexander, had returned to Iona after an accident while an engineer at sea. Along with his wife, a former student of art, he became interested in handicrafts using the interleaved Celtic designs of ancient manuscripts and carved stones. He began with leather, wood and brass and made bags, boxes, crosses, plates, candleholders and mirror frames before expanding into silver jewellery. They set up a stall for 'Iona Celtic Art' inside the Nunnery gate a few years before the First War and a Ritchie brooch or ornament became one of the most frequently sought local souvenirs. Alex also followed John MacDonald as official custodian of the ruins and was to produce his own guide book of Iona, incorporating a map of Gaelic place-names, in 1928.[20]

Early in the spring of 1906 quarrying of Iona marble began again. A Swedish company took a lease of the quarry at first but they were subsequently replaced by a London-based firm, Iona Marbles Ltd.[21] The managerial and skilled part of the workforce were incomers, the head man Mr Edgar having been previously in the slate quarries of Easdale. Some unskilled labouring, and the transportation between tender and cargo steamer of machinery or finished marble, provided occasional local work. A crudely constructed quay and a derrick were used to ship directly from the quarry and the first cargo, 130 tons of marble, was loaded in July 1907 bound for buyers in Belgium. In 1911 new cutting machinery was installed, to respond to an anticipated demand for more slabs than blocks. These will have been for the ornamental facings and surrounds which were fashionable in domestic interiors of the time.[22]

The War brought an end to operations, however, and they were never revived. The workers may have all joined up and the economic effect was, in any case, severe. A letter from the company's solicitors in August 1915 explained that after a strike in the building trade, followed by the start of the war and the loss of their large Belgian trade, the company's funds were entirely depleted.[23]

Links of Custom and Community, at Home and Abroad

The proportion of Iona's population who were long-established on the island remained relatively stable. Of the people resident in the 1890s, fifty per cent bore one of the core surnames which had been present since 1779: Black, Cameron, Campbell, MacArthur, Mac-Donald, MacFarlane, MacInnes, MacLean. Furthermore, families which may be traced through the male or female lines back to the early years of the nineteenth century, and probably in many cases to the 1779 list, constituted seventy-five per cent of the population.

From the start of the OPR in 1804 it has been possible to chart marriage patterns and, with the additional aid of family trees, the extent of intermarriage between families and between Iona and other districts. As Figure 7 illustrates, fifty-eight per cent of marriages in the first half of the century were contracted within the island itself. Neighbouring islands provided almost all remaining partners. This reflects the limited social horizons of the period and also the fairly easy communication by sea between Iona, Ross and Tiree and the events such as cattle fairs and peat cutting which drew these three communities together. In the second half of the century, due to increased mobility among the young people, a larger number of marriage partners (fifteen per cent) came from further afield. Yet fifty-one per cent were still from Iona and thirty-three per cent from the Ross and Tiree.

In the early part of the nineteenth century weddings were usually held in the winter months, particularly January to March with December and April following in popularity. When writer Malcolm Ferguson was staying on Iona in 1893 he asked his guide Calum Bàn to recount some of the old customs of the place and these included a lively description of wedding festivities. The ceremony generally took place on a Thursday, he was told, and on the preceding Monday both bride and groom would issue invitations in person to each house, starting from opposite ends of the island. The next day all the women would go to the bride's house 'loaded with nice, plump, nine-month-old chickens, big kebbucks of sweet milk cheese, mutton, hams and innumerable other dainties for the marriage feast'. On the wedding day, each party lunched on bread, biscuits, cheese and

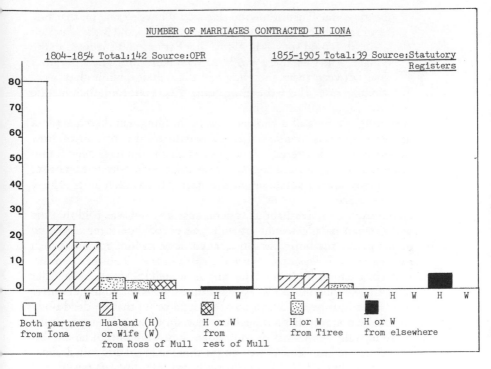

Figure 7. Number of marriages contracted in Iona.

whisky and then set off from their respective dwellings preceded by a
piper to the church. The ceremony was followed by a barn dance, a
'sumptuous supper' at the bride's house about ten o'clock and then
further singing and dancing until daybreak.

This description accords in the principal details with newspaper
accounts and oral tradition concerning weddings towards the end of
last century and the beginning of this. There was always a procession
led by a piper, then a meal and a dance, sometimes in the schoolroom.
Occasionally the whole event was at the bride's home, as in 1911
when Euphemia Campbell married Colin MacInnes at Cùldamph on
the evening of 31 May. The service was held on the hillside, the food
was served in a large tent and there was dancing on the Machair all
night.[1]

Angus MacKay's main recollection of weddings was the music
associated with them:

There was a lot of singing, at weddings or whatever. There
would be so many at one table and so many at another table and
one would say 'Tha am bòrd seo gur beatadh' – this table is

beating you. Then someone else would have to sing on that side
. . . I remember being between two cailleachs, old Mary Curlach
– oh, she could sing – she was a MacFarlane and she lived in the
village. And then there was Mrs. MacPhail – Mòr NicMhurain. I
was between them and they had the hankies, while they were
singing, just to keep the thing going. Everyone took their hankie
out. I remember that fine.

Beating the time of a chorus song by holding handkerchiefs in a
line or circle was mentioned in de Saussure's description of Iona
singers in 1807. Scattered references to this custom have been found
in a number of Highland areas over the last two hundred years or so.
Its origin is unclear but it may be the remnant of a much older type of
song or dance.

Ferguson also asked about funeral customs and was told that the
wake, when people would sit with the corpse for three days and
nights before the burial, had not taken place in Iona for more than
twenty years. It was during a wake early in the nineteenth century
that a blacksmith (Rob MacLachlan) outwitted the watchers in order
to fulfil his dying mother's last wish that she be buried in her native
Mull. The Iona people had a strongly held belief that no dead body
should be removed from the island. The smith supplied those at the
wake liberally with whisky and, when they were asleep, he and his
friends hoisted the coffin through the thatched roof and sailed under
cover of darkness to Mull. Ferguson heard that this supersition was
due to 'some unexplained fear that seven years of famine would
follow in consequence'. Sarah Murray had been given a different
explanation by the Mull minister when she visited Iona in 1802 : '. . .
for ages no corpse has been suffered without force to be carried out of
the island ; for as long as that custom is maintained, say they, no I-
onian can be drowned in the Sound between I and Ross'.

Following Highland tradition, only the menfolk of the community
attended funerals in Iona and carried the coffin to the graveyard. The
turn for each to do this was announced with the words : 'Seasamh a
mach, ceithir eile' (stand out, four others).

No strong tradition of singing or song-making has come down to
the present day in Iona yet it must have existed as part of the oral
culture common to Gaelic-speaking communities. Regrettably, the
great collector John Francis Campbell of Islay did not appear to
gather any material on a brief visit to Iona in 1870, although a
tantalising passing comment in his journal was : 'In the evening came
Dr. Black who sang Gaelic songs well'.[2] This was Donald Black, born
at Cnoc Cùl Phàil in Iona in 1839.

Singing undoubtedly accompanied work, as it did in many rural areas. In 1788 a visitor near Port a'Churaich 'heard for the first time an earse song performed by the women who were burning kelp, a melancholy ditty'.[3] Those who hired boatmen from Iona or Ulva mentioned the rhythmic 'iorrams' or rowing songs which accompanied the beat of their oars. In similar fashion, the teams of women who performed the long hard task of shrinking or 'waulking' newly woven tweed would sing as they pounded the cloth on a wooden board. Two guidebooks mention waulking songs in Iona, the 1831 edition of *Lumsden's Steamboat Companion* and W. Keddie in 1850 who stated: 'A friend who has witnessed the waulking in Iona informs us that as the work grows warm the song waxes louder and louder . . .'. Willie and Annie MacDonald's mother Catherine Fowler, who was a niece of the Dr Black who sang to J. F. Campbell and who was born in 1867, could sing snatches of waulking songs and knew of their being sung in Iona. Although the regular practice had died out even by her day when the tweed was sent away to be shrunk, the art had not been forgotten and was occasionally revived. Catherine Campbell of Lagandòrain for example, along with Marion MacKay and some others, held at least one waulking within living memory, sometime in the 1920s.

What is recalled more vividly by many Iona natives is dancing. Before the village hall was built in 1927, the boatshed in the village was used regularly for dances and, before that, the open air. It was the main form of entertainment for young people. Marion MacArthur from Clachanach used to organise dances on the flat grassy field above Burnside cottage in the 1890s. Mary Ann MacLean, born in 1884, remembered dancing on the road at the Nunnery corner, a favourite meeting place for the young, and also on the Machair at Sithean and Cùldamph. These were especially popular spots as May Powell also recalls: 'Old Neil MacCormick loved nothing better than to play his fiddle at the door of the old house, near Sìthean hill, for all the children to dance to'. And a verse of the song about Iona made by bard Teònaidh Chailean (John Campbell), who was born at Cùldamph in 1905,' captures the scene:

> Bha e air innse iomadh àm dhuinn
> Cuirm-chiùil bhiodh aca san t-samhradh,
> Air an rèidhlean chìte stampadh
> Far an do dhanns iad anns an ridhil.

> (It was told to us many a time
> they used to have concerts in summer,
> on the grassy plain you can see the
> stamp of where they danced the reel.)[4]

Duncan MacDonald from Ardionra croft played the pipes on many of these occasions. An *Oban Times* report of 1896 talked of his skill on the instrument:

> Iona this year can boast of a musical prodigy in the shape of a boy piper . . . a bareheaded, barefooted boy performing with wonderful grace on the national instrument while a dozen or so children squat or stand . . . Duncan MacDonald, his new set of Highland bagpipes the gift of Lord Archibald Campbell. The boy's musical talents have so much attracted the attention of Lord Archibald that he is to be forthwith placed under the tuition of one of the best exponents of pipe music in the country.

Others had also taken an interest in promoting musical education on the island. The previous year Allan MacBeth, Principal of the Athenaeum in Glasgow, presented a set of pipes and two chanters, one for the East End and one for the West End. Neil MacCormick was made custodian of the pipes and a committee was formed to deal with applications for loaning out the instruments.

Concerts of the period, which were numerous and usually raised money for a local cause, had full programmes and often included piping, fiddling, melodeon-playing, readings, recitations and songs in Gaelic and English. A long newspaper report of one such, in January 1890, concluded:

> Mr. A. MacPhail – a host in himself – completely brought down the house by his rendering, in character, of the Irish comic song 'Killaloo' . . . cheers of the audience were equally great when he gave several Gaelic comic songs. Pithy addresses, suitable to the occasion, were delivered by Messrs. N. MacKay and M. Ferguson. The Chairman (Captain George Ritchie) in his concluding remarks drew attention to the happiness, enjoyment and instruction to be drawn from social gatherings such as the present.

Satirical poems and songs about local events and personalities were regularly made up by Angus MacPhail and others. One such commemorated the occasion when a boat with Calum Bàn and Neil MacKay was driven off course on the way back from Bunessan and ended up in Ulva. Parodying a popular Gaelic song, it began: 'A Chaluim Bhàn, a' Chaluim Bhàn, a' Chaluim Bhàn, a' laochain'.

Summer visitors were enthusiastic supporters of the concerts, often helping to organise them and contributing to the entertainment. The regattas and games, revived in 1897, also brought visitors and islanders together. These annual events continued until the early 1920s with a gap during and immediately after the War years, and are recalled with evident zest by any who still remember them. The

Dowager Duchess of Argyll was present in 1904 when, as usual, the most keenly contested race was by skiffs of over fifteen feet for the silver challenge cup she had donated. The previous year Hugh Mac-Innes of Salum in Tiree won this race, reportedly in spectacular fashion, and he used to talk of how friendly and sporting the Iona people were.[5] The event attracted people from the Ross of Mull as well as Tiree, emphasising further the close social links throughout the district.

At the close of each school year the Duke of Argyll gave a picnic for the children and a second one was sometimes organised during the summer by lady visitors. The children would assemble in the village and march 'with banners flying' to the picnic site, alternately Calva or Traighmòr or the Machair. In the Coronation year of 1911 the Duke added gifts of mugs and more flags. For many years a Mrs and Miss Pettigrew provided apples, food and decorations for a children's Hallowe'en party in October. Older boys, and sometimes girls, celebrated this festival by dressing up and going out in small groups to play practical jokes, such as moving carts or gates. Hallowe'en was kept 'old style' on 11 November until well into this century, whereas New Year on 1 January became firmly adopted by around 1900.

In 1886 English guests at the Columba Hotel introduced Iona to the game of golf and a nine-hole course (later eighteen) was laid out on the Machair.[6] The men who had been shinty players in their youth took to it well and it became very popular. By 1897 a committee was set up to collect subscriptions and organise occasional tournaments.

There were always simpler diversions to be found too, as Angus MacKay recalled: 'We used to go down on a moonlight night to a place when you're just beside the Calva fence and the ice would be quite good there. You'd get a slide . . . you had boots, tackety boots. Aye, we did that often, it must have been the fellows from the East End who told us about it'.

On 29 March 1913 the *Oban Times* carried an editorial about the new ripples of emigration affecting Scotland. Four thousand people had left the Clyde the previous Saturday for Canada and one hundred and sixty thousand were expected to go by the end of the year. This was attributed in part to the lack of smallholdings which the Highland Congested Districts Board, set up in 1897, had not been able to expand to any significant degree. An Act of 1911 transformed this Board into the Board of Agriculture and also changed the Crofters Commission into the Scottish Land Court, which continued to consider questions of fair rent.

A steady trickle of young people departed from Iona during the two decades prior to the First World War. Some sought training and employment in the cities, as has been noted earlier, but an equal number at least went overseas. The death notice of James MacArthur, Sligineach in 1912 added : 'American and New Zealand papers please copy'. This kind of instruction was by this period a regular practice in the *Oban Times* and other Highland papers.

By the 1870s the Canadian mid-west was being opened up for farming by the Government. Some of the Iona settlers in Ontario moved west in response to this, for example Malcolm MacInnes and Catherine MacArthur, and Catherine's brothers Peter and Duncan, who all took up land in Calgary. Manitoba became a focus for new waves of Scottish emigrants during the 1870s and 1880s and large numbers of Tiree people claimed land there, many of them stopping for a few months first with friends in the established settlements of Ontario.[7] The Vista and Basswood areas of Manitoba drew most of the Iona emigrants from this period too. The Calva MacDonalds settled there, as did Alexander Black from Clachancorrach and his sister Catherine who married Sandy MacDonald, a Tiree emigrant. The Atlantic crossing was faster and more comfortable than forty years earlier and visits back and forth from the old land to the new were not uncommon. Catherine MacMillan from Lagnagiogan in Iona went to visit her good friend Catherine Black in Manitoba in 1899 and there met and married John MacPhail from Tiree. Their daughter Marion was to marry Coll MacCormick, who emigrated from Sìthean in Iona as a young man. A brother and sister of his also left home for Manitoba and eventually married a sister and brother of the Calva MacDonalds. Flora MacDonald of Sandbank in Iona had been widowed in 1888, as the result of a tragic gun accident, and when she decided to go to Canada with her grown-up family of seven in 1902 it was natural that they chose the same area of Manitoba.

The pattern of close settlement and intermarriage of the earlier generation of emigrants was thus repeated. So too were the traditions of working together to build a house or barn, helping each other in times of hardship or illness and keeping alive bonds of kinship and community. Marion MacPhail, interviewed in Canada in 1979, vividly recalled the attachment of families to each other and those still in Scotland :

> If somebody got a letter from Tiree from their people, they came to tell the news. You had a visit. And it was the same when my people got a letter from Tiree or Iona. The news was relayed.
>
> It was a very congenial thing . . . When an *Oban Times* came it was shared with everybody and it didn't matter even if it was months old. . . . They were all so clannish, they looked out for

one another. When there was trouble or sorrow, they were there.

Marion's brother, Alexander MacPhail, knew from his father the hard work faced by the first homesteaders. Around 1880 John Mac-Phail had made the long journey from Ontario, partly by boat up the Red River and then two hundred miles by ox and cart to Vista. A settler could register initially for a quarter of a surveyed section of land, that is for 160 acres. To claim for a further quarter he had to show that he had broken ten acres of land a year for three years, got five head of cattle, built a barn for oxen and a house for himself.[8]

This effort was usually rewarded with considerable success. The *Oban Times* reported in 1905 that 'Iona Farm' in Manitoba, run by the MacDonald family from Calva, was estimated to have 200 acres under crop and to yield 600 bushels of wheat. By 1912 it had 500 acres. Archie MacDonald in Iona remembered being told by a cousin Archie MacCormick, who took over part of this huge holding, that they could plough twelve furrows at a time with the horses. Accounts from Australia were in similar vein, as when James Campbell wrote to Dugald MacArthur in 1884: 'I sold a bit of ground bigger than Clachanach about two years ago and now I have a bigger bit, bigger indeed than one half of Iona'.

Such letters and newspaper reports confirmed the common perception at home that these new lands held unlimited space and unbounded opportunity for advancement. Sometimes the concept of such a difference of scale was clearly too hard to grapple with and had to be expressed in imaginative terms, as when Martha MacLeod said to her daughter one day at Greenbank: 'You know, some of my ancestors left here and went to Canada and they became very prosperous. They even had a house eventually with 365 windows, one for every day of the year'.[9]

Those who went to Australia and New Zealand were scattered more widely. Close-knit settlements of people from one area of Scotland were much less common in these countries. From correspondence it is clear, however, that many did keep in touch both with each other and with relatives at home. Neil MacArthur Sligineach who married in New Zealand in 1894 remained up to date with brothers at sea, in America and in Iona. Later in life he even had as a neighbour the Rev. John MacArthur, who had come there from Canada in 1901 but whose father Malcolm had left Iona in the 1840s. John was still known to Neil as a 'cousin'.[10] From the records it is clear they were not first cousins but the term is applied much more widely in Highland families where knowing who fourth and fifth cousins are is quite usual. They clearly knew they were related, an example of the strong persistence of kinship ties as John's family had emigrated from Iona ten years before Neil was born.

John MacDonald had gone out to Australia on the *Marmion* in 1852 and, according to his obituary, was 'a pioneer who well performed his part in the building up of Mount Gambier'. He had set up in business there, opening Mac's Hotel, had started the movement to establish the first Presbyterian church in the town, had helped launch a reading club and was a chieftain of the local branch of the Caledonian Society. All of this was despite an inauspicious start when, during a hazardous overland trek of a hundred miles from their port of entry, four of the party had drowned. John MacDonald brought his children back to Iona in the 1880s, so that they might be educated in Scotland. Two studied medicine and, even after returning to Australia, they all kept in touch with their relatives at Lagnagiogan.

Others had no communication with home from the time they sailed. On one of his spells farm labouring in Australia George Ritchie chanced upon a family who had emigrated from Iona. He was flatly disbelieved when he announced that was where he was from too : 'There is no-one of that name there' he was told.

Tales of sailing, emigrating and making a fortune are curiously blended in the tradition of Pàraig an Oir (Peter of the gold). It was a well-known story in Iona, told in several different versions one of which was published by John MacCormick under the title 'Calum an Oir'. Pàraig was, however, the more common local name. The basic thread was the kidnapping of an Iona fisherman by a passing ship, ostensibly to navigate her through the treacherous rocks at the south end of the Ross of Mull. He was held on board, made to work without reward and abandoned at their destination in America – or, in one version, Spain. Eventually, with the help of other Highland sailors, the captain was forced to recompense him with a bag of gold pieces and Pàraig made his way back to Iona, by which time there was a dent in his shoulder from the weight of his spoils. The surnames attributed to him most commonly were MacArthur or MacInnes.

In 1985 American descendants of James and Catherine MacArthur, who had emigrated in 1847, visited Iona. Through official and family records they had accurately reconstructed their links to a branch of MacArthurs of whom no trace had remained in the island itself. In Canada, they had become connected through marriage with a MacInnes family, also from Iona. A brother of Catherine, Peter MacArthur, had gone first to Canada and then Australia for a year, to work in the gold mines. He returned to Iona in the mid-1850s and married Mary MacDonald, a sister of Archibald MacDonald, of Martyrs Bay croft. (The ruins of that house were often pointed out to one informant by her mother as the spot where the kidnapped Pàraig an Oir of her story had lived.) Peter emigrated a second and final time, with Mary, in 1859. His descendants in the USA have always known him by the nickname of 'Peter the Gold'.

This Peter's exploits may have become elaborated in the retelling over the years after his departure. Or it may be that the nickname was transferred to him, as his adventure to seek gold recalled an earlier episode, involving the captured fisherman. The different versions are summarised in Appendix IV. Whatever the origins of the nickname, its independent survival on both sides of the Atlantic bears witness to the enduring character of the oral tradition.

Another, grimmer cause to leave Iona came with the outbreak of war in 1914. It is not known how many enlisted in total, but in 1915 the Mull and Iona Association published a 'Roll of Honour' of those currently serving from the two islands. Most of the fifteen Iona names were connected through a parent by then living on the mainland or because they had been boarded-out children. One from a native family was Lachlan Maclean of the 1st Battalion, Royal Scots Fusiliers, who wrote to his sister in Iona Cottage in the village in December 1914:

> I arrived in France with the first party of British troops and went right through the war up to September 14th. I was wounded . . . my Colonel ordered me to retire and it took me five hours to get to the hospital. . . . I rejoined on 14th November and have now been appointed Quarter Master Sergeant. At present I am working full pace reclothing and equipping the battalion as they are having a short rest after their hard work in the trenches. You can rest assured we are winning all along the line. Of course, we are losing men but there is one consolation – the Germans are losing three times as heavily. I am proud to be a soldier, especially a Scotch one . . . We are getting looked after like lords thanks to the people at home and we all appreciate it.
>
> What we want now is more men as we are at present living in the trenches for three weeks at a stretch. This is no exaggeration; and if you pop your head up you stand a good chance of getting shot by some German sniper. Don't worry about me as I suppose my proverbial luck will bring me through safe.[11]

Lachlan's luck did hold and he remained in the army for the rest of his career. But the War Memorial in Martyrs Bay, unveiled in 1921, bears the names of eleven sons of islanders or Iona emigrants who fell in the 1914–1918 conflict. This was not as high a loss as that suffered by many Highland communities, but the emotional and economic repercussions of these destructive years left few corners of Europe unscathed.

In 1897 the eagerly awaited telegraphic service had been opened in Iona, in the new Post Office built the same year. Sixty-six messages were sent and twenty-five received on the first day.[12] Throughout the War, courtesy of a generous gesture by a Dr Dewar from Dunblane, a Reuters telegram with news from the front was pinned up outside the Iona Post Office every afternoon. On 11 November 1918 the telegram arrived early and school was closed. As usual, the children ran down to read the message and then home to spread the word. Coll MacDonald went up to ring the Cathedral bell. It was the end of the War.

Parish Life:
Learning and Worship 1774–1843

In 1772 Thomas Pennant noted, with regret, of Iona: 'At present this once celebrated seat of learning is destitute of even a school-master; and this seminary of holy men wants even a minister to assist them in the common duties of religion'. A year later Dr Johnson made a similar observation. It must indeed have seemed strange to these men of letters that a place which had inspired such scholarship and Christian faith down the ages should now have neither school nor church. In fact, by 1774, the year after Dr Johnson's visit, a school was established on Iona but it was to be a further half-century before the island had its own parish church.

Since the last Bishop of the Isles was deposed in 1638, Iona had had no resident clergyman. There were occasional visits by a minister from Seil and Luing islands in the Firth of Lorne and, for a brief period in the 1640s, a Martin McIlvra was appointed by the Synod of Argyll to a charge which encompassed Iona and Kilviceuen in the Ross of Mull. It would appear that the Protestant faith had been adopted without undue resistance in Iona at the Reformation in 1560, aided no doubt by the Campbell nomination to the Bishopric of the Isles of John Carswell, a staunch defender of the reformed church. When Irish Franciscan missionaries were active in Scotland in the early part of the seventeenth century, they recorded some success in the inner Hebrides including on Mull. But their reports indicate only a few conversions to Catholicism on Iona, three in 1625 and four in 1630. On the former visit mass was celebrated on the island, for the first time since the Reformation.[1]

By the eighteenth century Iona was served by the minister for Kilfinichen and Kilviceuen, one of the three Mull parishes. This is a large area, thirty kilometres in length from the head of Loch Scridain plus the extra kilometre of water across to Iona. The minister's visits to the island were officially four times a year – but may have been even fewer when bad weather prevented a crossing. The absence of a resident minister led to the schoolmaster playing an active part in the religious, as well as the educational, life of the people during the late eighteenth and early nineteenth centuries.

For the year beginning 1 May 1774 a salary of £10 was allocated by the Scottish Society for the Propagation of Christian Knowledge (SSPCK) for a schoolmaster in Iona. The first appointment was that of Robert Colquhoun, who had come from Kerston school near Dunoon.[2]

The SSPCK was established in 1709, modelled on a similar English organisation, in order to combat the illiteracy and ignorance that were considered prevalent, particularly in the Highlands and Islands. The founders were also openly opposed to continuing Catholic missionary activity in the north and west of the country. By 1758 the Society had 176 schools, raised with money from supporters as it did not receive any Government funds. The Gaelic language was at first forbidden in SSPCK schools, as it was thought to be allied to the superstition the Society wished to stamp out. This rule was relaxed from the 1760s, however, and the early teachers in Iona school certainly spoke and used Gaelic. A visitor in 1788 mentioned that Mr Colquhoun taught it along with English, writing and the five rules of arithmetic.

The school roll in 1775 totalled forty. In the school returns of the following century the attendance was often entered as 'erratic', many fewer being regularly present than were formally on the roll. This was almost certainly the case from the beginning. The 1788 journal gave the number of scholars as twenty-five whereas the previous year's roll was officially forty-eight. Over the first twenty years the number of boys appears to have been disproportionately higher than that of the girls. At this period practical, domestic skills were considered more useful for girls and a spinning school plus mistress was proposed for Iona by the Duke in 1790; wheels would be provided by the Trustees for Fisheries and Manufactures. He had already received a request from an Alexander Campbell in the Ross of Mull to appoint his wife to 'set up a sewing school at Icolmkill for which he represents her as well qualified'. There is no further record of either of these ventures but they may have lasted for a short while. Special provision for spinning and sewing was not made by the SSPCK itself until the 1830s.

In return for providing a salaried schoolmaster the SSPCK normally negotiated with the landlord for land to build a schoolhouse, fuel to heat it and grazing for a cow. A plot was allocated to Colquhoun in Iona in 1776 and he built his own house, a rough construction using materials to hand such as stone and turf and 'a logg of fir that came upon the coast' for which he asked the Duke's permission. During the 1790s the improvement of this accommodation was the subject of considerable correspondence between the Duke, his Chamberlain and the Secretary of the SSPCK.[3] The Duke did not wish the latter to dictate terms or impose on the islanders the task of providing peat for the teacher. In response to the Secretary's proposal that 'a comfortable stone and lime house' be erected along with 'the other usual accommodation of grass and fuel', he replied:

> I am still willing to be at the expence of building a school and schoolhouse in that island, Icolmkill but it must be a plain building of one story with a thatch or heather roof, the whole expence not to exceed £50. I will give no cow's grass, neither will I lay any servitude on the tenants with regard to furnishing fewel to the schoolmaster but I will allow him five pounds yearly to purchase milk and fewel. After having given up every sort of servitude to myself over my tenants, the Christian Society on reflection will not wish or expect that I am to continue them in favour of schoolmasters.

In 1794 agreement was reached 'that a plain house of common drystone walls, pointed and harled with lime and covered with a thatched roof, should be built at Icolmkill for the accommodation of the schoolmaster'.

At the end of 1792 Robert Colquhoun was superannuated, retaining a salary as catechist until his death in 1799. His successor Allan Maclean had come in 1792 as assistant and the salary was raised to £15 on his full-time appointment. Also acting as guide to the ecclesiastical ruins, Allan Maclean was to feature in many travellers' accounts during his long career of over forty years. Robert Colquhoun is mentioned by name in only one, the Bute journal of 1788. The writer commented that the schoolmaster was not liked by the farmers who considered that he led an idle, subsidised existence. Colquhoun, however, had sufficient pupils to give up £2 of his salary to an assistant. He also had duties on behalf of the minister. From 1776 the schoolmaster's house was 'to answer for a preaching house also when Mr Macleod minister of Ross happens to go there to preach'. Once every two years the schoolmaster renewed the 'list of souls' for the minister and each Sunday he acted as catechist, read scripture to the people, said prayers with them and sang psalms in Gaelic. He was obliged to make a report every year of these proceedings which were, of course, in line with the religious objectives of the SSPCK.

Despite the infrequency of the minister's visits, then, the people maintained habits of religious observance. Even before the advent of a schoolmaster, according to Dr John Walker in 1764, it was their custom 'to repair on the Sabbath to their Devotions in the ruinous Abbey, to Columba's tomb and to the Chapells of several different Saints'.

The lingering superstition that so concerned the SSPCK was by no means dead in Iona however. Several eighteenth-century accounts mentioned customs and beliefs with clear magical or pagan undertones. 'They have all of them a remarkable Propensity to whatever is marvellous and supernatural' wrote Walker of the people; 'They are famous for the second Sight; full of Visions seen either by themselves or others; and have many wild and romantick notions concerning Religion and invisible things'. The then minister, who had taken up the charge in 1756, had been the first to abolish the practice of carrying a corpse around the whole Cathedral precincts before burial. (Martin Martin had noted a similar custom by the people of Colonsay who turned sunwise around their church on Oronsay Isle before any kind of service.)

Near the Machair is a small, green, smooth hill usually called in Gaelic Sìthean Mòr (large fairy hill) but which has the alternative name of Angel Hill. Here St Columba is said to have seen a vision of angels and it was here too, so Bishop Pococke was informed in 1760, that the people 'bring their Horses on the day of St. Michael and All Angels, and run races round it; it is probable this custom took its rise from bringing cattle at that season to be blessed, as they do now at Rome on a certain day of the year'. This was Pococke's interpretation but the practice echoed the pre-Christian ritual of dedication to the sun by turning a circle sunwise. There was evidently a small structure on top of the hill, described variously as 'a little cairn in the middle evidently druidical' or 'the ruins of a chapel' or 'a grand place of worship to which they went on white horses mounted. They said an angel sent them here, on a small Hill called Angel's Hill'.[4] This mingling of pagan and Christian beliefs has been widely commented on by folklorists. Investing places or practices with its own religious symbolism was one way the Church sought to neutralise the old creeds, which retained such a strong hold on the minds of the people.

In and around the Cathedral on Iona were stones attributed with a range of powers. A piece of the marble altar was said to be an antidote to disease in either man or beast. Martin Martin, in 1695, was the first of many travellers to mention the Black Stone on which any oath sworn was most solemnly binding. He also recorded a local belief in another stone which, if an arm was stretched over it three times in the name of the Trinity, would grant skill in the steering of a ship. The most famous were the Clachan Bràth or Judgement Day Stones, described as three globes of white marble to be turned sunwise in their stone basin by every passer-by. When the basin was finally worn through, this would herald the end of the world. The original stones had disappeared by the time John MacCulloch was in Iona in 1819 but such was the fascination of visitors for this doomladen custom that the village boys took care to substitute another stone when they saw the boats arriving! One or more stone fonts were said to stand between the Cathedral and the Nunnery which, if emptied of rain water by a virgin, would ensure a fair wind for sailing. Almost all travellers' accounts include a note about Iona's great variety of coloured pebbles, usually offered to them upon landing by the local children. A piece of translucent green serpentine rock, commonly found at the bay where Columba is believed to have landed, guaranteed the bearer immunity from drowning.

The power of the spirits to affect stock and crops was a common belief in the Highlands. J. Gregorson Campbell, who gathered oral tradition in the Hebrides while minister in Tiree from 1861 until 1891, noted: 'There are old people still living in Iona who remember a man driving a nail into a bull that had fallen over a rock, to keep away the Fairies'.[5] And Iona was one of many places where folklore collector Alexander Carmichael saw a 'leac gruagach'. This was a flat stone onto which a little milk was poured when the girls returned from tending the cows on the outlying pasture. It placated the 'gruagach' or guardian spirit of the cattle. In Iona the 'Clach a'Bhainne' or milk stone, as it was also called, lay on the edge of the eighteenth century village, a few yards from the site of the present day telephone boxes.

In two places, Iona and Lewis, Carmichael also recorded the custom of casting oatmeal or ale into the sea in order to assure a plentiful supply of seaweed to enrich the soil for the year's planting. He claimed that in Iona in 1860 he had talked with a middle-aged man whose father, when young, had taken part in the ceremony. It happened on Thursday before Easter, 'Diardaoin a Bhrochain Mhòir' (Thursday of the great porridge): 'As the day merged from Wednesday to Thursday a man walked to the waist into the sea and poured out whatever offering had been prepared, chanting

> A Dhè na mara
> Cuir todhar 's an tarruinn
> Chon tachair an talaimh
> Chon bailcidh dhuinn biaidh

> (O God of the Sea,
> Put weed in the drawing wave
> To enrich the ground,
> To shower on us food.)

Those behind the offerer took up the chant and wafted it along the seashore . . .'.[6] Local tradition connects this event with Dùn Mhanannain on the west coast, the hill of Manann who was a god of the sea.

Allan Maclean's long career as schoolmaster and official guide spanned the entire period from 1792 until 1840. For generations after that Iona people knew of him by the name Ailean Sgoilear (scholar Alan) and it is clear that he commanded respect and affection from islander and visitor alike. Many accounts talk of him as the 'Cicerone' of Iona. He was also referred to as 'the king of the island', 'the greatest personage, 'a mystagogue' and 'the village pedagogue and antiquary'. Robert Carruthers described the first sight of Allan Maclean in 1835:

> In a few minutes a little round-faced man appeared, his chin new reaped and on his head a smart beaver hat that shone conspicuously among the bare heads or blue bonnets of the fishermen. He had a staff in one hand and a little book 'The Historical Account of Iona' in the other.

On this occasion there was a warm altercation with a rival guide, probably Angus Lamont, who was to be officially appointed to this post by the Duke from 1840. Local people backed the schoolmaster's claim, joining noisily in the war of words between the two, and the writer concluded: 'It was obvious that the schoolmaster was the real Simon Pure and that his rival was an idle, talkative old fellow, who envied the dominie his glory and his gains'.

For many years Maclean was the only English speaker among the inhabitants and impressed many people with his knowledge, not only of Iona but of the wider world. He engaged the Swiss Necker de Saussure in intelligent conversation about Mont Blanc and its perpetual snow and ice. He also showed a pride in the antiquities under his care which at times bordered on the possessive. An effort by a Mr Rae Wilson to clear rubble from the sculptured stones met with '. . . violent opposition from the schoolmaster who was anxious that not a stone should be removed'.[7]

Maclean had good cause to be watchful, however. Increasing numbers of visitors brought an increased risk of theft or damage to the stones. Already by the 1770s the large marble altar described by early writers had been reduced to fragments, whittled away to provide visitors with souvenirs and locals with talismans to cure disease. Abbot MacKinnon's tomb was another target. In 1819 a group of sailors broke off the sculptured hands and crozier, reportedly 'at the instigation of one of the officers who gave them a double allowance of grog'. In subsequent years the nose was broken and three of the lion pedestals supporting it were stolen. The last lion nearly suffered the same fate but the culprit was caught red-handed by Maclean, who thereafter kept it stored under his bed for safety.[8] One account gave him credit for the improved state of the ancient buildings:

He had caused walls to be propped, rubbish to be cleared away, and many a beautiful old fragment to be brought to light. So strong was his feeling for his darling ruins that he could not speak with any patience of an Englishman having clandestinely carried off one of the figures that graced a tomb. I liked the old man, his energy and simplicity which was quite child-like.[9]

Allan Maclean's respected stature in the island was well deserved. Up until 1828 his school duties were combined with many of the minister's tasks, as his predecessor's had been. For a few years he also taught an evening Gaelic school for about thirty adults, to help them read and write in their native language.

The school roll totalled a hundred pupils or more for fifteen out of the twenty years between 1820 and 1840. In 1831 an application for an assistant teacher was accepted. From that same year until 1841 the SSPCK also ran a school for 'Spinning, Sewing and other Branches of Female Industry', allowing £5 a year to a Mrs MacInnes and then a Mrs MacColl, probably both local women. The schoolmaster's returns show that actual attendance by pupils was often 'irregular' or 'middling' with many fewer present in summer, reflecting the need for children to help with harvest and other farm work. Fees were payable but the extant returns for 1827–40 indicate that they were received erratically and often not at all.

SSPCK Inspectors, visiting in 1824 and 1828, gave excellent reports of the standards achieved by the Iona pupils and the character of their teacher:

I found 66 scholars present and upwards of 100 names on the roll. I was very well pleased indeed with the appearance and proficiency of the children. Mr. Maclean the teacher is an excellent man, has been 36 years at this station and has been extremely useful in the island and is much respected by the people.

Yet another of the schoolmaster's duties was that of librarian. The collection dated from around 1819 when books were donated by several visiting clergymen, concerned about the spiritual and educational welfare of the people. The best known of these was the Reverend Legh Richmond, whose short stay in 1820 inspired him to raise money to replace the dilapidated schoolhouse. He preached several times to the population, Mr Maclean translating sentence by sentence, and took a particular interest in the children. He composed a special hymn for them which was sung, again with instant translation, at the feast he organised as a farewell gift to the islanders:

The best sheep to be found in the island was purchased for the sum of six shillings. . . . The children assembled on shore and picked up shells, to answer the purpose of knives and forks.

How interesting a scene! Two hundred children and their parents assembled on the sea-shore every countenance beaming with delight! At the conclusion of the festivity all sung the hymn which Mr. Richmond in the glow of his benevolent feelings had instantaneously composed ... He left Iona amidst the tears of its population, nearly the whole of whom attended him to the seashore with more lively demonstrations of gratitude and love.[10]

Mr Richmond's enthusiastic plans for a new school did not, however, meet with the approval of the Duke of Argyll. It may be that the Estate was stung by the implicit accusation of neglect on their part. A letter from the Chamberlain to the Duke's lawyer refers to an explanation being available for the school's state of disrepair, in response to 'the insulting paragraph which Mr. Richmond or some of his friends had put into the newspaper'.

By 1822 a new schoolhouse had been erected at the Estate's expense and the Richmond funds were diverted to the SSPCK for augmenting the collection of library books. Further rebuilding took place around 1840–1, as the 1841 Census notes the presence on the island of 'seven males from other places working at building schoolhouse and stone dykes'. And in 1840 two instalments of £113.6.8 were paid to a contractor for this purpose, in addition to small sums for architect's plans and for a garden wall at the schoolhouse. This fairly substantial expenditure suggests a new and bigger building, with attached or nearby garden. It was probably on the site of the present school. It is not known where the earlier schools were although one account implies that Allan Maclean's house, where he lived and taught, was at the east end of the original village, i.e. between Maclean's Cross and the Cathedral grounds.

It seems that an infant school operated for a time, due to a further display of generosity by visitors. In 1832–3 an English lady and an Edinburgh lady collected £25 and £27 respectively for this purpose and presented it to the minister.[11] There is no record of how long the school lasted or who taught it.

In addition to daytime classes, Allan Maclean taught an evening Sabbath School for children, of whom fifty to a hundred sometimes attended. On those Sundays when the minister did not come over from Mull, in other words on all but four in the year, he read scripture to the people and he also held fellowship prayer meetings twice a week. It was small wonder that the SSPCK Inspector wrote: 'I have reason to believe there are very few more worthy characters on the establishment of the Society'.

Visiting clergymen such as Legh Richmond helped to fill the gap in the spiritual needs of the people. And there was the influence of the several dramatic evangelical movements which swept the Highlands in the early nineteenth century. Congregationalist and Baptist preachers were particularly active, travelling in all weathers, often holding services out of doors and drawing huge numbers. These spiritual revivals have been credited with creating a sense of unity and purpose among the small tenantry at a time when the familiar social order was rapidly disintegrating and their traditional superiors, including very often the minister, were becoming distant and neglectful of their interests. The religious experience, especially Old Testament themes such as the freedom of a people from bondage, helped them to understand their own experience and, later, gave them confidence to stand up to the landlords.[12]

Dugald Sinclair was one of the best known of the full-time itinerant missionaries, who undertook extensive tours of the Hebrides and the north-west mainland for the Scotch Itinerant Society between 1810 and 1815 and then for the Baptist Missionary Society, after his ordination in Lochgilphead in 1815. He twice visited Iona, in 1812 and 1814, preaching on one occasion to four hundred people: 'Here they seldom hear a sermon: and the poor people were much pleased when they heard of my intention to remain with them over Sabbath'.[13]

Alexander Grant, based in Tobermory from the 1820s, did much to build up a strong Baptist congregation in Bunessan and Ardalanish in the Ross of Mull and was one of several elders who went regularly to Iona. On one such visit in 1834 (which took place after Iona had its own parish church and resident minister) he reported:

> The people received us most kindly and manifested greatest eagerness to hear the gospel. They attended from the farthest part of the island in the darkest and wettest night, crowding the largest house in the place and listened with profound attention. When going to the place of meeting, it was truly pleasing and amusing to see the people coming from every quarter, each carrying a burning peat instead of a lantern. We remained in Iona seven days and preached ten times.

In 1839 a young woman was baptised in Iona, noted as perhaps the first ever adult baptism in that famous and holy island.[14]

As a dissenting movement from the established Church, the Baptists encountered opposition and harassment in many of the areas where they tried to make a base. Allan Maclean certainly did not approve, according to one account: 'He complained to me in course of conversation of the progress of Baptists in his neighbourhood'.[15]

In 1837 Allan Maclean was superannuated when Dugald Mac-Innes, a native of Iona, was appointed to the schoolmaster's post. The SSPCK files note that Maclean had been forty-seven years in the Society's service and they continued to pay him a retirement allowance for several years. His duties as tourist guide also continued until around 1840. Allan had been born in Kilninian parish in the north of Mull and clearly had no wish to move from the area where he had worked with so much dedication for so long. He died in Iona in 1853 at the age of ninety-two. A widower, he left no direct descendants but in 1880 a relative named Dugald Campbell, a banker in Tobermory, erected a handsome red granite obelisk over his grave in the Rèilig Orain, in memory of Ailean Sgoilear.

The medieval parish church of St Ronan, which stands in the Nunnery precincts, was probably abandoned as a place of worship in the early seventeenth century. The building of their own parish church and manse after two hundred years must thus have been a notable event for the people of Iona. It formed part of a Parliamentary scheme set up in 1823, with a grant of £50,000, to build extra churches in areas of the Highlands and Islands where large or remote parishes, served by a single minister, had left much of the population without regular pastoral care. The minutes of the Presbytery of Mull record the application from Iona for inclusion in the scheme, in a letter dated 21 September 1824. The certificate of completion of the church and manse there bears the date 7 November 1828.[16]

Thomas Telford furnished the plans and specifications for the whole scheme and directed the design work. The contractor for the area which included Iona was William Thomson. Iona was the smallest of the thirty-two churches erected and it followed Telford's standard design, with reduced wall and window height, but without a central rear wing or a gallery. The material used was pink Ross of Mull granite. As a parliamentary report noted a few years later: 'The front of the new Church is comprised of polished granite, which gives it a handsome appearance. The Garden and Glebe consist of two acres, two roods, seventeen falls of good land, which is under cultivation and already greatly improved'. Along with this land, conveyed to the Commissioners by the Duke, came the privilege to the minister of cutting peats on Ross and of grazing a horse and two cows on the village pasture. The six-roomed manse was of the single-storey design. An upper room was added many years later. The total cost for the two buildings was £1503.4.0, a little over the set contract price for each locality of £1500.

The interior of the church was originally designed with the pulpit placed between the two windows of the East wall. Below it was a chair for the precentor who, in the days before organ accompaniment, read out or sang each line of the psalms for the congregation to follow. The pews were placed around a long central communion table. (This table, the pulpit and one of the traditional collection boxes on poles have been preserved in the Highland Folk Museum at Kingussie.) This arrangement lasted until extensive renovation was carried out on the church in 1939.

The first minister of the new parliamentary church was Dugald Neil Campbell, a son of the Reverend Dugald Campbell who had served the whole parish of Kilfinichen and Kilviceuen from 1780 until 1816. Another son, Donald Campbell, had succeeded his father and continued as minister of the Bunessan district when Iona became separate. The Iona charge included the Creich district of the Ross of Mull and the minister's travels were now in reverse. He crossed to Mull twice a year to hold services and more frequently for pastoral duties. About twenty of the Ross congregation came regularly to the service in Iona, those without boats being obliged to go to the church in Bunessan in the next parish.

In May 1835 the Reverend Donald McVean from Kenmore in Perthshire was ordained in Iona. That same year the Royal Commission on Religious Instruction, Scotland (RCRI) was appointed to inquire into the provision for public worship and religious instruction throughout the country, with particular reference to the needs of the poor. Mr McVean argued that the size of his scattered parish made proper pastoral care very difficult. His suggestion, which was never taken up, was that the island of Iona should form a separate parish and that Creich should be joined with a portion of Bunessan district to form a new parish. Pressure on the space within the new church was another reason advanced. He estimated that three-quarters of the population of Iona were 'in the practice of occasionally attending church' and when 250, on average, attended in summer months the aisles, as well as the pews, were crowded.[17]

Mr McVean had arrived in Iona when the population was nearing its peak. Early in his ministry, the harvest failure of 1836–7 provoked a destitution crisis for his poorest parishioners. And as we have seen in earlier chapters, he was to be actively concerned in events following the disastrous potato famine of 1846. Before that, however, his attention was claimed by a crisis within his own calling, the church.

14

Parish Life:
Church, Cathedral, School 1843–1914

On 23 May 1843 the Rev. Donald McVean was present at the momentous proceedings of the General Assembly of the Church of Scotland. These were the culmination of nearly half a century of growing conflict within the ministry between two main factions, termed Moderates and Evangelicals. Issues of dissension included greater financial support for the Church from the State, the extension of mission work and, in particular, the practice of patronage, which had been restored in 1712. The Evangelicals wished to see this reversed and congregations rather than patrons, who were usually the landlords, once again granted the right to choose their own ministers. The ten years leading up to 1843 were especially stormy, with the Moderates' long dominance over the General Assembly finally shaken. The prospect of secession became increasingly likely.

In the event, around one-third of the Church's clergymen walked out of the General Assembly that year, in what became known as the Disruption, and formed the Free Church of Scotland. One of them was Mr McVean. He and the Coll minister were the only two in the Presbytery of Mull to come out. The Free Church clergy were initially drawn mainly from the Lowlands. In parts of the Highlands many fewer ministers deserted the Established Church, less than fifty per cent in the Synod of Glenelg for example and only twenty per cent in the Synod of Argyll, which stretched from Kintyre to Fort William. One of the new Church's first tasks was to train and send out men to these parishes where the great majority of the people had flocked to join them. Their schooner the *Breadalbane* became a well-known conveyance for this purpose up and down the west coast.[1] The mass popularity of the Free Church among the small tenantry of the Highlands and Islands owed much to the work of the itinerant evangelical missionaries and local lay preachers, who had filled a spiritual gap in the early decades of the century and built up a committed following. The Free Church was perceived as inheriting this tradition of dissent and identifying with the people rather than with the forces of establishment.

Despite the lead taken by their own minister, the Iona congregation acted against the general trend in the Highlands by dividing fairly equally between the two denominations. Each church attracted roughly similar numbers from cottar and tenant households. There were five examples of divided families. According to lists drawn up by both ministers at the request of the Duke of Argyll in 1845, a majority over the whole parish remained with the Established Church – 112 families as against the eighty who joined the Free Church. In Iona itself there was a small balance in favour of the Free Church, forty-seven families to thirty-six. The Reverend Alexander MacGregor had been appointed to the Established Church charge in December 1843.

In common with the experience throughout the country, Iona's Free Church minister and congregation faced considerable hardships in the early years. A site for a church was denied by the Duke and worship had to be in the open air. A visitor wrote in 1844: 'In the burying ground of the kings near the chapel of St. Oran is a sort of sentry box from which a non intrusion minister preaches to his followers, the church question, as our guide said, having penetrated even into these remote districts'.[2] The 'sentry box' refers to the tall wooden preaching tent used widely as a substitute shelter by ministers at this time. A hollow near the Machair, Poll Dubhaich, is also said to have been used for open-air services.

Ousted from the manse, the McVean family had to move dwelling-house four times, enduring damp and miserable conditions which one winter led to the death of a child. In 1845 the Duke relented and gave permission for a church to be built at Martyrs Bay and for a manse, just south of the Rèilig Orain.[3] The Disruption had repercussions in the school too. In 1841 the heritors had taken up the Government grant by then available, to obtain a salary for a Parochial School. Responsibility for its administration, and the appointment of its teachers, thus passed from the SSPCK to the Mull Presbytery of the Church of Scotland. In 1843 the schoolmaster, George Ross, newly appointed in June 1842, was dismissed from his post as he had seceded from the Established Church. His successor, John Fisher, also incurred the Presbytery's displeasure when he allowed the homeless Mr McVean of the Free Church to live in the schoolhouse. He agreed eventually to end this arrangement and was let off with an admonishment.

Very little evidence has come to light about relations between the two denominations on Iona in the years after 1843. A visitor in 1848 gained the impression that the split had led to serious divisions within the community: '. . . we were informed that, few and mutually dependent as they are for comfort, those visited by the new light will scarcely recognise their former friends as beings of the same species with themselves! This sad state of things is to be observed throughout the whole of the Highlands'. The same account reports a collection on board the steamer towards the setting up of a Free Church school on the island, implying that Mr McVean wished the children of his congregation to be educated separately. But there is no record of it ever coming into being.[4]

Neither H. D. Graham nor the Rev. J. C. Richmond, both of whom wrote in some detail about life on Iona in the late 1840s, mentioned major discord among the inhabitants over the church question. Perhaps the common experiences of coping with the potato failure, the rent rises and the pressure to emigrate during that period were stronger factors in drawing the people together.

In Mull the Baptists continued to thrive during the middle years of the century, attracting very large gatherings to the meeting-house they had now obtained at Ardalanish in the Ross. Meetings in Iona in the late 1840s and 1850s also reported good numbers and friendly co-operation from the Free Church, who allowed them the use of their building.[5]

No more than two or three Iona residents appear to have been formal members of the Baptist Church but one of them stands out in local lore as 'am Baisteach' (the Baptist). He was Archibald MacDonald and was quite active within the church, acting as visiting elder to Tiree at least once. At 1851 he worked one and a half holdings at Martyrs Bay and his house was described in the McNeill Report as having 'every appearance of comfort; a number of fowls about the door and a good supply of meal or grain stored in one part of the kitchen'. MacDonald emigrated to Canada in 1858, to be followed by his sister Mary and her husband Peter MacArthur the next year (one of the individual cases assisted by the Duke). He did not have a family of his own to support and the size of his stock did not indicate undue financial difficulty. Indeed, in 1856 he received five pounds from the Duke as 'prize for the best managed croft' in Iona. It is very possible that he was attracted by the large emigrant Baptist community in Ontario, founded by Dugald Sinclair the former itinerant missionary.

Whatever the reason, MacDonald did not leave without becoming immortalised in the only one of Angus Lamont's poems which is still readily recollected.[6] Lamont was his neighbour and they shared a skiff which came to grief after the Baisteach moored it carelessly when hurrying to a service in Ross. The poem recounts the episode in satirical style, the refrain being:

'S coma leam fhìn do chompanas bàta;
Bha thusa ga bristeadh 's mise ga càradh;
'S coma leam fhìn do chompanas bàta.

(I don't care for your boat partnership;
You broke it and I mended it.)

The Baisteach seemed to have been prone to marine disaster as in another incident a neighbour borrowed his horse to cross to Mull for peats and the horse drowned. On hearing the news, MacDonald's reply was to make a play on words, using the Iona people's nickname of 'na h-eich' (the horses):

Thàinig an t-each ag iarraidh each air an eich agus thug an t-each seachad an t-each don eich agus bhàthadh an t-each an t-each 's an t-each a nis gun each idir air tàilleamh an eich.

(The horse came to ask the horse for a horse and the horse gave the horse a horse and the horse drowned the horse and the horse is now without a horse at all on account of the horse.)[7]

When the lease of the Free Church manse in Iona ran out in 1865, the McVean family moved to Achabàn, a house built for them outside Fionnphort in the Ross of Mull. The minister continued to be actively involved in many aspects of parish life. He was keenly interested in education and was himself widely read. Both he and his sons contributed to the talks and debates of the island's Mutual Improvement and Debating Society, he ran Sabbath Schools for the young and he built up a valuable collection of books on the history of Iona. He was said to have been a guiding influence on several of the young men who decided to follow the learned professions.

When Donald McVean retired in 1878 he had served the parish for a total of forty-three years, thirty-five of them for the Free Church. He died two years later and was buried close to St Oran's Chapel in the historic burying ground of the kings. His personal standing in the community was such that at the funeral, old dissensions set aside, the island people turned out *en masse* to pay their last respects.

A call from the Iona Free Church in 1890 has survived.[8] The minister to whom it was addressed did not, in the end, accept the charge but the document shows the names of eighty-four elders and members, indicating that the adult population was still fairly evenly divided between the two churches. That year it was decided to have a separate minister for Iona and although the charge was reunited with Ross by 1906, a new manse was built at Martyrs Bay on the island in 1894. The church became the United Free Church in 1900 and its last resident minister was the Rev. Archibald Dewar, from 1891 until

1918. After that the congregation was served by lay missionaries and visiting ministers until the union of the U.F. Church and the Church of Scotland in 1929.

Meanwhile, the Established Church congregation had experienced a series of disputes during the latter part of the nineteenth century with their minister, the Rev. John Campbell – known locally as the Ministear Bàn – who had come to the charge in 1876. He had in fact been deposed from a charge earlier in his career, perhaps due to his argumentative nature which the discord in Iona certainly revealed. The main complaint, which was finally taken to the General Assembly by a congregational deputation, centred on Mr Campbell's absence from Iona during the summer of 1881 without explanation or provision for a supply minister. This charge was found proven, although other complaints, which included assault, falsifying parish information, and non-payment of debts, were found not proven and the Presbytery let the defendant off with a stiff censure.[9]

Relations appeared to continue scarcely less stormily until Mr Campbell eventually retired in 1889. Things even came to the point where the precentor, in a silent but noticeable protest, refused to lead the first line of the psalms and on two successive Sundays worship was conducted entirely without praise.

The Gift and Restoration of the Cathedral

The congregations of both churches in Iona were considerably swelled by summer visitors. This was one reason why the island was made a separate charge by the Free Church in 1890 and, in the same year, the question of supplying extra assistance to the minister during the tourist season was raised by the Church of Scotland. It was not only the two hotels that were doing good business. It was by now common for the islanders to move into outhouses or smaller cottages during the busiest months and let the whole house to visitors, who brought their families, their provisions, their maids and in one case at least, even their piano.[10] As the example below shows, a large number were from Glasgow and the houses that particular month were almost equally divided between crofts or farms and the village.

Surnames of visitors and the houses where they were staying in Iona. Published in *Oban Visitors' Register*, 4 August 1897:

Kirkwood (Glasgow)	Bishops Walk	Lang (London)	Roseneath
Navlin (Glasgow)	Dùnagan	Kirkpatrick (Glasgow)	Knocknacross
Kyle (Glasgow)	Greenbank	Rankin (Glasgow)	Lovedale

Macbeth	Maol	Turner	Lorne
(Glasgow)		(Glasgow)	
Brown	Sìthean	MacKechnie	Victoria
(Glasgow)		(Glasgow)	
MacCulloch	Sligineach	Bryson	Staffa
(Gourock)		(Dundee)	
Gilmore	Burnside		

Tourists were among those who continued to express concern about the need to preserve and maintain the historic buildings on Iona. The voices raised included that of the *Scotsman* newspaper and the Society of Antiquaries who, in 1870, appointed a committee to approach the Duke of Argyll on the matter. The Duke responded positively and in the mid-1870s a considerable amount of work was done, under the direction of architect Sir Rowand Anderson, to clear the interiors of rubbish and to strengthen the walls of both the Cathedral and the Nunnery.

From family memoirs it appears that from around this time the permanent future of the Iona ruins began to preoccupy the Duke. He kept his thinking close to himself. Even his daughter Lady Victoria, who had a particular love for Iona and the Cathedral, knew only the day before it was made public that he had decided to relinquish ownership of all the ecclesiastical remains on the island and hand them over to a public trust linked to the Church of Scotland.[11]

The Deed of Trust was signed at Inveraray on 22 September 1899. The *Scotsman* of 30 September quoted extracts from it in a leading article and praised the 'noble and generous thought' which had motivated the gift. The *Glasgow Herald* of the same date and the *Oban Times* of 7 October both published the text in full. The Duke prefaced the conditions of the transfer with his stated belief that the fickle fortunes and character of one family, however illustrious and long-established, could afford 'a very imperfect security for the protection and appropriate use of the buildings of such great historic interest to the Christian world'. His declared wish was 'that the Cathedral shall be re-roofed and restored so as to admit of its being used for public worship . . . and the other ruins carefully preserved' and he desired that the Trustees 'will and may occasionally allow, as it may be convenient, the members of other Christian churches to hold services within the Cathedral, as I have myself allowed during my ownership thereof'.

This ecumenical clause was of central importance to the Duke. He was a staunch supporter of the presbyterian Church of Scotland but was said to be wearied and aggravated by inter-church strife. The keen interest of other denominations in Iona had not escaped him and

two years before, on the 1300th anniversary of the death of St
Columba, there had been ironic comment on the fact that three
separate celebrations were held on the island. On 9 June 1897 two
services in Gaelic and two in English were conducted in the Cathedral, under a temporary roof, for a very large gathering of Protestant
clergy and churchgoers from all over the country. On the same day
the Bishop of Argyll and the Isles, along with other clergy of the
Episcopal Church, held a quiet commemoration in their new House
of Retreat on the island. And on 15 June over six hundred Roman
Catholic pilgrims came by special steamer and sang a Mass in the
Cathedral. Their initial request to arrive on 9 June had been turned
down in favour of the Church of Scotland event already planned.

There had long been misgivings in the local community about the
intentions of visiting Catholic or Episcopalian clergy, perceived by
many within Presbyterian denominations to be the same. The belief
that their ultimate aim was conversion was deep-rooted. Permission
had previously been given, in June 1888, for another Scottish Catholic Pilgrimage to Iona and a reporter from the *Glasgow Daily Mail*
judged from his samples of the popular feeling that 'it would be safe
to say that a plebiscite of the resident population would not have
supported the permission given by the Duke of Argyll to hold a
service within the ruined walls of the Cathedral'. After a visit to Iona
in 1869, a Catholic priest J. S. McCorry published his lament that 'no
altar was there for the Eucharistic sacrifice . . . that the poor people
from the cradle to the grave were living without graces and dying
without the blessing of true religion !'.[12] The following year a brief
note in folklorist J. F. Campbell's journal commented : 'Conclusion
of all that the Romans want a footing in Iona. A party came last year
in procession through Mull and held high mass in the Cathedral'.

Some twenty years earlier, Bishop Ewing and a small congregation of Episcopalians caused no little consternation during a visit to
the island. H. D. Graham heard first from the village children that
the 'pàpanaich' (papists) were preaching in the 'Eaglais Mhòr' (great
church, the usual local term in Gaelic for the Cathedral). The visiting worshippers were outnumbered by a crowd of curious locals
who 'looked on some with a smile and some with a sneer but
otherwise were perfectly well behaved'. The Free Church minister,
also present, had to be forcibly restrained when the Bishop ended
the service with a Latin prayer and said 'among other offensive
things . . . that God had removed his candlestick from Iona and that
its light and glory were gone'. It was a local lad named Charles
MacInnes who reportedly flummoxed the Bishop by challenging
him afterwards on the differences between his ceremonies and those

of the papists: 'Ah, said the Bishop, if you had attended to my prayers you would have perceived a vast difference. Well, said Charles, referring to the unfortunate Latin prayer, why don't you pray in a language that we can understand?'.[13]

A more public controversy with the Episcopal Church came in the early 1890s when Alexander Chinnery-Haldane, Bishop of Argyll and the Isles, applied for permission to build a chapel and retreat house on Iona. Vigorous opposition was mounted by the Established Church minister who raised a petition of one hundred and fourteen names against this scheme which threatened, he asserted, to 'outrage the religious feelings of the people'. Caustic rejoinders in the press pointed out that the number of signatures was greater by three than the number of adult residents on Iona and that the Presbyterian community was itself a divided house. The Duke held firmly to the principle that all who visited Iona should have the opportunity to worship in their own way and the feu was granted in 1893. The Bishop remained adamant that proselytising for the Episcopalian faith was not intended: '(he) knew the people well enough to be aware that any such attempt would produce no valuable result . . . he meant the House to be a House of prayer and Eucharist, of study and meditation'. For this purpose it was offered into the care of the Society of St John the Evangelist from 1897 until 1909 and a few of their members, known as the Cowley Fathers, were resident all the year round between 1906 and 1908. They invited local people to meetings and social functions in 'The Bishop's House', as the building came to be known, and the speculation was that this was an effort to attract converts. The Fathers' own letters, however, give an impression that local participation in their services, though welcome, was a lesser preoccupation than the pursuit of a contemplative life and the solution to practical problems, such as how to heat a large stone house and keep sheep out of the vegetable garden.[14]

Between 1902 and 1905 the new body of Trustees oversaw the restoration and reroofing of the Cathedral choir and transepts. The opening service on 14 July 1905 was attended by around 300, including many local people. The Dowager Duchess of Argyll was present and the preacher was Rev. Dr J. C. Russell of Campbeltown. Over the next few years a Miss Campbell of Blythswood was the moving spirit in efforts to raise money for restoration of the nave. She succeeded with the active help of Woman's Guilds throughout Scotland, and of Scots overseas, and this further work was completed between 1909 and 1910. Craftsmen and labourers were drawn from neighbouring areas of Mull during this period, including John

MacCallum the Kintra mason and Neil and Archie Graham, joiners from Ardtun. The nave was reopened for worship on 26 June 1910.

In the Deed of Trust the Duke specifically excluded the parish minister and kirk session of Iona from involvement in the management of the historic ruins. The wording included the phrase 'for the time being' and may not have been intended as a permanent injunction. It is thought that the Rev. Archibald MacMillan, who had come to the charge in 1890, had fallen out of favour with the Duke. It was he who had led the attack on the building of the Bishops House. The 'Ministear Mòr' (big minister), as he was known, also agitated strongly for the repairs now urgently needed to the Parish Church and organised a fundraising drive for a place of worship on the Ross side of the parish. St Ernans Church, on the shore of Loch Pot I, was completed in May 1899. The involvement of the Parish Minister in the work of the Trustees might have avoided the unfortunate breaks in communication between that body and the local people which occasionally arose. In 1908 there were strong objections from the parishioners to a ruling by the Trustees that prohibited upright tombstones and railed enclosures in the Rèilig Orain.[15] This was the graveyard not only of kings and chieftains but also of the local inhabitants and they claimed that they had not been consulted.

Whatever reason lay behind the Duke's exclusion of Mr MacMillan from the Trusteeship it did not, happily, prevent the involvement of his parishioners in the restored Cathedral. Permission was granted by the Trustees for parish services to be held there in the summer months after 1905 and from shortly before the First World War until 1930 the congregation used it in preference to the Parish Church all year round. The marriage of Archibald MacArthur, Clachanach and Janet MacNiven in the Cathedral in March 1909 drew a headline in the *Oban Times* of 'First for 300 years' and was described as a novel event 'well worthy of being recorded in the annals of the island'. The Cathedral became strongly identified in the minds of the local community as *their* place of worship and with the addition of summer visitors was often full to overflowing. The eighth Duke had died in 1900, but his wish that the ruins be reclaimed for full public use was realised.

Schooling – late nineteenth century

We left the story of Iona school at the time of the Disruption, soon after it had become a Parochial School under the authority of the Mull Presbytery of the Church of Scotland. In 1851 'an English tourist' wrote in querulous tones to *The Witness*, asking why the minister or the Duke did not provide education for the children in

Iona and so stop them assailing the unsuspecting visitor with their pebble trade. He had asked a small girl why she was not at school and had been told that the teacher had been absent for a year. The Presbytery had spent nearly ten months deliberating a case of alleged adultery between the schoolmaster John Fisher and a visiting married woman. They eventually dismissed him in 1849 and the post had been left vacant, although the Duke had paid for an interim teacher, Donald Campbell, for a while in 1850.

The long era of stability under Ailean Sgoilear was past. The next decade saw a high turnover of schoolmasters, beginning with brothers James and then John Barnett who taught in succession between 1851 and 1856. Both went on to become ministers. John MacDonald and Donald Ferguson were then appointed in turn, each for just under two years. In 1861 Angus MacInnes, who had been born at Greenbank croft, came back to Iona from a teaching post at Kilmore in Lorn and was schoolmaster until 1868.

The schoolmaster regularly enlisted older scholars to act as assistants or 'pupil teachers'. Dr Duncan MacArthur, born in 1839, was to recall on the occasion of the opening of Iona's public library that 'he had got instruction from about twenty different temporary teachers' in the nearby school. There is a record of Charles MacDonald, Ardionra being succeeded a pupil teacher in 1892 by Hector Maclean, Sligineach. The former would have been about twenty then, the latter fourteen. And in 1893 Jessie Dinah MacDonald, aged seventeen, was first appointed as a pupil teacher. Better remembered by the older generation of Iona natives as 'Jetta', she was to have a long association with the school, eventually presiding over the infant department until well into the 1920s.

Her father had been Allan MacDonald, a brother of Alexander whose wizardry with figures had long outlived himself in his nickname, 'The Mathematical Weaver'. Allan had succeeded Angus MacInnes as schoolmaster, until his death in 1876 when Jetta was still an infant. Church and school were interlinked in this family as Jetta's mother was Jessie MacGregor, a niece of the Rev. Alexander MacGregor who served the Church of Scotland congregation from 1843 until 1875. He was unmarried and had brought his brother and family from Perthshire to help run the holdings he rented from the Duke. Mr MacGregor, like Mr McVean of the Free Church, was a minister actively involved in working the land in addition to participating in the educational and recreational life of the island.

During Allan MacDonald's tenure the Education Act of 1872 was passed, making school attendance compulsory for children aged five to thirteen, the leaving age being raised to fourteen in 1883. Each parish or burgh had to elect a School Board who were responsible for the appointment of teachers and the management of the school and its buildings. At the first meeting of the Kilfinichen and Kilviceuen School Board, on 20 May 1873, the following were present: James Wyllie, Chamberlain of Argyll; Alexander MacIntyre, Ardalanish; Dr Donald Black, Bunessan (a native of Iona); Rev. Archibald Campbell, Assapoll; Rev. Donald McVean, Ross and Iona.

From the education census taken by the new Board, seventeen boys and sixteen girls were reported as attending school regularly in Iona. Only three boys and two girls were never present. This total of thirty-eight is rather less than the fifty of school age recorded in the population Census of 1871. The earliest surviving Admission Register dates from 1877 and shows that fifty-seven were entered between July of that year and November 1878. Many were well over five years, however. The average age at admission was ten and the average number of years on the school roll was three and a half. By 1885 a sample of the Register reveals that the average age at admission had fallen to six and a half and the average length of attendance had gone up to four and a half years. The annual fees were set as follows: 1/- for children preparing for Standard I, 1/6 for those in Standards II and III, 2/6 for Standards IV, V and VI. It was also agreed that the fourth and subsequent child in any family would not be charged.[16]

An early task for the Board was to undertake repairs to the school and schoolhouse. These took place during the winter and spring of 1878/9 during which time pupils were taught in the Free Church. Unfortunately, this too was in a dilapidated condition, which roused the ire of Neil MacKay and gave him an opportunity to urge active protest by the parents in his *NBDM* column of 27 December 1878:

> ... it is rather too much of the Board to expect that the children though hardy, can endure day by day the piercing currents of North winds that pass through paneless windows ... Why the repairs of the school house were not executed in the summer vacation we fail to see; but it is certainly in keeping with almost every action of the Board in relation to Iona since they accepted office. It is to be hoped that the ratepayers will earnestly study the interests of education at the approaching election and choose good men and true who will do their duty.

The parents did indeed exercise their right to approach the Board on several occasions with complaints, suggestions and sometimes praise. A petition from nine of them in 1890 hoped that the Board would 'establish a school in the parish where secondary education could be given and also hoping that the time will soon come when only Gaelic speaking teachers will be employed by the Board'. Gaelic had

certainly been stressed in earlier years. The advertisement for the post
of teacher in 1876 stated 'Applicants must have knowledge of Gaelic'
and an appointee, D. M. MacDonald of Stirling, subsequently with-
drew as his ability in the language was not sufficient. Teachers up
until 1882 will all have spoken Gaelic. David Kirkpatrick from Alex-
andria, appointed from then until 1892, probably did not – hence the
1890 petition – but parents expressed considerable satisfaction with
his general teaching abilities and with the very popular music class
which he began for adults as well as for scholars.

School Inspectors' reports continued to be satisfactory. Seventy-
four pupils were present on the day of inspection in September 1896,
forty-one from the island and thirty-three from Glasgow. This high
proportion of boarded-out children was one reason why an extension to the school was urgently needed by the 1890s and the alterations
were eventually completed by 1903. A surviving merit certificate
shows a pupil of fourteen in 1897 as having passed in the subjects
of Geography, History, English, Mathematics and Latin. In 1907 the
Inspector stated: 'The school is conducted with very good results.
Nature knowledge is all over a particularly strong subject. Singing
also deserves a word of praise'. It was noted that ten candidates had
passed the qualifying examination for secondary school that year and
by 1909 seven Iona children were attending secondary school on the
mainland. From 1894 until the War the teacher also conducted an
Evening Continuation Class for young people up to the age of
eighteen. This included practical subjects such as navigation.

The medium of teaching was now exclusively English. Most children who entered school in the first two decades of the twentieth
century spoke Gaelic as their first, or only, language. But a significant
side-effect of the number of Glasgow children was that the language
of the playground became predominantly English. In 1892 there
were thirty-four boarded-out children in Iona, most of them of
school age and the total roll then stood at eighty-two. This proportion was clearly higher than that earlier recommended by the Board
of Supervision who had stated that not more than a fifth, or a quarter
at most, of the children in a school should be boarded-out.[17] Overall
numbers fell substantially during the next two decades, to forty-
three scholars by 1913–14, but the proportion of Glasgow children
remained high. That year only one of the eight new admissions were
native to the island.

15

Conclusion:
Change and Continuity

The century and a half covered by this study brought changes of a more profound character than any witnessed in the previous few hundred years to the Highlands of Scotland. They altered radically and permanently the basis on which the land was held and worked. They were not, however, unique to the area but were part of a wider transformation in the countryside throughout Britain and much of Western Europe. In this examination of one small Hebridean community some aspects of the broader experience are mirrored, while the local factors that diverge from the general pattern are highlighted. Through certain periods the effects of the changes were slow and barely perceptible. At other times they impinged with sudden force on the economic and social life of the people. The turning points for Iona were clearly the making of the crofts in 1802, the destitution crisis of the late 1840s and the Napier Commission, followed by the Crofters' Act, in the mid-1880s.

The period from about 1750 until 1850 is identified by agrarian historians such as Slicher van Bath as one of agricultural boom in most West European countries.[1] It followed a hundred years of general stagnation in the rural economy. Up until the mid-seventeenth century the need to feed the people of the Continent had been largely met by expanding cultivated areas, rather than by improving production or developing specialised crops. From around 1650 grain prices fell and arable farming was neglected in favour of animal husbandry. But by the mid-eighteenth century there was the start of a population upsurge throughout the Continent. The chief cause is considered to have been a fall in the death rate due to slight improvements in diet and hygiene. Land began to be reclaimed in order to grow more cereals whose price was rising fast, communal farming was gradually abandoned in favour of individual units, and there was rapid innovation in agricultural tools and techniques.

A similar pattern of demographic and economic growth was at work in Britain and in some regions changes in the countryside were already underway before the mid-century. The enclosing of common land in England proceeded swiftly from the 1720s. It had begun in Galloway from 1710, for commercial cattle rearing, and the expansion of arable land also spread gradually through north-east and south-east Scotland. Up until the mid-eighteenth century, however, the Highlands presented a marked contrast to the rest of Scotland. Geographically and culturally they lay farthest from the influences permeating the landscape elsewhere. The traditional clan-based society of Gaeldom, supported by a predominantly pastoral economy, still prevailed.[2]

In the aftermath of the two Jacobite uprisings, the British Government made a conscious effort to assimilate the region. Neither the Wade military roads nor the plans of the Commissioners of the Annexed Estates were sufficient in themselves to make the Highlanders conform, politically or socially. But the severing of the old links between the people and their chiefs, the drawing of the latter into an anglicised society, and the growing demand from the south for the northern commodity of black cattle, all combined to move the tenurial relationship on the Highland estates from one revolving around kinship and mutual support to one stimulated by commercial concerns. This crucial shift was what James Hunter has called 'the great fact of eighteenth century Highland history. From it all else follows'.[3]

On the Argyll Estates, which had sided with the Crown and thus not been forfeited, the process had begun even earlier than the Forty-Five. As has been described in Chapter 1, the second Duke introduced competitive bidding for leases in Mull, Morvern and Tiree in 1737 with the prime object of increasing the rental income. Clan allegiances did not become irrelevant immediately. Indeed, the third Duke restored a degree of political loyalty to the system from 1743 and Eric Cregeen has identified him as playing a dual role, part traditional chief and part modern landlord.[4] By the time the fifth Duke succeeded in 1770, the Argyll Estates were at their most extensive and his role was primarily that of economic leader. The reforms he initiated, in their scope and their style, were a formative influence in the 'improving' ethos of the age.

The fifth Duke's attempts to broaden the economy beyond subsistence living off the land, which had for centuries been the norm, did not differ in any major ways in Iona from elsewhere on the Estate. Nor were their varying degrees of success unusual. The flax-spinning trial was short-lived in both Iona and Tiree but, with the notable exception of Islay, linen manufacture was not a thriving enterprise in any part of the west Highlands. Fishing on a substantial, commercial scale never prospered in the Argyll islands as it did, for example, in Barra or Lewis or on the

H

mainland around Loch Broom, although even in those places there were considerable fluctuations in fortune from year to year.[5]

Kelping was an ancillary activity that did last longer and contributed more significantly in Iona than either linen or fishing. Argyll was one of four landlords identified by Malcolm Gray as accounting for almost half of the total kelp output of the Highlands. The others were Seaforth in Lewis and, more importantly still, Lord MacDonald in Skye and North Uist and Clanranald in South Uist. The ability of kelpers to pay higher rents was certainly one determining factor in the expansion of the crofting system by the Duke of Argyll in Tiree from 1799. What part this thinking played in the dividing up of farms on the Mull Estate is less explicit, although it probably weighed to some extent. There was a long correspondence between the Duke and his Chamberlain of Mull and Morvern in the late 1790s about whether control of the kelp manufacture should be left wholly or partly in the hands of the tenants. As other kinds of seaware were used widely as fertiliser, the Chamberlain argued that there was a 'necessary connection' between the management of the shores and the cultivation of the soil which should be maintained in order to keep both rents and incentive to industry high. The specific instructions to apportion Mull, including Iona, make no reference to kelping as the sole or main reason for creating crofts. Indeed, the relatively good size of the crofts in Iona, plus the granting of leases to encourage improvement, imply that it was the land that was intended to provide the tenants' basic means of living.

The abandonment of runrig in favour of individual lots was to change the face of the Highland and Hebridean landscapes. The transformation made rapid progress through the first half of the nineteenth century. In some areas, particularly in the north-west, it coincided with the advance northward of 'Na Caoraich Mòra', the larger and hardier Lowland sheep introduced into Perthshire in the 1760s. The higher rents to be gained from sheepwalks run by a single grazier led landlords in Sutherland, Skye, Lewis and elsewhere to clear their inland straths and relocate the people on the coasts.

From the outset, the plots of land they received were too small for full-time agriculture. These crofters were expected to supplement their living from kelping, fishing or, in the case of Sutherland, various new manufacturing or industrial activities. The making of Iona's crofts was not part of this pattern. Neither it nor the island's later loss of population can in any way be directly attributed to the invasion of the Big Sheep, as at least one popular historian has inferred.[6] The advent of crofting in Iona is placed clearly within the context of the fifth Duke's agricultural reforms, which were underpinned by his firm belief that the existing cattle-rearing and crop-growing economy of his tenants would be sounder and more profitable based on individual lots.

The Duke was not universally successful. The plan for separate lots on nine-year leases in Morvern does not appear to have been carried out and the Argyll lands there continued to be worked on the old communal basis, either by small-tenants' farms or by larger tacksmen.[7] Whether resistance to change on the part of the Morvern people was a factor is not known. The conservatism of the Highlanders in clinging to their outmoded ways was commented upon by several eighteenth century observers and the hostility of Argyll's tenants in Tiree to his reforms is regularly cited in support of this view. It was, however, the Duke's *first* proposal for Tiree that was unpopular. He intended initially to remove small tenants to fishing villages and let their lands in larger units to better-off tenants, a plan which foreshadowed the clearing of the glens farther north to make way for sheepfarmers. The people were not inherently opposed to all reform and in the end showed less resistance to what did happen, the division of the land on long leases among them. The Chamberlain's correspondence during the time of similar reorganisation in Mull and Iona described the people there as entering 'very heartily' into the new scheme.

Another notable difference on the Argyll Estate was that the crofters were generally allocated the existing arable land. This was also the case in some other areas, for example in parts of South Uist where former communal farms were split up or in the division made much later, in 1845, by Dr John MacKenzie on the Gairloch Estate.[8] Far more typical of the crofting communities which emerged over this period, however, particularly in the north-west islands and mainland, were townships placed on thin, rocky soil or reclaimed moorland. The natural advantage of the former method is obvious. The comparison of Map 3, which reconstructs the crofting layout in Iona at 1802, and the 1769 map (Plate 1) illustrates the straight transfer of the new lots onto most of the formerly cultivated portion of the island.

This leads directly to the central question of the balance between Iona's population and the land required to support it. Did the many travellers' comments about abundant grain and livestock mean that Iona was never short of food? Were the material conditions of its people therefore better than elsewhere in the eighteenth and nineteenth centuries? The population of 1779 had access, theoretically, to eight acres each of Iona and even the greatly increased total of 1800 still had six acres each. This contrasts with the most congested parts of the north-west where as little as one or two acres per whole family, for instance in Assynt or Tongue, were not unknown.[9] More significant, however, was the amount of cultivated land in proportion to the whole. Dr Walker's estimates of land areas in 1764 are, unfortunately, not reliable but if the ratio he calculated for Iona was even near accurate then the agricultural portion was over sixty per cent. Sir John Sinclair's report of 1814 did not specify the percentage in Iona, merely noting that 'the island is either all arable or consists of good pasturage'.[10] Judging from the Douglas map, however, it is fair to claim that Iona will have been level with, or higher than, places noted by Sinclair as having a good proportion of cultivable land: for example, Colonsay at forty per cent or Lismore at forty-five per cent. Iona was certainly well above Sinclair's average for Argyll of 11.6 per cent or Lewis at 8.4 per cent.

Throughout the Highlands the people lived by any standards in hard and miserable conditions. Pennant's description of the Islay inhabitants as 'a set of people worn down with poverty' is well known and he continued: '. . . but my picture is not of this island only'. There was a high degree of self-sufficiency in basic foodstuffs, dictated partly of course by the inaccessibility of these areas before improved roads and the advent of steamship links. Even after the potato provided a cheap and easily grown supplement to a meagre diet, however, Gray asserts: 'But far more characteristic of Highland conditions was the steady year-by-year import of meal'. Pennant's account and the *OSA* are the main sources backing up this claim and the minister for Kilninian and Kilmore in north Mull was one of many recording the regular buying-in of oatmeal and seed corn.

It does appear, however, that Iona was a rare exception in its ability not only to raise enough grain for its own needs but to generate income through exporting a surplus along with its cattle. (Gigha also stands out in the *OSA* of 1793 and other sources as a small, fertile place whose arable produce was 'more than sufficient for the maintenance of the inhabitants'.) It has been demonstrated that extra cash for the Iona rents still had to be met from non-agricultural sources, such as kelp while it lasted and seasonal work in the Lowlands. And fertile though Iona was, it will not have been exempt from the consequences of harsh weather and low yields from time to time. If the need actually to import food, however, was restricted to occasional bad years, then the community's economic circumstances may be considered perceptibly better than those faced by many others in the Highlands.

The wealth of a people cannot, of course, be measured in economic terms alone. As this study shows, it was clear to several visitors that the inhabitants of Iona, though in poor material surroundings, placed considerable value on their songs and dances, on the convivial exchange of the ceilidh, on the bonds of kinship and the age-old traditions that held them together. The part played by these factors is touched on further below.

Iona's transition from the old agrarian order to the new began in 1802 and appears to have been fully effected before 1820 as dykes, croft houses and the relocated village were built. There was some dislocation of the population, especially among the cottar class, but it was very largely the former joint tenants who inherited the crofting system. Their principal · preoccupation as the nineteenth century opened up was to establish and maintain that system. They did not share the jolts experienced by communities elsewhere as the increasingly lucrative sheep farms encroached upon populations made redundant by the collapse of the kelp boom. There were over two thousand summonses of removal served in Lewis, for example, between 1813 and 1832. Around 350 families were evicted from Strathnaver in Sutherland, in favour of sheep, between 1807 and 1822. In Morvern in the 1820s and 1830s new proprietors, such as Miss Stewart of Glenmorvern and Patrick Sellar of Acharn, undertook wholesale clearances. Emigration, no longer voluntary, was stepped up. Between 1826 and 1827 1300 people left Skye for North America; 600 from North Uist did the same in 1828; and that year Maclean of Coll shipped 300 from the isle of Rum.[11]

What Iona did share with the areas undergoing these traumatic events was an upwardly spiralling population. The graph illustrates the same steep rise as the whole of the north-west Highlands from 1755. Where figures have allowed detailed comparison, Iona shows even more rapid acceleration at some stages than the Argyll Estate average: a thirty per cent increase from 1779 to 1792, as against twenty-five per cent in Mull, Morvern and Tiree and twenty per cent over the whole Estate.[12] Iona was also one of the last places to reach a peak, almost certainly two or three years beyond 1835. At this point Iona had as many inhabitants as the island of Eigg at its peak, an area three times larger, and its population density was greater than, say, Kilmuir parish in Skye or the whole of Harris.[13]

It was noted in Chapter 5 that there was little evidence of evictions in the first half of the nineteenth century and that voluntary migration or emigration was slight. Rents appear to have been fairly stable. Documentary detail on individual rents is not available prior to 1846 but estimates by observers indicate that the total rental for the island rose from £200 to about £300 between 1800 and around 1820 and then only gradually to £400 sometime in the 1830s. There were some rent arrears but not on a scale large enough to make them an intolerable burden on the tenants or to incur retribution from the landlord. This again provides a contrast with many places where debt was becoming a severe problem, even despite the rent abatements made by some proprietors. Iona's good agricultural base may in fact have disguised for slightly longer the precarious foundations on which its rental income stood. As late as 1835, when the population was near its height, a traveller commented on the island's ability to feed itself, although he did note that 'sometimes' the people imported a little oatmeal.[14]

There is no precise date from which the whole downward trend in the economy of the Highlands may be measured. The end of the Napoleonic Wars in 1815, however, is regarded as a general watershed. It marked the end of military service for many young men and accelerated the slump in kelp manufacture. Over the following two decades, any remaining linen industry in the Highlands disappeared and wages for summer harvest work were depressed by competing Irish labour. Fishing remained unreliable, an additional rather than a central occupation for much of the west coast. Most critically of all, the crofters' main asset, black cattle, fell sharply in value in the 1830s.

By this time a further factor must be weighed in the equation of population and resources, namely the mushrooming of the landless class. In Iona the cottars had accounted for twenty-two per cent of the population in 1779. By the 1841 Census this proportion was forty-two per cent and by 1851 it was forty-four per cent. It may well have shot to this level much earlier, perhaps even from when the crofts were made. Recorded totals for 1804 and 1808 were already over 380 and a rough calculation based on thirty or thirty-five crofting families puts the tenantry at no higher than about fifty-five per cent of the whole population. It has been noted that the Iona holdings were never on the tiny three- or four-acre size of places such as north-west Sutherland or Lewis. They averaged seven or eight acres of arable, plus individual pasture and there was only one instance (in 1860) of the reduction of any common grazing.

Yet, in addition to the subdivision within families that continued unchecked up to the 1840s, all crofters will have borne their share of providing the customary support, in food or a patch of potato ground, to the cottar section of the community. The balance between the crofters and cottars on Iona did not return to approximately eighteenth century levels until 1881. By the mid-nineteenth century, over the Argyll insular estates, the proportion of crofters to cottars was almost exactly equal, implying that the burden of a landless population was as bad or even slightly worse in the Ross of Mull and in Tiree.[15] And throughout the north-west the picture was the same: congested, poverty-stricken communities where even those who technically possessed resources, in the form of stock and land, were caught in the vice of debt and diminishing returns.

The crisis provoked in Iona by the potato famine of 1846 and succeeding years was almost universal in the north-west Highlands and Hebrides. It had been foreshadowed by the famine of 1836/7 when nearly forty per cent of the island's inhabitants, overwhelmingly from the landless class, were affected. The entire population suffered a decade later. The complex attitude of the people themselves to their predicament has been explored in Chapter 8, along with the difficulty of gauging the degree to which coercion by the Estate played a part in the dramatic exodus from Iona in the post-famine years. The decline in the island's population was steeper than the average in the Highlands and Islands area. Yet it did not undergo the same kind of wholesale, often brutal, evictions that swept the north-west and the islands in the wake of the destitution. The infamous clearances by Gordon of Cluny in Barra and South Uist, for instance, took place from 1848 through to the early 1850s and, much nearer home, Francis Clark reduced Ulva to a virtually deserted state. Across the Sound of Iona treatment also appears to have been more sweeping and severe. Oral tradition in the Ross of Mull has retained to the present day memory of the total clearance of fertile Shiaba township and of the time when the Factor's men came with dogs and sticks to burn cottages at Ardalanish. The Napier Commission evidence for the Ross and for Tiree provides further testimony to such events. It may be that the numbers of Iona people willing to leave proved sufficient to meet the Estate's aim of a reduced population. Another element that may well have been at work was awareness on the part of the Duke that any policy too heavy-handed in relation to such a famous spot would risk a storm of public outrage.

It should not be forgotten, however, that the agricultural potential of Iona *was* good. Despite the crisis of the famine years, the Estate clearly believed that the holdings could be made to pay more as they stood and the Duke must have resisted the Factor's pressure to consolidate the entire island into two large farms. The crofting pattern remained largely intact, serving a population that was smaller but similarly structured to the pre-1840s period. Those who remained managed to survive, despite being forced even more abruptly into a money-based economy by the steep rent rises of 1847 and later.

It was the resulting financial strain that, for the Iona people, linked the crisis of the 1840s directly to the crofters' agitation of the 1880s. Their evidence to the Napier Commission made it clear that the days of near-total self-sufficiency in food had long gone and that their own produce could not even support a population half that of forty years before for more than three months of the year. By this time the arable acreage had declined too, as a result of fewer people and an increase in sheep stocks, to form around twenty-six per cent of the total land.[16] The central position of agricultural output in the people's case to the Napier Commission also made Iona atypical. More common was the small plot rendered viable only by support from elsewhere, especially the sea, as the Reporter noted: 'By far the greater number of the crofters and cottars of the Highlands and Islands of Scotland are wholly or largely dependant for their subsistence on their earnings as fishermen'.

A fundamental objection by the Duke of Argyll to the provisions of the 1886 Act was that they interfered with the landlord–tenant relationship. The intervention of legislation finally effaced any remaining traces of the old, special sense of obligation between the head and his people. Eric Richards notes that this subtle shift could be seen at work in the gradual cessation by many landlords of small, but useful, forms of support for crofters: 'In 1889, for instance, the Duke of Sutherland chose no longer to respond in the accustomed way to the requests of his small tenants for building materials with which to improve their houses'.[17] Similarly, the Duke of Argyll replied in the following terms to a request from William MacFarlane and Dugald MacArthur in Iona when their barn burned down: 'You ask for my help in building a new one which I should be most glad to give you at once if our relations on such matters of business had been left on the old footing'.

Yet, although keen to make this point clear, Argyll did not appear to end totally his grants for minor improvements such as lime for houses.[18] And towards the end of the nineteenth century there is evidence of close interest taken in the island by various members of the Duke's family and the cementing of a fairly cordial relationship between people and landlord. (This positive feeling lasted, indeed, through to the sale of the island by the twelfth Duke in 1979.) For example, an *OT* report in 1895 stated: 'The poor people of the island are much indebted to Lord Archibald Campbell and his son Mr. Neil for having their houses made more comfortable and weather-proof – floors, roofs, lofts and other conveniences having been provided by these gentlemen in several cases'. Ten years earlier Lord Archibald, who was a brother of the ninth Duke, was declared 'a great favourite' when he stayed for several days on Iona, visiting almost every household and organising two dances 'in which he joined with great spirit'. Lady Victoria Campbell, a daughter of the eighth Duke, was devoted to the islands and, despite being lame from childhood, made the journey many times to Iona, Mull and Tiree. She took a particular interest in young people, starting a branch of the YWCA in all three islands.

The sole ownership of Iona by the House of Argyll throughout the whole period of this study provides one important line of continuity. It was also unusual. The great ducal families of Argyll and Sutherland stand out as examples of reasonable stability as around them Highland estates changed hands, often in rapid succession, and a new breed of proprietors took over. Many of these were from a business background and a few were immensely wealthy. In the twenty years after 1813 every one of Morvern's properties was sold and by 1850 only one out of the ten was held by the same family as in 1800. Also by 1855, the entire Long Island had passed out of hereditary ownership.

Argyll's association with the Mull lands, of course, dated only from the end of the seventeenth century and it did not appear to be followed, in the case of Iona at least, by any major transplanting of Campbell kin into the tenantry. There was certainly movement in and out of the island during the eighteenth century but an attachment to their former Maclean chiefs evidently remained constant among the population, as Dr Johnson noted in 1773. The incident in 1799 when Iona people flatly refused to send their sons to the army may be another indication that traditional allegiances, such as military service, had never fully transferred. Similar ties to the Macleans lingered too in Tiree, probably even more strongly. It may have been this, rather than innate conservatism, that lay at the root of the people's slow acceptance of the fifth Duke's reforms there.

Clues as to the Iona tenants' changing attitude to their landlord may be pieced together from the turn of the nineteenth century. They reveal a note of growing respect, even goodwill. In 1802 Sarah Murray understood that the fifth Duke was viewed as a 'benign father' by his people. An eyewitness account of the sixth Duke's visit to Iona in 1807 talked of the scrubbing of the historic tombs in preparation, of the schoolmaster's nervousness when trying to deliver his speech of welcome, of the men and women dancing 'an Iona fandango' for their guest and of the children pressing forward to touch his coat.[19] In 1844 Neil MacDonald held a celebration in his home for the majority of the Marquis of Lorne (later the eighth Duke) and a bonfire was lit in front of the Argyll Hotel to mark the election to Parliament of Lord Colin Campbell in 1878 and 1880.[20]

Local tradition is consistent that it was not the Duke but his underlings, particularly the Factor, who were to blame for particular episodes of hardship or injustice. This dual attitude has been

mentioned in Chapter 10 and there can be no clearcut conclusion
about how the people responded to any of their overlords. A refusal
to be cowed and a respectful deference both feature in different
stories. Donald MacDonald at Machir was issued with a veiled threat
about the continuing occupancy of his croft when he refused to sell a
beast to the Factor's man. His father-in-law, a former gamekeeper on
the Inveraray Estate, was staying with the family at the time and he
was promptly despatched to intercede with the Duke. No more was
heard of the threat. This was probably in the early 1880s.[21] Also
around that time, Henrietta MacInnes, recently married into the
Greenbank croft, could not believe her eyes when one rent-collection
day she saw the Iona crofters, all in their best clothes, rush into the sea
and lift the Factor bodily from the boat onto dry land. As a child in
Greenock she had helped her father collect rents and the reception
normally met with had been of a quite opposite kind.[22]

The confidence to assert their own voice and stand up to authority
grew in Iona in the latter part of the nineteenth century as it did
throughout Highland communities. A remnant of the older, more
wary, perceptions comes through in a letter from emigrant James
Campbell who had left Iona for Australia in the 1840s or before. He
had heard about the Land-Leaguers and warned his relatives not to be
involved: 'You will get on just as well without it; everybody that
rises this agitation are spotted, you may be sure'.[23] There was,
however, a lively branch of the HLLRA in Iona, who supported
MacFarlane as a crofters' MP and in 1885 openly condemned the
actions of Sheriffs in Skye and Lewis who were suppressing popular
protest. Two years earlier, the locals had been swift to pass a vote of
censure on their School Board for demonstrating 'the impertinence
of officialism' by refusing permission to use the school for a meeting
to be addressed by John Murdoch. That campaigner awarded the
Iona people a word of praise for their spirited show of independence.[24]

A factor that may have contributed to the clear sense of common
purpose among the islanders was that the tenantry had not been split
into the extremes of very substantial and very tiny. The norm, as
Gray has observed, was that the process of clearance had created 'a
simple two-class antagonism, of small farmers and large farmers,
mutually isolated in economic status, everyday operation and out-
look'. The farming families who came into Iona – MacPhail, Ritchie,
Sinclair – vere not Lowlanders but Gaelic speakers, either from Mull
or with a Mull connection. None of the three consolidated farm units
rented at over £100, the level generally regarded as the middle rank of
holding. In 1883 islander Peter MacInnes moved from the tenancy of

a croft to Cùlbhuirg farm, with the approval of the Duke who preferred this to his alternative option of letting to a non-resident farmer.

The institutions of school and church usually provide a focus for community life in rural areas and Iona was no exception. The ministers of both the Established and the Free Church demonstrated consistent concern for the educational and material, as well as the spiritual, welfare of their parishioners although, as has been argued in Chapter 8, their stance leaned undeniably toward that held by the Duke on the question of emigration in the destitution years. In the 1880s, on the other hand, the Rev. John Campbell, whose reputation as pastor became somewhat tarnished by the end of his controversial ministry, spoke out for the rights of the small tenant in the Highlands. He expressed this view, for example, when presiding at an election meeting for MacFarlane in Iona.[25] There is only a little evidence by which to judge relations between the two congregations in the years after 1843. Some initial strain must have been inevitable. There are one or two indications, however, that the ministers did interchange if necessary – an OPR entry notes that the Established Church minister married a Free Church couple; there is an anecdote about a wedding procession headed by a piper, despite the Free Church minister's objection to bagpipes being played on the road beyond Maclean's Cross, and the quip of an Established Church member, 'If your minister doesn't marry you, our one will'. It does not appear that there was major or long-lasting friction between the denominations and Lady Victoria Campbell was agreeably surprised to find good relations between the ministers in 1886.[26]

Differences in religious adherence were not enough to impair seriously the stronger bonds that held the small community together. Ministers and schoolteachers took active parts in the social life of the island. The numerous accounts of debates, talks, concerts, picnics, sports, regattas and gatherings to mark personal events give an impression of a close-knit and thoroughly enjoyable community spirit. Nor did organised functions detract from the more traditional forms of exchange and entertainment – the ceilidhing at the tailor's house or at the smiddy or in each other's homes.

Maintaining customs and celebrations associated with periodic events, such as weddings, or with the turn of the seasons, such as at harvest, Hallowe'en and New Year, also provided a link throughout the community. Moreover, they point backward through many generations to the rituals bound in with the rhythms of nature which were common to all races living close to the land and sea. Such people were dependent, of course, not only on their natural environment but also on each other for the mutual support and co-operation that made easier the essential tasks of providing food and shelter. Some communal practices in Iona have been described in the later chapters of this book, but they will have been a continuous part of the people's way of life right through the period covered.

The traditional beliefs described earlier, however, in Chapter 13, did disappear some time in the nineteenth century. Along with them went all but a few traces of the heroic and supernatural tales that formed an integral part of Gaelic oral literature. These have been found alive well into the twentieth century in places as near to Iona as the Ross of Mull and Tiree. The reasons why it is thought oral tradition of this kind died out more rapidly in some parts than in others have been noted in the Introduction. The attitudes of the educational establishment and the Church harboured definite undertones of 'old-fashioned' and 'uncivilised' in the pressure they exerted. It seems extremely probable that this pressure was heightened, in a place so frequented by visitors as Iona, by a desire – conscious or subconscious – not to be seen as such by the outside world. This is precisely the impression gained from an article by John MacCormick in the *Oban Times* of 15 June 1889 when, clearly for the benefit of tourists, he described several old customs and stories from Iona's past including the casting of porridge or 'am brochan mòr' into the sea in spring, in the hope that seaware for the fields would be cast on the shore. He then added: 'All such superstitious practices are now quite forgotten in Iona. Civilisation has firmly established itself . . . and many strangers visiting the island during the summer months are surprised to find it quite a nineteenth century place'.

It could be argued, in this respect at least, that the impact of tourism on Iona was an impoverishing one. It would be harder to attribute directly to visitors the decline in the Gaelic language, the medium through which the culture naturally flourished. Spoken Gaelic remained strong on the island up until the First World War, long after improved communications had made the influx of thousands of tourists an annual summer event. Permanent links with the Lowlands were probably more significant, as greater numbers of young islanders went away to study, train or work. There was also the influence of the large numbers of boarded-out children in Iona school in the first two decades of the century, who generally did not learn Gaelic.

There was also, of course, the economic impact of tourism throughout the nineteenth century. This included practical help, such as the fishing boats scheme of the 1850s, regular donations to the poor, the selling of pebbles and other mementoes or of foodstuffs to private yachts. All of this was undeniably of benefit and may well have eased difficult conditions from time to time. It was never enough to make a permanent difference, however, and could not avert the worst moments of hardship. Of more importance, from the 1870s onwards, was the letting of rooms or cottages during the summer months. This came into the category, which it still holds in many crofting districts, of an ancillary occupation whose returns could go toward the rent and other living expenses.

In 1914 twenty-one families on Iona could have claimed descent from people living on the island at the end of the eighteenth century, most of them from 1779 or earlier. In a few cases the name had changed through marriage. By far the majority, seventeen, were from the crofting and farming tenantry. This core of families working the land over a century or more is one of the clearest lines of continuity running through this study.

It is very likely that the heads of those twenty-one households could have recited their genealogy back through this hundred years at least and could perhaps have added knowledge of further interrelationships on the island, which may now be lost. Family history is one aspect of the oral tradition that has lasted most vigorously in Iona. This tradition may not be quite as rich, nor reach so far back, as in some places such as Tiree, where the ability to trace kinship links over two and even three hundred years has been found. But all my informants for Iona have been able to provide at least a few, often very valuable, genealogical details.

Iona's small population remained fairly close-knit throughout the period under study, due to the high degree of intermarriage within the community. The custom of naming children after the grandparents, who in turn had been called after earlier generations, was very commonly observed. This recurrence of Christian names in the family records reinforces the sense of lineage over a long period. In the settlements of Iona emigrants in Canada, similar links of marriage, social life and community spirit have been noted. It would not, of course, be realistic to paint a picture of constant social harmony. But none of the rivalries and tensions that naturally arise among humans in the course of day-to-day living ever emerged with sufficiently disruptive force to mar the much clearer image of a people solidly rooted in a common history, culture and way of life. As one informant put it, reflecting on his parents' generation: 'People were happy in the old days, content with what they had I think. Everyone knew each other in those days, it was like a big family'.

The late-nineteenth century poet William Sharp, better known as Celtic mystic 'Fiona MacLeod', once wrote:

I have nothing to say of Iona's acreage or fisheries or pastures; nothing of how the islanders live. These things are the accidental. There is small difference in simple life anywhere. Moreover, there are many to tell all that need be known.[27]

For him as for many others, the island was primarily a place of spiritual pilgrimage and this is a deeply felt personal view that it would be discourteous to decry. To take as the corollary, however, that the secular life of the island was merely accidental is, in my judgement, misleading.

This book has attempted to demonstrate that Iona underwent changes and hardships, some of them dramatic, which were shared by communities throughout the Highlands in the eighteenth and nineteenth centuries. It is true that much of this experience showed marked similarities from place to place. Yet the overall picture of Highland history is more complex than is sometimes realised. It is precisely the 'small difference' in emphasis or consequence that provides interest for the historian and helps illustrate the broader trends. In some respects Iona was favoured, with good natural resources and, on the whole, sympathetic and energetic landlords. At some points it suffered as acutely as elsewhere, for example during the potato famine years. Meanwhile, through times of stability and of transition, the institutions of parish life established themselves and flourished.

The entire process of moving this one community of people from the old clan society to the new crofting system, and thence through the struggle to keep that system alive and viable, unfolded in Iona against the background of intensifying public interest – not, generally speaking, in the people but in the historical monuments alongside which they happened to live. That this public interest turned at times to Iona's advantage has not been overlooked. And it is through the eyes of many outsiders that such a wealth of detail on aspects of life there has been gathered. But the people's survival never hinged on the concern of visitors. Nor can their authentic identity be fully grasped through that lens alone.

Moreover, the fame of Iona may itself be said to derive from a chance of history. This is in no way intended to diminish the great importance of Columba's mission and all that flowed from it. Had his monastery been established on any other part of the Scottish west coast, his work would still have been of immense significance in historical and religious terms. It is important to emphasise, however, that with or without the Columban settlement on Iona – and the medieval and modern foundations that followed in its train – the history of the island's people would have been substantially unaltered.

It is inconceivable that such a fertile spot as Iona, lying in the centre of the main west coast sea route, would not have been populated and cultivated from the earliest days of human movement among these islands. The ups and downs of Highland history would have affected this population in largely the same way, while those factors identified as ensuring continuity and stability would still have done so. There has been the relationship between the tenantry and their landlord. There has been the cohesive force of language, tradition, custom and communal practice. Most clearly of all, there has been the landscape itself and the families who have lived in and from it over many centuries.

This book has traced the story, over a period that saw particularly significant change, of the inhabitants of Iona's crofts, farms and village. It is this community, and their link to the land they have worked, that – far from being incidental – has provided the fundamental and enduring strand in the history of the island.

References

Introduction

1. *Adomnan's Life of Columba*, edited by A. O. Anderson and M. O. Anderson (London 1961), p.525.
2. See RCAHMS, *Argyll. An Inventory of the Monuments*, Vol.4, Iona, (Edinburgh 1982); Vol.3, Mull, Tiree, Coll (Edinburgh 1980).
3. See RCAHMS, *Argyll*, Vol.4, p.251; *Collectanea de Rebus Albanicis*, edited by the Iona Club (Edinburgh 1847), pp.1–4; *Highland Papers Vol.1 1337–1680*, edited by J. R. N. MacPhail (SHS, Edinburgh, Second Series, Vol.5, 1914), p.315.
4. John MacInnes, 'Population Changes in a Hebridean Island. A Demographic Study of Iona 1800–1860', unpublished dissertation, Queen Mary College, University of London (1986).
5. Dr John Leyden, *Journal of a Tour in the Highlands and Western Islands in 1800* (Edinburgh 1903), p.252.
6. George Douglas, 'Tour in the Hebrides A.D. 1800', NLS ms.213.
7. Anonymous, 'Tour of my Native Country particularly of the Highlands' (1806), Aberdeen University Library ms.1023.
8. *Handbook for Travellers in Scotland*, 6th edition (John Murray, London 1894).
9. J. G. Lockhart, *Memoirs of the Life of Sir Walter Scott*, 5 volumes (London 1900), Vol.II, pp.142, 433.
10. John 1st Marquess of Bute, 'Journal of the Tour round the Western Islands of Scotland 1788', NLS ms.9587. John Phillips, 'Tour in Scotland' (1826), Mitchell Library ms.24080o.
11. See Dr John Walker, *Report on the Hebrides of 1764 and 1771*, edited by Margaret M. McKay (Edinburgh 1980), pp.140–1; Thomas Garnett, *Observations on a Tour through the Highlands and part of the Western Isles of Scotland*, Vol.I (London 1810), p.269; W. Maxwell, *Iona and the Ionians* (Glasgow 1857), p.35.
12. *Popular Tales of the West Highlands*, collected and translated by J. F. Campbell, facsimile 2nd edition., Vol.I (Hounslow 1983), pp.v–vii.

Chapter 1

1. William Reeves, *Adamnani Vitae Sancti Columbae* (Dublin 1857), pp.421–2.
2. Thomas Pennant, *A Tour in Scotland and Voyage to the Hebrides 1772* (London 1776), Part 1, p.278.
3. MacPhail, *Highland Papers 1*, 'Caption, the Earl of Argyll against John McLean and others, 1675', p.298.
4. Dr W. Sacheverell, *An Account of the Isle of Man . . . with a voyage to I-Columb-Kill* (London 1701), p.143.
5. Rev. Dugald Campbell, 'Parish of Kilfinichen and Kilviceuen' in *OSA*, Vol.XIV (1795), p.188.
6. SRO, SC.54/22/52, 'List of men delivering up their arms upon solemn oath in Mull, Ulva . . . 2nd April 1716 at Duart Castle'.
7. Note that *NSA*, Vol.VII, p.338 makes an error in attributing a total of

277 for Iona to Dr Webster's return for 1755. That figure refers to a total noted by the minister in 1782 and recorded in the *OSA*.

8. *The Clan Campbell . . . from the Campbell collections formed by Sir Duncan Campbell of Barcaldine and Glenure*, edited by the Rev. Henry Paton, 8 volumes (Edinburgh 1913–22), Vol.1 (1913), pp.42, 160.

9. See Eric R. Cregeen, 'The Tacksmen and their Successors' in *Scottish Studies*, Vol.13 (1969), pp.93–144 and 'The Changing Role of the House of Argyll in the Scottish Highlands' in *Scotland in the Age of Improvement*, edited by N. T. Phillipson and R. Mitchison (Edinburgh 1970), pp.5–22.

10. Sir Bruce Seton and J. G. Arnot, *Prisoners of the '45*, *Vol.III* (SHS, Edinburgh, Third Series, 15, 1929), pp.150–1; Lord Archibald Campbell, 'The Caves of Iona' in *Records of Argyll* (Edinburgh and London 1885), p.363; SRO, GD.14/100, 103, 118, Campbell of Stonefield papers.

11. James Boswell, *Journal of a Tour to the Hebrides*, edited by F. A. Pottle and C. H. Bennett (London 1936), p.331; Dr Samuel Johnson, *A Journey to the Western Islands of Scotland 1773* (Philip Allan & Co., London 1925), p.206; Bute 'Journal', ff.45–6.

12. Johnson, p.211; Boswell, p.337.

Chapter 2

1. Boswell, p.331. Robert Heron, *General View of the Natural Circumstances of those Isles adjacent to the North West coast of Scotland, which are distinguished by the common name of Hebudae or Hebrides* (Edinburgh 1794), p.43.

2. Donald Monro, *Description of the Western Isles of Scotland called Hybrides in 1549* (Edinburgh 1774, 1st edition; Glasgow and London 1884), p.31.

3. John Fraser, 'A short description of I or Iona, 1693' in *MacFarlane's Geographical Collections*, *Vol.II* (SHS, Edinburgh, Vol.LII, 1907), pp.216–17.

4. Walker, pp.139 and 186.

5. Pennant, p.277 and *OSA*, p.194.

6. *OSA*, p.191 and J. Smith, *Agriculture in the County of Argyle* (London 1813), p.79.

7. The Hon. Mrs Sarah Murray of Kensington, *A Companion and Useful Guide to the Beauties in the West Highlands of Scotland and in the Hebrides*, Vol.II (London 1803), p.225.

8. James Bailey, 'Journey in Scotland', Vol.2 (1787), NLS ms.3295.

9. *Pococke's Tours in Scotland*, edited by D. W. Kemp (SHS, Edinburgh, 1, 1887), p.88.

10. Boswell, p.331.

11. Garnett, p.243; Murray, p.226.

12. AEP.

13. See Malcolm Gray, 'The Kelp Industry in the Highlands and Islands' in *Economic History Review*, 2nd series, 4, no.1 (1951), pp.197–209; and Alexander Ross, 'Old Highland Industries' in *TGSI*, Vol.XII (1885–6), p.407.

14. *OSA*, pp.182–3.

15. AEP, Report from James Maxwell to Duke of Argyll.

16. *AEI*, p.122.

17. British Fishery Society Papers, SRO GD.9/1. Information on fishing taken from these papers, from the *AEI* and from receipts in the AEP.

18. Information from Calum Cameron, Iona, 1985.
19. *AEI*, p.173.
20. A E P.
21. A E P. See also D. J. Viner, *The Iona Marble Quarry* (Glasgow 1979).
22. *OSA*, p.189.
23. *AEI*, p.195.
24. *OSA*, pp.189, 193.
25. *AEI*, p.138.
26. Garnett, pp.271–2.
27. Smith, *Argyle*, p.79.
28. *AEI*, p.196.
29. S R O, S C.54/1/4, Inveraray Sheriff Court 1796–1803.
30. Murray, p.254.
31. Cregeen, *AEI*, Introduction.
32. Duke of Argyll, *Scotland As It Was and As It Is*, 2nd edition (Edinburgh 1887), p.430.

Chapter 3

1. L. A. Necker de Saussure, *A Voyage to the Hebrides* (London 1822).
2. A E P, Mrs D. Maclean of Torloisk, letter relating visit to Iona 1814.
3. S R O, H D.7/9, letter from R. Graham to F. Maule, 25 March 1837.
4. Anon., 'Tour', 1806.
5. A E P, letter from Chamberlain.
6. A E P, memorial from Chamberlain.
7. Anon., 'Tour', 1806.
8. James MacDonald, *General View of the Agriculture of the Hebrides or Western Isles of Scotland* (Edinburgh 1811).
9. de Saussure, p.36; Dr John MacCulloch, *A Description of the Western Isles of Scotland*, 3 volumes (London 1819), Vol.I, p.6.
10. Anon., 'Tour', 1806. Dugald Sinclair, *Journal of Itinerating Exertions*, No.V (Edinburgh 1816).
11. Murray, p.226. *Inverness Courier*, 26 August 1824.
12. Information on this event comes from the newspapers mentioned; also from the *Oban Times* of 1 June 1889, 19 April 1890 and 4 August 1928; also Calum Cameron, Iona, 1987.
13. T. M. Devine, 'Temporary Migration and the Scottish Highlands in the Nineteenth Century' in *Economic History Review*, 2nd series, 32 (1979), pp.334–59. And T. M. Devine, *The Great Highland Famine* (Edinburgh 1988), pp.146–70.
14. Phillips, 'Tour', 1826.
15. John MacCormick, article in *OT*, 15 June 1889.
16. Sir John Carr, *Caledonian Sketches or a Tour through Scotland* (London 1809), p.469.
17. Anon., 'Tour', 1806.
18. P. B Homer, *Observations on a Short Tour made in the Summer of 1803 to the Western Highlands of Scotland* (London 1804), pp.82–3.
19. M. B. Forman, *The Letters of John Keats* (Oxford 1952).
20. J. E. Bowman, *The Highlands and Islands. A Nineteenth Century Tour* (Gloucester 1986), pp.123–4.
21. D. Jenkins and M. Visocchi, *Mendelssohn in Scotland* (London 1978), pp.73–4.
22. *Lumsden*, 4th edition (1839), p.177.
23. Bernard Ducos, *Itineraire et Souvenirs d'Angleterre et d'Ecosse 1814–1826* (Paris 1834).

24. Bowman, p.119; James Johnson, *Recess in the Highlands and Lowlands* (London 1834).
25. Lord Teignmouth, *Sketches of the Coasts and Islands of Scotland and of the Isle of Man* (London 1836).

Chapter 4

1. Lockhart, *Scott*, Vol.II, p.433
2. AEP.
3. AEP Accounts 1826–36.
4. SRO, Gd.95/9/6, SSPCK Abstract of School Returns.
5. PP XLIX (1843), Return of the Population and Management of the Poor in each Parish.
6. SRO, HD.7/9, R. Graham's Report on the Highland Destitution of the Year 1837, entry of 6 May 1837.
7. *Greenock Advertiser*, 27 August 1822.
8. PP V (1833), Select Committee on Agriculture, p.128, Mr Thomas Oliver, farmer, Lochend, Midlothian.
9. Ms. list in possession of Dugald MacArthur, Connel.
10. Nominal list, Immigration Department, Vol.4/4780, pp.36–9, Archives Office, New South Wales.
11. Roderick Balfour, 'Emigration from the Highlands and Western Isles of Scotland to Australia during the 19th Century' (unpublished M. Litt. thesis, Edinburgh University, 1973). Also see *IC* advertisements August–September 1839 for passages to Australia.
12. A. Fullarton and C. Baird, *Remarks on the evils at present affecting the Highlands and Islands of Scotland with some suggestions as to their remedies* (Glasgow 1838).

Chapter 5

1. PP XXI (1844), PLIC, evidence from Iona, PP XXIII XXV (1844), questionnaire.
2. *NSA* extracts from Rev. Donald Campbell, 'Parish of Kilfinichen and Kilviceuen' in *NSA*, Vol.VII (Edinburgh 1845), pp.296–339. Account drawn up 1842–3.
3. G. F. Boyle, 'Journal of a voyage to Staffa and Iona' (June 1844), ms. St Andrews University Library.
4. PP XXVI (1851) McNeill Report, minutes of evidence p.5.
5. Robert Carruthers, *A Highland Note-Book* (Edinburgh 1843), p.243.
6. AEP.
7. PP XXVII (1841), Appendix No.1 to the report from Mr Elliott, Agent General for Emigration for the UK.
8. PP VI (1841), First and Second Reports from the Select Committee on Emigration, Scotland, para 3364.
9. PLIC evidence, p.130.

Chapter 6

1. *Oban Staffa and Iona*, Nelson's Handbook for Tourists (London 1859).
2. AEP.
3. See R. N. Salaman, *The History and Social Influence of the Potato* (Cambridge 1949).
4. SRO, CH2/557, Minutes Synod of Argyll, Vol.10, 2 September 1846.
5. SRO, HD.7/12, minute of public meeting, Salen.

6. PP LIII (1847), Correspondence from July 1846 to February 1847 relating to the Measures adopted for the relief of the distress in Scotland, p.24.
7. Statement by the Acting Committee of the Free Church on the Destitution of the Highlands and Islands of Scotland, 22 December 1846.
8. Unless otherwise noted, sources for information on famine relief and fisheries assistance taken from PP LIII (1847) Correspondence and from AEP.
9. Letter in possession of Robin Campbell, Surrey.
10. 2nd Statement of the Destitution Committee of the Free Church (Glasgow 1847), pp.15–16.
11. *Extracts from Letters to the Rev. Dr N. McLeod, Glasgow regarding the famine and destitution in the Highlands and Islands of Scotland* (Glasgow 1847), pp.41–2. Letter from A. MacGregor, Iona, 25 December 1846.
12. Central Board of Management, 1st Report. 2nd to 13th Reports run from May 1847 until December 1850.
13. SRO, H.7/6, letter from Sir Charles Trevelyan to Sir John McNeill, 31 May 1847; also SRO, HD.16/60, minutes of the Central Board Emigration Committee.
14. SRO, HD.7/26, letter Duke of Argyll to Mr Dobree, Commissary General, Oban, 29 May 1847.
15. T. M. Devine, *The Great Highland Famine* (Edinburgh 1988), pp.83–105.

Chapter 7

1. *The Globe*, Toronto, 3 February 1847, notice of public meeting to open subscription fund; 1 December 1847, report of relief consignment sent to Scotland.
2. SRO, HD.7/1 and 7/8.
3. AEP, letter from Duke of Argyll, 5 May 1851.
4. SRO, HD.4/5, list of emigrants, HIES; nominal list compiled on arrival at Portland Bay, Victoria, Archives Office New South Wales. Also letterbook of Sir John McNeill concerning selection and shipment of Highland emigrants, April–December 1852. Mitchell Library, ms.21506.
5. AEP list of warnings of removal; also SRO, SC.59/2/7, Tobermory Sheriff Court, 2 summonses of removal dated 20 March 1850 against 11 Iona crofters.
6. Devine, *Famine*, pp.146–70, Appendices 8 and 9, pp.317–22.
7. McNeill Report, p.xvi.
8. W. Maxwell, *Iona and the Ionians* (Glasgow 1857), pp.26, 42.
9. Manuscript census for Iona, 1855 and 1858, in possession of author.
10. Report covering Iona and minutes of evidence contained in PP XXVI (1851).
11. SRO, SC.59/15/5, Tobermory Sheriff Court papers, Meal Distribution 1848–53.
12. James C. Richmond, *A Visit to Iona: by an American Clergyman* (Glasgow 1849). Henry D. Graham, letters from Iona 1848–50, in the possession of Mrs Iona Chatterton, London.
13. H. D. Graham, *The Birds of Iona and Mull, 1852–1870* (Edinburgh 1890), pp.117–18.
14. J. D. Smith, article in *Ulster Journal of Archaeology*, I (1835), pp.79–91.

Chapter 8

1. Ian McCrorie, *Steamers of the Highlands and Islands*, (Greenock 1987) p.14.
2. J. A. MacKay, *Mull Iona Coll and Tiree*, Islands Postal History Series, No.9 (Dumfries 1979).
3. William Reeves, *Adamnani Vitae Sancti Columbae* (Dublin 1857), p.54 footnote.
4. AEP, letter from John Campbell to Duke, 24 November 1857.
5. BHMSS Report (1860).
6. Parochial Board minutes, 21 December 1848.
7. PLIC evidence, p.130.
8. Parochial Board minutes : a Mr Ronald MacCallum accepted as interim Medical Officer, 15 May 1848; a Dr Stewart appointed Medical Officer, 10 December 1852. Also AEP accounts.
9. Rae Fleming, *Eldon Connections: Portraits of a Township*, p.169 (no place or date of publication; material compiled for Eldon Township, Ontario in the late 1970s).
10. *A History of Glenelg Township*, edited by Mary Ann Neville (Owen Sound, Ontario 1985). *Greenock Township History 1856–1981*, edited by Laura M. Gateman (Greenock, Ontario 1981). Also family history from Shirley MacArthur Credo, USA.
11. Dr Margaret A. Mackay, Final Report on SSRC Project HR 5691, part of The Tiree Project, School of Scottish Studies, University of Edinburgh.
12. AEP, letter from Mr Thomson to Duke of Argyll, 31 October 1849.
13. *The Witness*, 2 January 1850 : referred to vessel which sailed the previous June with people from Mull and Tiree – 'All arrived safe in Quebec but after going up country most of them died. One lad returned to the ship before her voyage home saying he was the only survivor of his family and begged to be taken back to Scotland'.
14. Told to Dugald MacArthur, Connel by Dan Ogilvie, Kentucky, descendant of Donald MacInnes and Ann MacCormick who emigrated from Sithean, a West End croft, in 1847.
15. Mr McVean described his trips in a speech to the Mull and Iona Association, reported in the OT of 4 March 1899.
16. Told to Dugald MacArthur by his father, Archibald MacArthur, Clachanach.
17. Undated newspaper cutting, 'Mull and Iona Clearances and Poor Rates', probably 1880s.
18. Margaret MacDonell, *The Emigrant Experience: Songs of Highland Emigrants in North America* (Toronto 1982), pp.136–9.
19. Letter from Iona published in *The Scotsman*, 16 January 1847; 2nd Statement Destitution Committee (1847), pp.15–16.
20. Richmond, p.9; McNeill Report, evidence from Rev. D. McVean and Rev. A. MacGregor, p.2.
21. AEP accounts. These figures may have been slightly higher. Entries do not always indicate what expenditure was for the Tiree Estate and what was for the Mull and Iona Estate.
22. Letters from Mrs Flora Campbell to her son Donald, August and November 1863, in the possession of Robin Campbell, Surrey.

Chapter 9

1. *Slater's Royal National Commercial Directory of Scotland* (London 1867).

2. The Duke of Argyll, *Iona*, new edition (London 1889), pp.92–3.
3. MacDonald, *General View*, p.485 ; I. Levitt and T. C. Smout, *The State of the Scottish Working Class in 1843* (Edinburgh 1979), p.27.
4. Anonymous article 'Progress in the Hebrides' in *The Journal of Agriculture*, Series III (January–June 1868), p.17.
5. C. F. G. Cumming, *From the Hebrides to the Himalayas*, new edition (London 1883), pp.94–5.
6. James Miln, *Excavations at Carnac (Brittany)* (Edinburgh 1877), pp.20–1.
7. William Keddie, *Staffa and Iona Described and Illustrated* (Glasgow, Edinburgh and London 1850), p.121.
8. *NBDM*, 21 November 1877.
9. *NBDM*, 2 December 1881.
10. AEP, Report of losses by crofters in Iona 1881–2.
11. *NBDM*, 10 May 1872.
12. Tobermory Procurator Fiscal Files, 1868.
13. John Pudney, *The Thomas Cook Story* (London 1953), p.84.
14. G.T., *Three Days in the Highlands with the late Rev. Alexander Fletcher DD in the summer of 1858 with especial reference to his visit to the islands of Staffa and Iona* (London 1861).
15. *OT*, 22 August 1885.
16. *OT*, 18 May and 1 June 1867.
17. W. Reid, *William Black Novelist: A Biography* (London 1902), pp.280–1.
18. *OT*, 'The Weaver of Webs and Mathematics', 18 April 1936.
19. AEP, letter from J. Campbell to Duke of Argyll, 19 May 1869 re 'Alexander MacDonald, the Duchess's weaver as he is called . . .'.
20. F. Marian McNeill, *The Silver Bough*, 4 volumes, Vol.3 (Glasgow 1981), p.109.
21. *Tocher*, No.36–7 (School of Scottish Studies, Edinburgh University), pp.364–76.
22. *OT*, 11 July 1885, 'Life in Iona (by one who lives there)'.
23. *OT*, 12 August 1876, 125 August 1883, 16 August and 27 December 1884.
24 Coll A. MacDonald, 'Eilean I' in *Am Measg nam Bodach* (Glasgow 1938), pp.25–33. Text of series of Gaelic talks for radio, published by An Comunn Gaidhealach.

Chapter 10

1. Mentioned in the lease of Maol farm, 1878.
2. Tobermory PF files, March 1868, John Wilson kelp contractor cited as witness, residing in Iona village.
3. See Thomas Ferguson, *Scottish Social Welfare 1864–1914* (Edinburgh and London 1958), pp.522–9. Information on boarding-out in Iona comes from Strathclyde Regional Archives, D-CH1, City of Glasgow Parish Children's Committee Minutes 1852–97 and D-CH2.1–5, Parochial Board Barony Parish, Education (Children's) Committee minutes 1882–96. Also AEP.
4. Napier Commission evidence, para 44074 ; ms. statement by John MacMillan, c.1890 ; report of fair rents inquiry in *NBDM*, 19 April 1890.
5. Napier Commission evidence, para 44071.
6. See in particular (quoted below), The Duke of Argyll, *Crofts and Farms in the Hebrides* (Edinburgh 1883).

7. *Tocher*, No.24, 1976, pp.310–12, Donald Morrison, Ardtun, Ross of Mull (School of Scottish Studies, Edinburgh University).
8. Letter from Archibald Campbell, Ardfenaig, 13 September 1872, in possession of Robin Campbell, Surrey.
9. See Dr Margaret A. Mackay, 'The Famine that Vanished' paper to Oral History Conference, Cambridge 1987; Dr Alan Bruford, 'Factor Fiction' in *By Word of Mouth*, No.12 (Scottish Oral History Group 1986–7).
10. AEP, undated, but from the names it must be between 1881 and 1888.
11. Napier Commission information derived from SRO. AF.50 (papers) and from PP XXXVI (1884), pp.3036–54 (Iona evidence).
12. AEP, list of stock kept by EE tenants 1879–80.
13. Argyll, *Crofts*, p.74.
14. Napier Commission evidence, paras 3086–7.
15. SRO, LC.4/2/1, Crofters' Holdings Book; and *NBDM*, 19 April 1890.
16. *OT*, 8 September 1888. W. Black re an article in *Harpers Magazine* on the Hebrides by Mrs Elizabeth Pennell.

Chapter 11

1. Malcolm Ferguson, *A Visit to Staffa and Iona* (Dundee and Edinburgh 1894).
2. May Powell, Peterborough, 1987.
3. County of Argyll, Annual Reports on the Health and Sanitary Condition of the County and Districts. Roger McNeill, Medical Officer of Health (1891).
4. School Board minutes 1892–1901; School Log Book 1907–14.
5. County Council of Argyll, Committee for District of Mull, Minute Book No.1, 1904.
6. William Winter, *Old Shrines and Ivy* (Edinburgh 1897), p.122.
7. Recollections of the MacCallums come from conversations with Angus Mackay, Willie MacDonald and Dugald MacArthur.
8. Calum MacLean, 'The Last Sheaf' in *Scottish Studies*, Vol.8 (1964), pp.193–207.
9. Peter MacInnes, Iona, 1985.
10. Tobermory PF files, 15 March 1861.
11. Angus MacKay, Iona, 1984; *Cowley Evangelist*, 1907, p.19.
12. AEP, letter from Mrs Allan MacInnes, Iona regarding her right to receive payment as owner of a boar.
13. Coll A. MacDonald, in *Am Measg nam Bodach*, pp.31–2, translated from Gaelic.
14. Calum Cameron, Iona, 1985; John Campbell, Bunessan, 1986.
15. Description of swimming horses comes from these informants, also Calum Cameron.
16. C. L. F. Panckcouke, *L'Ile de Staffa et sa Grotte Basaltique* (Paris 1831), Plate 9 and p.16.
17. General information on potato varieties and history from the late Donald MacLean, Crieff, Chairman of the National Vegetable Society. Specific information on Iona varieties from MacMillan notebook.
18. Prospectus of The Iona Press, private collection.
19. Recollections of the Ritchie family from Dugald MacArthur, Connel.
20. A. and E. Ritchie, *Iona Past and Present*, 1st edition (Edinburgh 1928), 2nd edition (Edinburgh 1930) 3rd edition (Edinburgh 1934).
21. *The Celtic Monthly* (September 1905), p.233, 'Revival of old industry at Iona'.

22. *OT*, 13 July 1907 and 10 June 1911; *The Quarry* Vol.XIII (September 1907), p.410.
23. AEP, letter from Jenkins, Baker, Reynolds & Co., London to D. Cameron, Estate Office, Bunessan re Iona Marbles Ltd.

Chapter 12

1. Wedding recalled by Donald Morrison, native of Ardtun, 1983.
2. J. F. Campbell, Journal 10 September 1870, NLS ms.50.2.2, f.118.
3. Bute 'Journal', ff.26–7.
4. From the song 'Eilean I' by John Campbell, SA 1986/42.
5. From conversation with the late John Lachie MacInnes, Salum, Tiree, 1987, son of Hugh MacInnes.
6. *Oban Telegraph*, 11 June 1886.
7. Dr Margaret A. MacKay, 'Poets and Pioneers' in *Odyssey*, edited by Billy Kay (Edinburgh 1980), pp.59–69.
8. Information on this emigrant family from: Mary MacMillan, Balquidder, SA 1985/114; Alexander MacPhail, Shoal Lake, Manitoba, SA 1974/259; Marion MacCormick (nee MacPhail), Minnedosa, Manitoba, SA 1979/71. (MacPhail tapes part of the Tiree Project.)
9. May Powell, Peterborough, 1986.
10. Letters to author from Kathleen MacArthur, New Zealand, 1985–6.
11. *OT*, 19 December 1914, letter received 9 December.
12. Opening of service reported in *OT*, 1 May 1897.

Chapter 13

1. See Alan MacQuarrie, *Iona through the Ages* (The Society of West Highland and Island Historical Research, 1983); Cathaldus Giblin, Editor, *Irish Franciscan Mission to Scotland 1619–1646* (Dublin 1964).
2. SRO, GD.95 for SSPCK reports, minutes and school returns.
3. Included in *AEI*, from p.106.
4. Garnett, p.267; Bute 'Journal', ff.26–7; Anon., 'Some Account wrote by a Schoolmaster of Iona or I-Columkille' (1776), NLS ms.14876, ff.41–3.
5. J. Gregorson Campbell, *Superstitions of the Highlands and Islands of Scotland* (Glasgow 1900), p.93.
6. Alexander Carmichael, *Carmina Gadelica. Ortha nan Gaidheil*, 6 volumes, Vol.I (Edinburgh and London 1900), p.163; Vol.II (Edinburgh and London 1928), p.306.
7. *Lumsden*, 3rd edition (1831), p.176.
8. AEP, letter of 28 August 1819; *The Gentleman's Magazine*, Vol.CII (1832), part II, p.497; James Wilson, *A Voyage Round the Coasts of Scotland* (Edinburgh 1842), p.142.
9. Chauncy H. Townshend, *A Descriptive Tour in Scotland* (Brussels 1840), pp.136–7.
10. T. S. Grimshawe, *Memoirs of the Rev. Legh Richmond*, 5th edition (London 1829), p.459.
11. Lachlan MacLean, *A Historical Account of Iona from the earliest period*, 1st edition (Edinburgh 1833), pp.90–1.
12. See James Hunter, 'The Emergence of the Crofting Community: the Religious Contribution 1798–1843' in *Scottish Studies*, Vol.18 (1974), pp.95–116; Donald Meek, 'Evangelical Missionaries in the Early 19th Century Highlands' in *Scottish Studies*, Vol.28 (1987), pp.1–34.
13. Sinclair, Journal, No.V (Edinburgh 1816).
14. BHMSS, *Report*, 1836, p.11 and 1839, p.7.

15. MacLean, *Historical Account* p.89.
16. PP IX (1831), Sixth Report of the Commissioners for Building Churches in the Highlands of Scotland. See also: S. Hackett, and N. Livingston, 'Scottish Parliamentary Churches and their Manses' in *Studies in Scottish Antiquities*, edited by D. Breeze (Edinburgh 1984), pp.302–36; A. MacLean, *Telford's Highland Churches* (The Society of West Highland and Island Historical Research, 1989).
17. PP XXXIII (1838), 4th Report of the RCRI, Scotland, 1835. SRO, HH.37/124, ms. minute book of verbal evidence, Mull Presbytery, to His Majesty's Commissioners for Religious Instruction, 21 September 1836.

Chapter 14

1. Thomas Brown, *Annals of the Disruption* (Edinburgh 1877); *The Home and Foreign Missionary Record for the Free Church of Scotland* (December 1846), log of the *Breadalbane*.
2. Boyle, 'Journal'.
3. *Free Church Magazine*, Vol.2 (1845); AEP; and Richmond, *Visit*, p.18: he saw the roof going on to the new Free Church in July 1849.
4. Rev. Thomas Grierson, *Autumnal Rambles among the Scottish Mountains* (Edinburgh 1850). Iona section of journey in 1848.
5. BHMSS *Reports*, 1846–60.
6. See Appendix IV for further information on Lamont and his poems.
7. Recalled by Donald Morrison, native of Ardtun, 1983.
8. Call to Rev. A. S. MacIntyre, copy passed to D. MacArthur, Connel, by descendant Mr C. Bannatyne, Connel.
9. SRO, CH2/273, Mull Presbytery Minutes, Vols 10–12.
10. *OT*, 7 August 1897. One of a series of articles observing the arrival of visitors by 'The Man on the Dyke'.
11. Lady Frances Balfour, *Lady Victoria Campbell. A Memoir*, 2nd edition (London, New York, Toronto 1911), pp.283–5.
12. J. S. McCorry, *The Monks of Iona* (London 1871), p.157.
13. Graham, Letters, 14 August 1848.
14. *The Scottish Guardian*, 1892–3; T. I. Ball, *A Memoir of Alexander Chinnery-Haldane* (London 1907); *Cowley Evangelist*, reports from Iona 1901–9.
15. *OT*, 7 November 1908.
16. School Board of the Parish of Kilfinichen and Kilviceuen, minutes run from 20 May 1873 to 25 March 1919.
17. T. Ferguson, *Scottish Social Welfare*, p.525.

Chapter 15

1. B. H. Slicher van Bath, *The Agrarian History of Western Europe AD 500–1850* (London 1963).
2. See Bruce Lenman, *An Economic History of Modern Scotland 1660–1976* (London 1977), Chapter 4; Eric Richards, *A History of the Highland Clearances* (London 1982), Chapter 1.
3. See Lenman, Chapter 4; James Hunter, *The Making of the Crofting Community* (Edinburgh 1976), Chapter 1.
4. Cregeen, 'Changing Role', p.16.
5. See Malcolm Gray, *The Highland Economy 1750–1850* (Edinburgh 1957).
6. John Prebble, *The Highland Clearances* (London 1963), p.267.
7. See Philip Gaskell, *Morvern Transformed* (Cambridge 1968).

8. Hunter, *Crofting Community*, p.29 mentions Kildonan and Geirinish in S. Uist as examples : J. B. Caird, 'The Creation of Crofts and New Settlement Patterns in the Highlands of Scotland' in *Scottish Geographical Magazine*, Vol.103, No.2 (September 1987), pp.67–75, writes about the Gairloch estate.

9. Gray, p.30.

10. Sir John Sinclair, *General Report of the Agricultural State and Political Circumstances of Scotland* (Edinburgh 1814), p.97.

11. See Donald MacDonald, *Lewis. A History of the Island* (Edinburgh 1978), p.160; Malcolm Bangor-Jones, 'The Strathnaver Clearances' in *North Sutherland Studies* (Scottish Vernacular Buildings Working Group, 1987), pp.23–37; Gaskell, pp.33–42; Hunter, *Crofting Community*, Chapter 3.

12. Cregeen, *AEI*, Introduction.

13. Population comparisons taken from *NSA*, written early 1840s; also S. Wade Martins, *Eigg. An Island Landscape* (Dorking 1987).

14. Carruthers, p.248.

15. PP LIII (1847), Correspondence, letter from Marquis of Lorne, 6 January 1847.

16. *Ordnance Survey Book of Reference to the Parish of Kilfinichen and Kilviceuen*, surveyed 1878 (London 1879).

17. Richards, *Clearances*, Vol.I, p.501.

18. AEP. Cited letter undated but probably 1885–6. Various requests for lime, draining tiles etc. on file, which appear to have been granted.

19. Carr, *Caledonian Sketches*, p.485.

20. Mull Presbytery Minutes, Vol.6, 1 March 1849, citing the occasion in Spring 1844 when 'Neil MacDonald went to Bunessan to get whisky to celebrate the event. Several of his neighbours gathered in his house for that purpose'. *OT* for reports of bonfires.

21. Told to Dugald MacArthur by Coll A. MacDonald.

22. May Powell, Peterborough, 1986.

23. Letter from James Campbell to Dugald MacArthur, Clachanach, 15 March 1885.

24. *OT*, 25 August 1883. *For The People's Cause. From the Writings of John Murdoch*, edited by James Hunter (Edinburgh 1986), p.198.

25. *OT*, 15 August 1885.

26. Balfour, pp.196–7.

27. 'Iona' in *The Works of Fiona MacLeod*, arranged by Mrs William Sharp, Vol.IV (London 1919), pp.94–5.

Bibliography

An extensive bibliography of manuscript, published, oral and photographic sources, primary and secondary, is included in the author's Ph.D. thesis 'The Island of Iona: Aspects of its Social and Economic History from 1750 to 1914' (Edinburgh University, 1989). The tape recordings which form part of the oral material are lodged in the sound archives of the School of Scottish Studies, Edinburgh University. Below is a selection of the main primary sources used.

From Archive offices

Argyll Estate Papers, Inveraray Castle:
  Miscellaneous rentals, accounts, correspondence, maps.
Argyll & Bute District Council Archives:
  Parish of Kilfinichen & Kilviceuen – Parochial Board Parish Council Minute Books, 1842–62, 1873–1914; School Board Minute Books, 1873, 1919.
  Iona School Admission Register 1877–1926, Log Book 1905–79.
  Tobermory Procurator Fiscal files 1850–80.

General Register Office for Scotland, Edinburgh:
  Old Parochial Registers, Kilfinichen (542/1 & 2), Iona (538/1).
  Statutory Registers of Births, Marriages, Deaths, 1855–1914
  Census Enumerators' Schedules, Iona, 1841–91.

Scottish Record Office, Edinburgh:
  AF.50: Royal Commission on the Highlands and Islands 1883, miscellaneous papers.
  CH2/273: Presbytery of Mull minutes, Vols 1–13.
  GD.9: British Fishery Society papers.
  GD.95: Scottish Society for the Propagation of Christian Knowledge papers.
  HD: Highland Destitution papers.
  HD.4/1–6: Highland and Island Emigration Society papers.
  HH.37: Royal Commission on Religious Instruction, Scotland 1835, additional papers and verbal evidence.
  LC.4: Land Court papers.

Aberdeen University Library:
  Anonymous diary, ms., 'Tour of my native country particularly of the Highlands' (July–August 1806), 132 pages, ms.1023.

National Library of Scotland:
  Bute, John 1st Marquess, ms. diary including 'Journal of the Tour round the Western Islands of Scotland 1788', ff.26–7 and 45–6, ms.9587.

225

Books, reports, articles

Anonymous, 'Progress in the Hebrides' in *The Journal of Agriculture*, 3rd series (January–June 1868), pp.7–26.

Argyll, Duke of, *Crofts and Farms in the Hebrides, being an account of the management of an island estate for 130 years* (Edinburgh 1883).

Baptist Home Missionary Society for Scotland, reports, 1829. 1831–4, 1836–46 in Glasgow University Library; 1853–64, 1890–1971 in Baptist Church House, Glasgow.

Boswell, James *Journal of a Tour to the Hebrides* edited by F. A. Pottle and C. H. Bennett (London 1936). First published London 1785. Tour in 1773.

Bowman, J. E., *The Highlands and Islands. A Nineteenth Century Tour* (Gloucester 1986). Tour in 1825.

Brown, Thomas *Annals of the Disruption* (Edinburgh Parts 1 and 2 1877, Part 3 1881, Part 4 1883).

Carr, Sir John. *Caledonian Sketches or a Tour through Scotland in 1807* (London 1809).

Carruthers, Robert *The Highland Note-Book or Sketches and Anecdotes*. (Edinburgh 1843). Tour 1835 – first appeared as series of articles in the *Inverness Courier* of 8, 15 and 22 July that year.

Central Board of Management reports 1847–50. NLS Y.59.d.18 and 19.

Cregeen, Eric R., Editor, *Inhabitants of the Argyll Estate, 1779* (Scottish Record Society, Edinburgh 1963).

Cregeen, Eric R., Editor, *Argyll Estate Instructions Mull, Morvern, Tiree 1771–1805* (Scottish History Society, Edinburgh, 4th series, Vol.I, 1964).

Cumming, Constance F. G., *From the Hebrides to the Himalayas*, 2 volumes 1st edition (London 1876); 1 volume 2nd edition (London 1883). Tour in 1876.

Destitution Committee of the Free Church, Statement 22 December 1846 and *Free Church Assembly Proceedings*, May 1847. NLS Y.59.d.19. *Destitution Committee of the Free Church*, 2nd statement, 1847. New College Library, Edinburgh University, A.a/6.112.

Ducos, Bernard, *Itineraire et Souvenirs d'Angleterre et d'Ecosse 1814–1826*. 4 volumes (Paris 1834). Visit to Iona 1826.

Ewing, William, Editor, *Annals of the Free Church of Scotland 1843–1900*. 2 volumes (Edinburgh 1914).

Ferguson, Malcolm, *A Visit to Staffa and Iona* (Dundee and Edinburgh 1894). Visit 1893.

G.T., *Three Days in the Highlands and Islands of Scotland with the late Reverend A. Fletcher in 1858 with especial reference to Staffa and Iona* (London 1861).

Garnett, Thomas, *Observations on a Tour through the Highlands and part of the Western Isles of Scotland*, 2 volumes (London 1810). Tour in 1798.

Grimshawe, Rev. T. S., *Memoirs of the Reverend Legh Richmond*, 1st edition (London 1828), 5th edition (London 1829).

Johnson, Dr Samuel, *A Journey to the Western Islands of Scotland (1773)* (London 1925). 1st edition (London 1775). Tour in 1773.

Lumsden & Son's Steam-Boat Companion, 1st edition (Glasgow 1820), 2nd
    edition (1825), 3rd edition (1831).
McCrorie, Ian, *Steamers of the Highlands and Islands: An Illustrated His-
    tory* (Greenock 1987).
MacCulloch, Dr John, *A Description of the Western Isles of Scotland,* 3
    volumes (London 1819); *The Highlands and Western Isles of Scotland,* 4
    volumes (London 1824). Iona visit c.1819.
MacDonald, Rev. Coll A., 'Eilean I' in *Am Measg nam Bodach* (Glasgow
    1938).
MacDonald, James, *General View of the Agriculture of the Hebrides or
    Western Isles of Scotland* (Edinburgh 1811). Visit to Iona 1808.
MacLean, Lachlan, *A Historical Account of Iona from the earliest period,* 1st
    edition (Edinburgh 1833), 4th edition (Edinburgh 1841).
MacLeod, Rev. Dr Norman, *Extracts from letters to the Rev. Dr. MacLeod
    Glasgow, regarding the famine and destitution in the Highlands and
    Islands of Scotland* (Glasgow 1847).
MacPhail, J. R. N., Editor, *Highland Papers Vol.1 1337–1680.* (Scottish
    History Society, Edinburgh, Second Series, Vol.5, 1914).
Martin, Martin, *A Description of the Western Islands of Scotland.* 1st edition
    (London 1703), 2nd edition (1716), facsimile of 2nd edition (Edinburgh
    1981). Tour c.1695.
Maxwell, *Iona and the Ionians* (Glasgow 1857).
Murray, The Hon. Mrs Sarah of Kensington, *A Companion and Useful
    Guide to the Beauties in the West Highlands of Scotland and in the
    Hebrides,* Vol.II, 1st edition (London 1803). Iona visit 1802.
Necker de Saussure, L. A., *A Voyage to the Hebrides* (London 1822) Tour in
    1807.
New Statistical Account of Scotland, Vol.VII (Edinburgh 1845), 'Parish of
    Kilfinichen and Kilviceuen' by Rev. Donald Campbell, written 1842–3.
PP IX 1831, *Sixth Report of Commissioners for Building Churches in the
    Highlands of Scotland.*
PP XXXIII 1838, *Fourth Report of the Royal Commission on Religious
    Instruction, Scotland, 1835.*
PP XX–XXVI 1844, *Poor Law Inquiry Commission for Scotland.*
PP LIII 1847. *Correspondence from July 1846 to February 1847,* relating to
    the measures adopted for the relief of the distress in Scotland.
PP XXVI 1851, *Report to the Board of Supervision by Sir John McNeill on the
    Western Highlands and Islands.*
PP XXXII–XXXVI 1884, *Report and Evidence of H.M. Commissioners of
    Inquiry into the conditions of the crofters and cottars in the Highlands
    and Islands of Scotland.*
Pennant, Thomas, *A Tour in Scotland and Voyage to the Hebrides 1772,* 2
    volumes (London 1776).
Pococke, Bishop, *Pococke's Tours in Scotland,* edited by D. W. Kemp
    (Scottish History Society, Edinburgh, Volume 1, 1887).
Reeves, William, *Adamnani Vitae Sancti Columbae* (Dublin 1857).
Richmond, James C. *A Visit to Iona: by an American Clergyman* (Glasgow
    1849).
Ritchie, Rev. Robert L., 'Some Unpublished Gaelic Songs from Iona' in

Transactions of the Gaelic Society of Inverness Vol.XXIV 1899–1901), pp.66–84.

Royal Commission on the Ancient and Historical Monuments of Scotland, *Argyll. An Inventory of the Monuments* Vol.3 Mull, Tiree, Coll (Edinburgh 1980), Vol.4 Iona (Edinburgh 1982).

Sacheverell, Dr W., Governor of Man, *An Account of the Isle of Man . . . with a voyage to I-Columb-Kill* (London 1701). Visit to Iona in 1688.

Scott, Hew, Editor, *Fasti Ecclesiae Scoticanae* (Edinburgh 1923), Vol.IV, Synod of Argyll.

Sinclair, Dugald *Journal of Itinerating Exertions in some of the more destitute parts of Scotland*, No.III (Edinburgh 1814), No.V (Edinburgh 1816).

Smith, J., *Agriculture in the County of Argyle* (London 1813).

Statistical Account of Scotland, Vol.XIV (Edinburgh 1795), 'Parish of Kilfinichen and Kilviceuen' by the Rev. Dugald Campbell.

Walker, Rev. Dr John, *Report on the Hebrides of 1764 and 1771*, edited by M. M. McKay (Edinburgh 1980); *An Economical History of the Hebrides and Highlands of Scotland*, 2 volumes (Edinburgh 1808); in ms. 'History of the Island of Icolumbkill', Laing Collection, University of Edinburgh. Walker visited Iona in 1764.

APPENDIX I

Lines of Continuity: Iona Surnames Charted

The following two charts indicate the surnames recurring on Iona. The continuity of certain names is shown by the arrows. The incidence of each name is shown in graph form. The sources are as follows:

Chart A

1716: List of men delivering up their arms upon solemn oath in Mull, Ulva and Icolmkill. (WRH SC.54/22/52)
1742/1744: Two rentals for Icolmkill. (AEP.757)
1755: Memorial to Duke of Argyll from West End tenants of Icolmkill. (AEP.757)
1779: List of the inhabitants upon Icolmkill from *Inhabitants on the Argyll Estate. 1779*

Chart B

1779: As above.
1841: Census.
1881: Census.

Notes

I have assumed the following to be different spellings of the same name: McKie and McKay; McPhilip/McGillip/McKillop; McKinvine and McIlichinvan.

McKinvine/McIlichinvan derives from MacGhille-naoimh and is equivalent to MacNiven.

McInleater derives from Mac an Fhleisdeir, equivalent to Fletcher.

The O Brolchan family were Irish stonemasons and churchmen, closely linked with the monastery at Derry. A Donald O Brolchan carved his name on the abacus of the capital of the south-east pier of the Cathedral. He was probably at restoration work there circa 1450.

The earliest extant list of names from Iona is contained in the letters of caption by the Earl of Argyll against rebels in the Mull lands, 1675 (Ref. MacPhail, *Highland Papers*, p.298). They are mostly patronymics:

Donald M'Lauchlan	Archibald M'Intyre
Donald M'Donochie vic Lavish	John M'Neel vic Neil
Charles M'Adam	Archibald Roy M'Donald vic Errochar
Angus Fleger	Donald M'Lean
Thomas M'Onohie vic Avish	Donald Dow M'Lean
Malcolm Charles vic Adam	John M'Eun ur vic Finlay
Archibald M'Lun	Neil M'Eun ur vic Finlay
Donald M'Charles Dow	Dougald M'Ronald

Patrick M'Donald Gregune   Donald M'Ronald
John M'Donald   Malcolm M'Finlay moir
John M'Donald vic Ean   Donald M'Ean vic Donald bean
Charles M'Lean   John M'Eun alias Fledger

IONA: INCIDENCE OF SURNAMES, CHART 4   □ = 1 household listed   P = partial list   * = first record of name

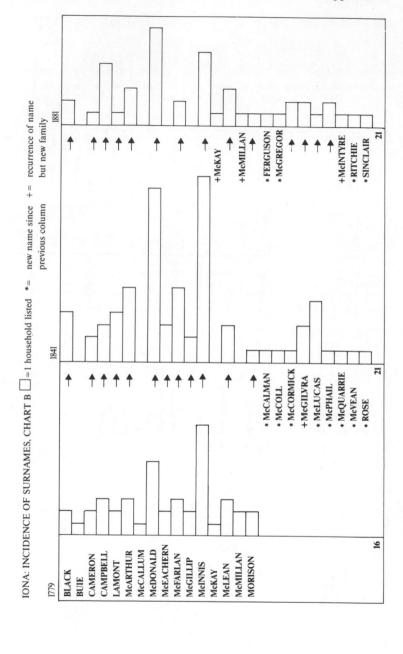

IONA: INCIDENCE OF SURNAMES, CHART B ☐ = 1 household listed   * = new name since   + = recurrence of name
previous column   but new family

APPENDIX II

Emigrants and their Ships

Below are listed the families that disappear from the Iona Census records between 1841 and 1861. Their occupation at 1841 is given, plus their destination on leaving the island where this is known, The source(s) of information about them are shown on the right.

Alexander BLACK and Janet McGilvray	Crofter/ shoemaker WE	New Zealand, 1859	AE Accounts – given assistance to emigrate
Donald BLACK* and Ann Cameron	Turner	Donald died 1851–61 ; five grown-up children all left island	
John CAMERON and Flora Black	Agricultural labourer '51	Canada, 1850s	Oral tradition, Camerons, Iona
Colin CAMPBELL and Margaret Beaton	Crofter EE	Australia, 1852	HIES records
Duncan CAMPBELL* and Flora Campbell	Cottar	?	Gone 1845–51
Donald LAMONT* and Catherine MacArthur	Crofter EE	?	Gone 1845–51
Alexander LAMONT* and Betty McKillop	Crofter EE	Canada, 1849	Shipping list
Robert LAMONT and Mary ?	Innkeeper/ crofter WE	Came in between 1845–51, left between 1851–5	
James MACARTHUR* and Catherine MacArthur	Crofter EE	Canada, 1847	Oral tradition, descendants ; + minister's testimony 1847
Charles MACARTHUR* and Isabella ?	Crofter WE	?	Gone 1845–51
Charles MACARTHUR* and Peggy MacInnes	Agricultural labourer	?	Gone 1845–51
Archibald McCALMAN* and Catherine Livingstone	Weaver	Australia, 1852	Oral tradition, descendants + shipping list
Donald MACDONALD and Mary MacDonald	Crofter WE	?	Gone 1845–51
Margaret MACDONALD	Crofter EE	?	Gone 1845–51
Alexander MACDONALD* and Catherine MacArthur	Agricultural labourer	Canada, 1849	Shipping list
Archibald MACDONALD	Crofter WE	Canada, 1858	Oral tradition, Iona. AE rentals
John MACDONALD* and Cirsty MacInnes	Crofter EE	? possibly Canada ; gravestone Argyll Cemetery, Ontario has name + age that fit, d.1858	

Duncan MacEachern* and Jean Cameron	Beadle WE	Canada, 1849	Shipping list
John MacEachern* and Ann Black	Weaver	Canada, 1849	Shipping list
Hector MacEachern* and Catherine MacLucas	Weaver	?	Gone 1845–51
Angus MacFarlane* and Catherine Bell	Crofter EE	?	Oral tradition, Iona, that they did emigrate
Neil MacFarlane and Margaret MacEachern	Weaver	Canada, 1840s	Glenelg, Ontario 1861 Census
John MacFarlane and Mary ?	Cottar	?	Gone 1845–51
Mary MacFarlane*	Widow of shoemaker	Australia, 1852 records	HIES
Hector McGilvra and Catherine McColl	Crofter WE	?	Gone 1851–5
Donald McGilvra and Ann MacDonald	Crofter WE	?	Gone 1841–5
Neil MacInnes and Mary Black	Infant teacher	Canada, 1849	Shipping list
Dugald MacInnes and Mary Campbell	Schoolmaster	Canada c.1843	Oral tradition, Iona
John MacInnes* and Ann MacArthur	Agricultural labourer	Australia, 1852	HIES records
Malcolm MacInnes and Ann MacInnes	Crofter WE	Canada, 1847	Glenelg, Ontario 1861 Census
John MacInnes Flora MacDonald	Crofter WE	Canada, 1840s	Glenelg, Ontario 1861 Census
Mark MacInnes* and Flora MacGilvra	Cottar	?	Gone 1845–51
Malcolm MacInnes and Effy MacLean	Crofter WE	America, 1847	AEP, assistance by Duke; shipping list
John MacInnes and Marrion MacFarlane	Crofter WE	Canada, 1847	Oral tradition, descendants; AEP rental
Charles MacInnes and Janet MacLean	Agricultural	Canada, 1840s	Oral tradition, descendants
Catherine MacLucas	Cottar and widow	?	Gone 1841–51
Malcolm MacLucas	Tailor	America, 1842	Oral tradition, descendants
Allan MacLucas and Catherine Cameron	Weaver	America, 1844	Ditto
Neil MacLucas and Margaret MacInnes	Crofter WE	America, 1844	Ditto – Malcolm, Allan and Neil were brothers
Malcolm MacLucas and Marion Colquhoun	Labourer/ cooper	Lorne, 1856	AE Accounts, assisted by Duke
Donald MacPhail and Catherine Macpherson	Crofter WE and spirit dealer	?	Gone 1849–51

| James MacQuarrie* and Catherine MacInnes | Shoemaker | Canada, 1851–5 | Oral tradition, descendants; gravestones in Victoria County, Ontario |
| Alexander Rose* and Marion Black | Tailor | ? | Gone 1851–5 |

The following definitely emigrated from Iona but they either did not appear as heads of household in the 1841 or 1851 Census or they were not listed at all. They may have been working away temporarily or they may only have moved into the island in the early 1840s.

Peter MacArthur and Mary MacDonald	He went first to Canada when other members of his family emigrated, late 1840s; then travelled to Australia for a year before returning to Iona to marry and emigrate a second time	Canada, 1859	A E accounts, assisted by Duke; oral tradition, descendants
John MacDonald and Marion MacPhail	Crofter's son '41 and '51	Australia, 1852	Shipping list; oral tradition, Iona
Dugald MacFarlane* and Catherine ?		Canada, 1849	Shipping list
Archibald MacInnes (aged 22, single)		Canada, 1849	Shipping list
Hugh MacPhail and Janet MacDonald + brother Colin MacPhail	Farmer's sons 1851	Australia, 1852	Shipping list
James Lamont and Catherine ?		Canada, 1849	Shipping list

Families known to have emigrated   30
Families known to have migrated   1
Disappeared – destination unknown   18

         Total   49

* The asterisk indicates that a member of this family signed the list of those wishing to emigrate from the Ross of Mull and Iona, 23 March 1847.

Note: The two families who emigrated to Australia on the *Brilliant* in 1837 are also known, from immigration lists preserved in the Archives of New South Wales. They were:

Hugh Campbell and Christina MacLean, plus their children Dugald, Donald and John
John MacDonald and Marion MacEachern.

Ships known to have taken Iona Emigrants

Sailing date	Name	From/To	Notes
27 September 1837	Brilliant	Tobermory to Sydney	7 from Iona. Others from Mull Coll, Morvern, Ardnamurchan: 315 in total. Government assisted
April 1847	Eglinton	Greenock to Canada	Unknown number from Ross of Mull and Iona. Argyll Estate (AE) assisted
9 June 1847	Jamaica	Greenock to Canada	Unknown number from Tiree, Ross and Iona. AE assisted
1 July 1847	Britannia	Greenock to Canada	Unknown number from Tiree and Iona. AE assisted
July 1847	Ann-Harley	Glasgow to New York	9 from Iona. Some assistance with passage money from AE. Other passengers mainly from Glasgow
June 1849	Barlow	Greenock to Canada	52 from Iona. Others from Mull and Tiree, total 254. AE assisted
21 July 1852	Flora	Liverpool to Port Henry, Victoria	8 from Iona (1 family)
28 August 1852	Marmion	Liverpool to Portland, Victoria	31 from Iona. Assisted by the HIES

Other AE assisted ships carrying emigrants from Tiree and Mull:

June 1849	Charlotte	Greenock to Canada	Definitely none from Iona
June 1850	Conrad	Greenock to Canada	Definitely none from Iona
July 1850	Cambria	Greenock to Canada	Definitely none from Iona
July 1851	Birman	Greenock to Canada	Definitely none from Iona
July 1851	Onyx	Greenock to Canada	Definitely none from Iona
July 1851	Conrad	Greenock to Canada	Definitely none from Iona

(Source: AEP, miscellaneous correspondence with Duke of Argyll from Alexander Thomson, Greenock; John Campbell, Factor, Mull; John Lamont, lawyer, Glasgow.)

APPENDIX III

Extracts from a Crofter's Notebook

A notebook kept by John MacMillan, crofter at Lagnagiogan, West End, Iona, has been preserved by a nephew. It covers the years 1883–96 and contains a wealth of detail, for example : notes on livestock (cows' names and calving dates, sheep sold and killed); the names and dimensions of fields; sowing, harvesting and yield of crops; the variety of potatoes grown; itemised income and expenditure for the household each year.

In the Return to the Napier Commission of 1883, this croft was listed as having 7 acres of arable land and 11 of pasture and stock of 8 cattle, 10 sheep, 1 horse and 3 pigs. Rent, including grazing rights was £21.18.0. After the fair rents' hearing of 1890, John MacMillan's rent was reduced to £12.0.0.

The following extracts from the notebook are attached :

A. Income and Expenditure accounts – a photocopy of the year 1889; typed copies of the years 1883, 1887 and 1896.

B. Crop production notes.

C. Potato production notes.

Notes on A

Rent is entered as such, or against item 'to J. Wyllie', who was then the Argyll Estate Factor for Mull and Iona. It is clear how the rent arrears, into which most crofters had fallen by the 1880s, built up. The full rent does not appear to have been paid in any of the years quoted – where most of it was settled, e.g. in 1883, this accounted for 47% of the total expenditure that year. In 1887 less than one-third of the due rent was paid and even with the much lower rent of 1896 only half appears to have been paid that year.

Of the *firms* mentioned the following can be identified : MacPherson & Buchanan were the livestock auctioneers in Glasgow; Archibald Hamilton & Sons were grain, flour and seed merchants in Glasgow; both Francis Spite & Co. and Cooper & Co. were general grocers in Glasgow; Robert Houston & Sons were woollen manufacturers in Greenock.

Most of the *individuals* named under 'income' may be identified as local crofters or farmers in Iona or Mull who, for example, would buy a young pig for rearing. Lachlan MacLean, merchant in Iona, did this regularly and he also bought occasional sheep or lamb carcases. In 1883 two donations appear from John MacDonald, an uncle emigrated to Australia, and Coll MacMillan, John's twin brother who was working at sea.

Under 'expenditure' the item 'Katie going to Tiree' probably refers to John's sister who may have been visiting relatives there. Their father came from Tiree. 'Marrion' in 1889 was John's aunt. John MacDonald ran the Post Office in Iona at this period, from where he also sold some goods.

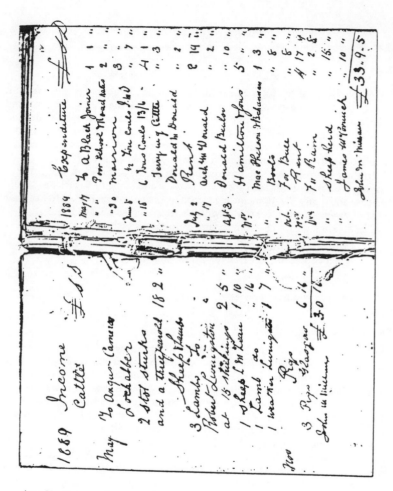

App. III. Extracts from a crofter's notebook.

Income 1883

		£	S	D
May	2 stirks	9	12	6
July	1 sheep L. MacLean	1	12	—
"	1 lamb Mrs. McKinnon	—	18	—
"	1 lamb L. MacLean	—	14	—
	Pigs:			
July	2 Rev. Campbell	1	—	—
"	2 Jas. McCormick	1	—	—
"	1 Macnabb	—	10	—
"	1 Jno. McGilvray	—	10	—
"	1 Duncan McInnes	—	10	—
"	1 Duncan McPhail	—	10	—
"	1 Duncan Campbell	—	10	—
Dec	2 Richard Sinclair	7	—	—
		24	6	6
May	John MacDonald, Australia	10	—	—
"	from Coll	10	—	—
		£44	6	6

Expenditure 1883

		£	S	D
July	6 tons coal	3	10	4
"	Hamilton	5	—	—
"	Poor, school & road rates	1	18	—
"	Houston	1	14	2
"	Rent	9	19	—
Aug	Scythe & sugar	—	18	—
"	D. McCormick rye	1	5	—
"	castrating 1/6, ferrying 2/1	1	3	6
"	D. McDonald, Bunessan	1	2	6
"	Hamilton	2	—	—
"	Katie going to Tiree	1	6	—
"	D. McCormick	—	10	—
"	sh.rts	—	10	—
"	paid John McDonald, merchant	2	10	—
"	paid Ballantine, Glasgow	2	3	—
Nov	buying rams	—	15	—
"	paid J. McFarlane for pig	—	10	—
Dec	Rent	9	19	—
		£42	13	2

Income 1887		£	S	D
May	1 stot stirk	3	–	–
„	1 3-year old	5	–	–
„	1 2-year old	3	–	–
June	Coll	–	10	–
Aug	3 lambs @ 9/-	1	7	–
„	1 cow at Glasgow	6	2	6
Oct	2 pigs L. MacLean	1	–	–
Nov	1 cow at Glasgow	6	3	–
„	2 pigs	4	9	–
		£30	11	6

Expenditure 1887		£	S	D
May	paid John McDonald	3	–	–
June	Hamilton & Sons	3	10	–
„	poor & school rates	1	8	5
„	Angus MacDonald	–	10	–
July	5 tons coal	3	–	–
„	road rates	–	5	11
„	sundries	–	2	–
Aug	scythe, stone & salt	–	6	6
Sep	to J. Wyllie	6	2	6
„	Donald Beaton	–	10	–
Nov	Spite & Co., Glasgow	1	10	–
„	Hamilton & Sons	3	–	–
„	blankets Houston	2	–	–
„	ironmongery	–	9	5
„	shirts & braces	–	12	6
„	repairing watch	–	2	6
„	tobacco	–	2	4
„	4 pairs boots	1	12	6
„	to Glasgow and back	–	7	6
Dec	J. Kennedy, Kinloch	–	10	–
„	sundries for New Year etc	–	10	–
		£29	11	1

Income 1896

Income 1896	£	S	D
Cattle:			
sold to Mr. Macpherson one stot stirk and two quay stirks at Bunessan market one two-year old heifer	12	–	–
Sept. to Donald McNiven 1 stot stirk	4	15	–
Sheep:			
July to L. MacLean 1	4	–	–
" to Mac & Buchanan four lambs 18/-	1	8	–
cleared	3	4	8
Pigs:			
May one pig Mac & Buch	2	8	–
June " " " "	2	13	–
	£31	12	8

Expenditure 1896

	Expenditure 1896	£	S	D
May	Paid A. Hamilton & Sons	4	10	–
"	sent Katie one pound going to the market and	1	–	–
"	litt.e account paid	–	10	–
June	paid Mac & Buchanan	2	18	–
July	Katie when going to Tiree	1	–	–
"	paid rent	6	–	–
"	sert Cooper & Co.	1	12	–
"	paid tailor	1	2	–
"	paid for shirting	–	10	–
"	paid J. MacInnes for coals 6½	3	14	9
"	Shepherd's year's salary	–	15	5
June	poor & school rates	1	1	8
"	Malcolm Beaton	–	10	–
"	pa.d for McDougall's dip	–	3	–
"	Duncan Campbell for pigs	1	–	–
Sept	sent Cooper & Co.	1	5	–
"	paid for repairing watch	–	5	6
Nov	gave Katie when going to Glasgow	1	–	–
"	paid tailor for trousers	–	3	–
Dec	paid Cooper & Co. for goods	1	9	–
"	dc. for New Year	1	1	–
"	road rates	–	4	10
		£31	14	2

No. acres under each crop :   Grass to be cut for hay this year :
Barley – 3   Oats – 2½   Rye Grass – ¾   Meadow – 1¼
Rye – 1   Potatoes – 2½   + 4 acres outrun not to be cut

AGRICULTURAL RETURN OF 4TH JUNE 1890

Sowing dates of crops :   *Oats*   *Rye*   *Barley*
          1891   6 May   7–8 May   22 May – 2 June
          1893   28 – 29 April 29 April   9 – 18 May
          1894   30 April   1 May   14 – 24 May
          1896   2 May   4 May   9 – 21 May
          1898   2 May   3 May   9 – 20 May
          1899   6 May   7 May   15 – 24 May

Harvesting of crops + no. of stooks : *Oats*   *Rye*   *Barley*   *Total*

1890 : begun 9 September
        finished 23 September
        secured 17 October   96   44   183   323

1891 : begun 10 September
        finished 26 September
        secured 2 October   66   58   197   321

1892 : (no dates)   58   52   167   277

1896 : begun 14 August
        finished 6 September
        secured 12 September   40   133*   202   365
                          * rye and small oats

Production of Potatoes :

1890   Digging 21 October – 13 November   57½ barrels
1893   Digging 2 – 19 October   104½ barrels
1894   Digging 5 – 18 October   88 barrels
1895   Digging 13 – 31 October   100 barrels

Potato varieties grown:

CHAMPIONS	1887–1895	Bred or raised in Scotland in 1863.
ROCKS	1887–1895	Very old, before Champions.
SNOWFLAKES	1887–1895	True name LANGWORTHY.
HEROES	1887	Little recorded.
MAGNUMS	1887	Short for MAGNUM BONUM, introduced 1876.
LAROCHELLES	1893–1895	No record.
PORRIMS	1893–1895	No record.
KIDNEYS	1893–1894	Referred to shape, several kinds.
VILLAGE BLACKSMITH	1893–1894	Very old, listed 1836, one of the first; true name FORTYFOLD.
BRUCES	1894–1895	Synonym for Magnum Bonum.
CALCUTTIES	1894–1895	No record.

(Source: Donald MacLean, Crieff, chairman, The National Vegetable Society.)

Below: Diagrams and notes on where potato drills or storage pits were; Lachlan Maclean, merchant in the village, had some drills on this croft. Also notes on making a potato creel.

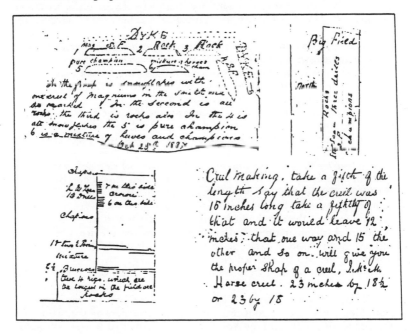

APPENDIX IV

Story and Song from the Oral Tradition

Gathered together here is a selection of Iona lore passed on, wholly or in part, by word of mouth. Traces of it may be found in the landscape itself as, at one time, every field, rock and gully will have had its own name, often commemorating a particular event, personality or tradition. Many of these names have never been recorded on maps but a list of the ones still recalled by Iona people has been included in an Appendix to the author's thesis, on which this book is based.

For example, the island abounds in wells. *Tobar Magh Luinge*, above Traigh Bàn nam Manach at the north end, must be a very old name as it is dedicated to Moluag, a seventh century Saint who founded a church on Lismore. *Tobar na Gaoithe Tuath*, south-west of Dùn I, means 'well of the north wind' and there were once south, east and west wind wells, their sites now forgotten. Certain people were said to have been endowed with the ability to raise the appropriate wind by chanting a rhyme at the well. And *Tobar a'Cheathain*, just below the Cathedral, was believed to have healing powers.

There are more down-to-earth associations with *Glac Domhain*, a deep gully on the western slopes of Dùn I, and *Am Briuthas Beag*, just south of Traigh Mòr, both sites for illicit whisky distilling. And *Lòn na Poit-Dhubh*, south-west of Dùn I, is a marshy spot where the 'black pot' (i.e. the still) was said to have been hidden from the customs men.

A family long gone from Iona is remembered in *Croit Eachairn*, a small plot of land where the road presently runs past the Cathedral. These Mac-Eacherns were herds to the other East End tenants and emigrated in the 1840s.

Accidents or shipwrecks often resulted in a new, or changed, name at the spot they occurred. The original name of *Geodha Ruaraidh* (Roderick's creek) on the north coast is no longer known. It was where Roderick Cameron drowned when his small boat fell foul of the rocks. It was a market day and most of the able-bodied men at the East End were away, so help could not reach him in time. Roderick Cameron married Marion MacKillop of Lagandòrain croft in 1807 and his death was probably in the late 1820s. Their daughter Marion married Neil MacKay, tailor.

Brown's Rock, off the Machair shore, commemorates what is perhaps the best known of the many shipwrecks that happened around Iona. It is named after Captain Charles Brown of the sailing ship the *Guy Mannering* bound from New York to Liverpool and which foundered here on the night of 30 December 1865. Fifteen of the American sailors drowned and were buried in the Rèilig Orain. Nineteen were saved during a rescue attempt by the islanders that lasted several hours. For their bravery the Royal Humane Society awarded bronze medals to Dugald Black, Neil MacCormick, Donald

MacDonald and John Campbell and testimonials to Malcolm Ferguson, John MacDonald and Duncan Campbell. A memorial to the victims was erected at the grave in 1882, on the initiative of the US Consul in Glasgow, Mr Bret Harte.

An accident of some kind must have claimed a lad named Dugald many years ago on the high ground known as *Druim Dhùghaill* above the south-east coastline. The way it was told by the old folk to Hector MacFarlane, who worked in Iona as a boy, was passed on to his son, the late Donald MacFarlane of Deargphort in the Ross of Mull : 'A young man had a fairy sweetheart and a smith made him a steel arrow so that he could not be harmed while carrying it in his garments. But he was to be best man at a wedding one day and changed out of his normal clothes. He went to hunt rabbits till the wedding began but he never returned. His body was found next day. She had killed him. The place where he was found was called after him, Druim Dhùghaill'. (Translated from Gaelic, s A 1963/30.)

Two places in the West End of the island, *Uamh a'Bhodaich* (old man's cave) and *Cnoc na h-Analach* (hill of the breath), are linked by the same story. The cave is also known as the Sheep Stealer's Cave. An outlaw, said to be an Islayman, was hiding in the cave and was in the act of killing a stolen sheep when a young girl, searching for it, chanced upon him. She fled back over the hills with the man in close pursuit and at Cnoc na h-Analach collapsed, out of breath, and expired. The man was chased by her brothers but escaped in a boat. The story was already known by 1848, when Henry D. Graham arrived on Iona, as he noted it down in a sketchbook (unpublished) along with a drawing of the cave.

The connections with both Christian and pagan belief of *Sìthean Mòr*, the grassy knoll just south of the road leading on to the Machair, have been mentioned in Chapter 13. It is also strongly associated with the world of the supernatural. Two fishermen were said to have been enticed inside the 'big fairy hill', as the name means, by the sound of music. One stuck his fish-hook in the door and so protected by this piece of metal, was able to escape. The other danced for a year before being allowed to leave. Another version is that the men were hunchbacks and that the one who left early did so free of his hunch while the other ended up with the two on his back. Over thirty similar 'hunchback' tales have been recorded from the Gaelic and Scots traditions by the School of Scottish Studies in Edinburgh University. One of these is located at Calva in Iona, where one man had his hunch removed by the fairies as thanks for completing their song 'Diluain, Dimàirt' (Monday, Tuesday) but the other spoiled the song and had his hunch doubled. (sA 1953/103, recorded from Duncan Cameron, Ross of Mull who heard it from Archibald MacArthur, Clachanach, Iona.)

Pàraig an Oir (Peter the Gold) is the central character in two stories – that of a kidnapped fisherman who subsequently returned to Iona, and in that telling the adventures of an emigrant who finally settled in North America. The merging of these two traditions is commented upon towards the end of Chapter 12. The story is published as 'Calum an Oir' in *Oiteagan o'n Iar* by John MacCormick (Paisley 1908), pp.114–23. It also appears under this name in 'Sgeulachdan Bhearnaraidh', an article in the *Transactions of the Gaelic Society of Inverness*, Vol.LII (1980–3), pp.145–7. The story reached

Berneray through Malcolm MacLeod, who was born in Berneray and married Martha MacInnes of Greenbank croft in Iona.

Why the main character's name in these sources was Calum (equivalent to Malcolm) is not clear. The emigrant Peter MacArthur, whose nickname in North America was 'Peter the Gold', had a brother, cousin and grandfather all named Malcolm. There were Malcolms too in the MacInnes family, also emigrants from Iona, to whom Peter's family became linked by marriage. The following are local, oral sources:

1. Angus MacKay (SA 1984/81/B)

MM : Calum an Oir – did you hear the story from your father?

AM : No, I heard it from Kintra. Well, I heard it here before but the one I heard in Kintra was a kind of different story. He said that it was a Spanish boat that went out and he was out fishing about Sandeels, out there somewhere, and they came on him and they wanted to get round . . . get round the Torran Rocks. And he was by himself and he went aboard and he had his own boat at the stern and he just took it with him. And whenever they got out they wouldn't let him go, they kept him on the ship and they took the wee boat on board and away they went. And they went to Spain and they were travelling about Spain and down about the Mediterranean there. And they were never letting him off the ship at all and he was kind of a prisoner and he was not getting any wages, he was only getting his food.

MM : He was being made to work?

AM : Aye, he was getting all the work. He was like that for a long time. And then he went up to the North of Spain, there's a place Bilbao at the very North. And a boat came in, a ship came in from Greenock and in alongside their ship and he noticed the men were speaking Gaelic. Oh, he said, I'll have to get in tow with these fellows, to get me out of here some way or other. So – he was a long, long time away, five or six years I think. He had got in tow with the boat that came from Greenock, there were a few Highlanders on her and he got in tow with them and they said, now the first chance you can get, if you can get aboard the ship they told him to get up to the British consul and he will do something for you. It was not easy . . . but I think they took him . . . he got aboard this other ship anyway and they must have showed him the way to the Consul anyway and then the Consul got on to the Spaniards that held him all this time and they had to pay him quite a lot of money . . . quite a lot of money to get back. And he came back on this ship and he was put off at Greenock. Then, they were saying, he came back and he had a fearful lot of money. They were saying there was a 'lag' (hollow) on his 'druim' (back), carrying the money, he carried it all in case he never saw it again. That's why they called him Calum an Oir – well, he was a Pàraig, I believe he would have been a MacInnes . . . no, it was a MacArthur at Greenbank but he married a MacArthur this MacInnes . . . and he lived happily ever after. Aye, Pàraig an Oir, that's the way I heard it but I think there was a few versions.

Angus MacKay also said that when Pàraig an Oir was an old man he would sometimes take a gold coin out of his pocket, to show to the children, and then put it back.

2. Johnnie Campbell, Bunessan (SA 1986/42)

This version is very similar to that published by John MacCormick. A fisherman is taken on board a ship to act as guide and his own boat, with his companions, then cut free. He is made to work without pay and set ashore in New York. He is spotted by the ship's owner, a Gaelic-speaker, who hears his tale and makes the Captain pay compensation in a bag of gold coins. The man then returns by the next ship to Greenock and Iona. Johnnie's name for him was Calum MacArthur.

3. May Powell, Peterborough (daughter of Malcolm MacLeod and Martha MacInnes), in conversation, July 1987.

May heard Angus MacKay tell the version involving the Spanish ship. The same story, but with the American ship, was told in her own family. Her mother often mentioned Pàraig an Oir, particularly when passing the remains of the houses at Martyrs Bay which, she indicated, was where he had lived. She also implied that he was a relative and had become very rich in the end.

4. The MacArthurs at Achabhaich have a tradition that Pàraig an Oir sent money home from Australia to help them, his relatives. The dent in his shoulder from carrying the bag of gold he had made also features in their story.

5. Calum Cameron, Iona, in conversation 1985.

Calum knew of Pàraig an Oir as a MacArthur but connects him with the Greenbank MacInneses and also with the MacInnes family who emigrated to Canada and married into Peter MacArthur's family.

In one story Pàraig an Oir is linked to the gold-digging and to another character who set himself up as a robber, got into a fight and let Pàraig through in the scuffle. Pàraig spoke or swore in Gaelic and so the robber told him to go his way.

Calum also has the story of an Iona man called 'Portugal' who was taken on board ship as a navigator but they cut the rope of his boat and kept him till they got to Portugal. A Skye man on the pier where they landed saw he was a Highlander and helped him get away.

A fragment of rhyme, said to be a drake talking to a duck, is remembered today as follows:

Thalamaid, thalamaid!
Càite? Càite?
Buntàta mòr tioram
Aig Aonghas MacLaomain.

[Let's go, let's go!
Where? Where?
Big dry potato
At Angus Lamont's.]

It may well hark back to the potato blight of the late 1840s, when the wet

A photograph of Peter MacArthur, supplied by a descendant in Canada – he is still known to her as 'Peter the Gold'.

rotten crop raised the spectre of starvation. And Angus Lamont was one of the local people charged with distributing the famine relief meal. Lamont himself was also a bard. He was born in Ulva in 1771 and came to Iona as a young man. He married a local girl Mary MacDonald and worked a croft at Martyrs Bay until his death in 1856. The Duke appointed him Guide to the Cathedral around 1840, after Allan MacLean retired.

    Eleven of Angus Lamont's songs were the subject of a talk by his great-nephew, the Rev. Robert Lamont Ritchie, to the Gaelic Society of Inverness and subsequently published in their *Transactions*, Vol.XXIV in 1899–1901.

No other work has been traced in either oral or written sources. Lamont's inspiration was often a local event or personality and his verses can thus yield snippets of information or anecdote otherwise unrecorded. His songs include a lament for his son Donald, who died in infancy in 1808, one dedicated to departing emigrant Neil Morison, another to Rob MacLachlan who was blacksmith in Iona for a time, and a rebuke to his herd, Dugald MacColl, whose haste drove the bard's sheep into a ravine.

The two examples quoted below are also in satirical vein. The first concerns a tiff between Lamont and his neighbour Archibald MacDonald (nicknamed am Baisteach, the Baptist). The lines of the chorus are still readily recalled by several Iona people.

Oran mu 'n Bhàta	*Song about the Boat*
'S coma leam fhìn do chompanas bàta; Bha thusa ga bristeadh 's mise ga càradh; 'S coma leam fhìn do chompanas bàta.	I don't care for your boat partnership, You broke her and I mended her, I don't care for your boat partnership.
I air tràigh agus *'slip'* oirre, Na sìneadh air sitinn; A beul mòr air a bhristeadh, 'S a clisnean cràiteach. 'S coma, etc.	She is beached with a slip-rope on her, stretched out on a midden, her gunwale broken and her ribs aching.
I gun stiùir 's gun taoman, Gun ràmh na gun aodach; A crannsach air sgaoileadh, As eugmhais nan tàirnean.	She is without rudder, without bailer, without an oar, without a sail; her hull split open being without nails.
'N uair a theid thu do 'n t-Searmoin, A dh'èisdeachd Mhic Fhearghuis, Bidh is ann an Dearg-Phort, Air laimhrig gun chàbal.	When you go to church to hear Ferguson, it is in Deargphort she will be, by the jetty with no cable.
Fhad 's a bh'agam làn choir oirr' 'S i fo shùil Dhòmhuill-ic-Dhòmhuill, Cha 'n fhàgadh e guilmean Bho 'fara-dhruim gu a h-àpruinn.	So long as I had full charge of her and she was under the eye of Donald son of Donald, he would not leave a reproach from her super-keel to her apron.
A Ghilleasbuig 'ic Dhòmhuill 'Ic Iain, 'ic Shòghain, Ged 's maith leam thu còmhl' rium Cha chòrd sinn mu 'n bhàta.	Archibald son of Donald son of John son of Soghan (?), though it is good to have you with me we cannot agree about the boat.
'S fàilt ort a Shlipeag Bho 'n thainig thu 'n 't-Shlignich; Bho 'n bhrist e do chlisneach, Cha chàirinn gu bràth thu.	Welcome to you, Slipeag, since you came to Sligineach; since he broke your frame I would never mend you.

Am Freagradh	*The Reply*
'S coma leam fhìn luchd cithean is cànrain,	I don't care for those
Ged nach ann sgìth de 'r comunn a tha mi,	who complain and grumble,
'S coma leam fhìn luchd cithean is cànrain.	though I am not tired of
	your companionship, I
	don't care for those who
	complain and grumble.
Och! eudail a dh'fhearaibh,	Och! my dear man, how
Bu bheumnach 'ur teanga,	cutting your tongue when
'N uair a theann sibh air gearan	you began to complain
Air fear nach robh làthair.	about one not even present.
'N uair a thainig mi 'n bhaile	When I came back to the
Mu 'n deachaidh mi dhachaidh,	village before I went home,
Chuala mi caithream	I heard the lads on the
Aig balaich na sràid air.	street noising it abroad.
'S fios aig a' bhaile	The whole village knowing,
Na 'n deanadh iad aithris,	if they were to mention
Nach fliuchadh sibh cas	it, that you would not
A thoirt aire do 'n bhàta.	wet a foot to look after
	the boat.
Ach 's tàlann fo thalamh,	But it is buried talent,
Gun bhuannachd gun mhalairt,	without profit or exchange,
'Bhi teannadh ri rannan	to start on making verses
Do ghlagraich bhàta.	about a worthless boat.

Notes

Duncan Ferguson, verse 3, was an elder of the Baptist Church in the Ross of Mull. Deargphort is a small bay in the Ross, opposite the north end of Iona. MacDonald crossed the Sound, to join the much larger Baptist congregation in Ross, in the boat he shared with Lamont.

'Soghan' in verse 5 is not a readily recognisable Christian name, unless it is possibly a form of 'Johnnie'. It may be a misprint in the printed text.

Oran do 'n Chladach Fheamuin

Ath-ha-a-lam, Ath-ha-a-lam,
Ath-ha-a-lam o Ceann Anndraidh,
B'e sid an t-àite còmhalach,
'N uair thig an ròd 's a' Gheamhradh;
Bithidh bodaich agus crògain aca,
Crios mu 'n còta teann orra,
Gheibh thu dòrn 's a'cheann bhuath.*

    Thoir fios gu Niall MacLaomuinn bhuam
    Nach 'eil mo ghaol 's an am air,
    Ged bhiodh pailteas feamuin aige,
    'S geamanta na 'ceann e;
    'S ann their e neo-aoigheil rium-

A shlaodair' fuirich thall uam,
Cha d' thugainn mìr de m' mhàthair dhuit,
Ged bhiodh a bàs na gealltachd.

Mo ghaol air Dòmhull Dòmhnullach,
Gur duine còir gach am e,
'S ann bheir e cuireadh sòlasach
Do 'n fhear tha 'n dìth le ganntachd;
Tha feamuin anns na ròidibh,
'S thig gu leòir oirnn fo Bhealltuinn,
'S gun toir mi iomadh lòd dhith
Do 'n ghille chòir mo chleamhuinn.

Bha Iain Dubh Mac Airtear ann,
Bu taitneach leam a chainnt-san,
Gu bheil againn pailteas dhith,
'S gun airceas thugaibh leibh i;
Cha 'n 'eil 'so ach càirdean,
Bithidh dian mu 'n tig an oidhche,
'S airbeulthaobh Aonghuis Làmoin,
'Ur diùltadh ni tha oilltcil.

Beannachd is buaidh làraich leibh,
Nach fhaca càs 's an am oirnn,
A leasaich am buntàta dhomh,
Gu 'n fhàilluing a Ceann-Anndraidh;
Tha e 'nis gu sàbhailt'
A' fàs le blàths an t-Samhruidh,
'S mur toir sinn tuilleadh pàidheadh dhuibh
Gu bràth gu 'm bi sinn taingeil.

Notes

Athaluim is a placename on the Sligineach shore and Ceann Anndraidh is a headland at the north end of the Machair. Both spots were good for gathering seaweed. This clearly did not happen without occasional squabbles over seaweed rights. There is reference to such disputes in Chapter 11.

* A line appears to be missing here from the printed text. It is otherwise an eight-line formula that is used.

Song to the Seaweed Shore

Athaluim from Ceann Anndraidh,
what a place of gathering that was
when the seaweed comes in winter;
there will be old men with pitchforks,
belts tight round their coats,
you will get a fist in the head from them.*

Send word to Neil Lamont from me
that I have no love for him at the moment,
although he has plenty of wrack
he is niggardly in the mind about it;

what he will say unwelcomingly to me –
Sluggard, stay away from me,
I would not give a particle of my mother to you
though she were on the point of death.†

I like Donald MacDonald,
he is a kindly man every time to me,
he would give a happy invitation
to the man in need because of scarcity;
there's seaweed in the shoreline,
plenty will come on us before Beltane (May),
that I will give many a bulky load of it
to that good lad my son-in-law.

Dark-haired John MacArthur was there
and agreeable to me was his speech –
indeed I have plenty of it,
and without difficulty take it with you;
there are none here but friends,
be brisk before the night falls,
and in front of Angus Lamont,
your refusal is horrible.‡

Blessing and good luck to you,
who did not see us in extremity,
who gave fertiliser for my potato crop,
without shortage
it is now safely growing with the
warmth of summer,
and if we don't give you any more pay
we will ever be thankful.

Notes

* A line is missing here. See note on previous page.

† The context of these two lines is not clear. Neil Lamont may have been related to the bard and it may thus be a private reference to the mother's health or to caring for her.

‡ Again, the meaning of these two lines is not entirely clear. From a note in the printed version, it seems that MacArthur set aside a share of seaweed for Lamont, who was late. The bard thus expresses gratitude to him in the final verse.

Another of Angus Lamont's songs was in praise of a Neil Morison, who had gone to the West Indies. Several of its verses bear close resemblance to lines in the song *Toirt m'Aghaidh ri Diura*, which appears in Archibald Sinclair's *An t-Oranaiche* (Glasgow 1879), pp.293–4. This song is not attributed to any composer in the published source but, according to informants, was made by an Iona bard *James Campbell*. (John Campbell, Calum Cameron in conversation 1988.)

James Campbell, also known as Seamas MacPhàraig (James son of Peter), is thought to have been in Iona around the mid-nineteenth century. He may have reworked part of Lamont's text into his own song or both songs may have used material from a common, third source.

Only one other of James Campbell's songs is recalled in oral tradition today. Calum Cameron knows it by the title of *An Anna Ghrand* (the *Ann Grant*). In it the ship of that name takes the bard from Greenock to the West Indies and he talks with nostalgia about returning to Iona. A fragment, probably the last four verses, is transcribed below from a recording with Peter MacInnes along with a brief conversation about the bard. (SA 1987/30)

> Nam bithinn mar bu chòir dhomh
> 'S gun ruig sinn air tìr an I Phort Rònain
> Bhithinn cinnteach tighinn am chòmhdhail
> Fleasgach bàn nam blàth shùil bhòidheach
>
> O gur gòrach mi le m' smaointinn
> 'S gun ann dhomh ach an fhaoineis
> A liuthad tonn tha an taobh seo Staoineig
> 'S barr orra cho geal ri faoilinn
>
> Nam biodh fhios aig nighean Ailein
> Seamas a bhith 'n eiginn-mara
> Chan e sùgradh a bhiodh air a h-aire
> 'S bhiodh na deòir a' ruith gu talamh
>
> Tha mi seo an Demcrara
> Fada thall air cùl na grèine
> Ach nam faighinn as mo dhèidh i
> Sheòlainns' i gu cùrsa Rèidh Eilean.

PM : Seamas MacPhàraig . . . Cò as a bha e? Bha e a I fhèin seo, tha mi smaointean gur ann as an linn againn fhìn a bha e, Seamas MacPhàraig. Agus bha e aig muir . . . 'S e fonn air a bheil, 's e Ho-rò 's hillinn òro, Ho-rò 's hillinn ì, Ho-rò 's hillinn òro . . . Chaneil cuimhne agam air a'phìos mu dheireadh. Ach bhithinn ga chluinntinn mar a bha mi nam bhalach.

MM : Cuin a bha e an seo? A'bheil fios aig duine?

PM : Well, chaneil mi cinnteach. Bhiodh e ann o chionn trì linn air ais, shaoilinn. Bhithinn a'cluinntinn mo mhàthair a'bruidhinn air agus bha i glè mhath air seinn cuideachd agus 's minig a chuala mi i aig an òran seo. Ach sin an aon òran a chuala mi aig Seamas MacPhàraig ach tha mi cinnteach gum biodh dorlach feadhainn eile. Bhiodh dorlach bàrdachd a bharrachd air a sin.

MM : An do dh'fhalbh e?

PM : Well, cho fad 's a tha fios agam, tha mi smaointean gun do rinn e dhachaidh thall thairis mu dheireadh. Chaneil cuimhne agam direach dè 'n dùthaich don do lean e nuair a dh'fhàg e na cladaichean seo.

Translation

If I were as I ought to be, and if we arrive on shore in Iona, Port Rònain, I would be sure, coming to meet up with me would be the fair-haired lad with the handsome warm eyes.

O foolish am I with my thoughts, since it is for me only foolishness, so many waves this side of Staonaig and a crest on them as white as the seagull.

If Alan's daughter knew that James was in distress upon the sea, her thoughts would not be full of mirth and the tears would be falling to the ground.

I am here in Demerara, far away beyond the sunset, but if I could get it behind me I would sail on a course for Rèidh Eilean.

PM : James, son of Peter . . . Where was he from ? He was from Iona itself, I think he was from our own family, James son of Peter. And he was at sea . . . The tune it has is Ho-ro hillinn oro . . . I can't remember the last bit. But I used to hear it when I was a boy.

MM : When was he here ? Does anyone know ?

PM : Well, I am not sure. He would be here three generations ago, I think. I used to hear my mother speak about him and she was very good at singing too and I frequently heard her at this song. But that is the only song of James's that I heard but I am certain that there would be a good deal more of them. There would be a good deal of poetry besides that.

MM : Did he go away ?

PM : Well, so far as I know, I think he made his home abroad in the end. I don't just remember which country he went to when he left these shores.

Note

Rèidh Eilean is a small, uninhabited island west of Iona.

Index